The Autonomy of the Self
from Richardson to Huysmans

The AUTONOMY of the SELF
from RICHARDSON to
HUYSMANS

FREDERICK GARBER

Princeton University Press

All Rights Reserved
Library of Congress Cataloging in Publication Data will be
found on the last printed page of this book

Publication of this book has been aided by a grant from the Paul
Mellon Fund of Princeton University Press
This book has been composed in Linotron Sabon

Clothbound editions of Princeton University Press books
are printed on acid-free paper, and binding materials are
chosen for strength and durability

Printed in the United States of America by
Princeton University Press, Princeton, New Jersey

For
Barney and Ida Garber
in memoriam

Contents

Preface

The dialectic of aloofness and association runs through this book from beginning to end. Our commonplaces about the period imagine a pure, willed apartness, embodied in figures who are irrevocably settled outside the social order, their minds set on their separateness. But such figures are more characteristic of the frontispieces to nineteenth century editions of Byron than they are of the texts themselves. Byron knew better and so did Goethe and Stendhal: they built worlds based on the dialectic, with all its opposing tugs and difficult alternations. Further, the willing of that separateness is itself a curious issue. Of course it was chosen; Rousseau argued that from the beginning, and so, for that matter, did Richardson. When the separateness happened it was seen, frequently, to be very good. Poe's heroes make it clear that they are happiest in their rooms or mansions, and the early Wordsworth was a great extoller of isolated cottages. But the dialectic—which few could ever escape—turns the willfulness into something tenser and grayer than our commonplaces would have it. Rousseau also said, in his first *Promenade*, that he was compelled into separateness, that he, "le plus sociable et le plus aimant des humains,"[a] had been driven out of society. If we recognize that he was, in fact, forced to do what he wanted to do, we can still see that the conditions are far more ambivalent than any unequivocal position, any Byronic frontispiece, can make them. Rousseau was a good deal less troubled by the ambivalence than most of his successors; he was not much of a model for such anguish. The disturbance was more purely expressed in Milton's Satan, who laid out the conditions for an interplay of warring desires with absolute clarity, though that was as far as he got with working out the problem. Others got further, sometimes with a signal success if not with a sustained one. Those efforts to work out the dialectic are a recurrent subject in the following chapters.

One term of the dialectic is a hunger for autonomy so pervasive and passionate that it has to be seen as one of the defining features of the age. The autonomy desired is, essentially, that of the self and its agents, particularly consciousness and the imagination, though an independence within (not merely from) the social order is part of the picture, and the sort of autonomy in relation to one's literary forebears that Harold Bloom has analyzed is still another part. The hunger is enormous, the impediments to its satisfaction are equally so. They come from within as well as without, from one's own possible inadequacies as well as all the familiar external pressures. The chapters that follow concentrate particularly—indeed, obsessively—on the question of adequacy: how can one organize the conditions of one's world so that the dialectic of aloofness and association, the need both to be and to be among, is handled without danger to the self? Put another way the question becomes threefold: what is it like, this cherished self-sufficiency? How can I bring it about, make it real? Can I bring it about at all?

The result of these explorations is a series of images of desire, that is, of what is desired as well as of the desiring itself. The period from Richardson to Huysmans is remarkably of a piece in its quest for such images, going from the opening out of self into the bourgeois order to the final encasement of self in a prisonership that had threatened it from the beginning. That danger had been apparent as early as Richardson, and it recurs with a chilling regularity in places such as Shandy Hall and in acts such as Werther's self-devouring. But the risks had to be run. The alternative to autonomy was a submission of self, which, to many, was as good as its death. Rousseau broods over these matters with a massiveness and intensity matched by no other: defining autonomy in him goes far toward defining it, if only by contrast, in those who follow. Earlier models, such as Satan and Quixote—an unlikely pairing only if we forget what they want—turn up occasionally.

If they were equivocal, as many saw them to be, that only adds to the ambivalence. Localized paragons, such as Schiller's naive poet, had special tasks in particular settings, and rarely went further than their home grounds. That there is no lack of instances, pervasive or parochial, shows the intensity of the passions with which the issues were broached, how much they were felt to be matters of the self's survival.

What these chapters chart, then, are aspects of self-making; more precisely, of the making of special modes of the self that were as difficult to sustain as they were to put together. The wisest among these artisans of consciousness knew that ambivalence was endemic to the situation because the self had to face discontinuities with which it could not always live comfortably. Conversely, they also knew that there could be enforced (and possibly unsuspected) continuities as well: Julie found out, at the end of her life, that there were links between strata of her subjective experience that she had assumed were safely insulated. Separateness is always equivocal, ambivalence is not peripheral or occasional but central and persistent. Autonomy, even of the finest quality, never comes without cost. Yet there were, after all, points of exquisite balance, moments in which the self came through in tentative but definite triumph. The chapters show these moments too, scattered as they are. It is, overall, a mottled picture, with some heroes, some villains, and an occasional fool. The chapters do not, however, put the figures into such categories. That is not an evasion of judgment but, rather, a recognition that those figures are sometimes in several categories at once.

Acknowledgments

I am grateful to the following journals for permission to reprint material previously published:

Canadian Review of Comparative Literature for "Richardson, Rousseau and the Autonomy of the Elect," 5 (1978), 154-68;

Comparative Literature for "Self, Society, Value and the Romantic Hero," 19 (1967), 321-33 and "Nature and Romantic Mind: Egotism, Empathy, Irony," 29 (1977), 193-212;

Nineteenth Century French Studies for "The Structure of Romantic Decadence," 1 (1973), 84-104.

Some material in the book was published as "The Autonomy of Consciousness and the Adequacy of the Imagination," *Neohelicon*, 3 (1975), 27-50.

Haskell Block and Lore Metzger were very generous with comments on the translations. Their help is warmly appreciated.

Vestal, New York   *September, 1980*

*The Autonomy of the Self
from Richardson to Huysmans*

∾ ONE ∾

An Autonomy for the Elect

The first letter in Richardson's *Clarissa* points out a curious set of qualities in the heroine's condition, a pairing of characteristics that are not so much opposites as incompatibles. Anna Howe, Clarissa's lucid and free-spoken correspondent, reminds Clarissa of what she already knows well, that she is a paragon to other women and under increasing constraint in her own household. Miss Howe puts the point precisely, and with an unknowing irony which needs the whole novel to reveal itself fully: "You see," she says, "what you draw upon yourself by excelling all your sex."[1] Somewhat later, she adds to the invisible ironies by telling Clarissa that "prodigies, you know, though they obtain our admiration, never attract our love" (I, 125). As both Clarissa and Anna perceive from the beginning, prodigies attract our desire to restrain them, to imprison their light if we cannot quite put it out.

Clarissa has her own kind of lucidity, not nearly as free-flowing as Anna Howe's but sufficient to show her that what she has now could easily, with only a slight adjustment, be made into an admirable pattern for living. All it would take, it seems, is a release from the necessity for marriage, not merely a freedom from engagement with the pudgy and muddle-headed Mr. Solmes but from any man at all, whatever his characteristics or the age of his fortune. It is not only the squat ugliness of Solmes that drives Clarissa into "declaring for the single life" (I, 117), though that is, of course, a way out of her current entrapment. She had sorted out her options some time before, asserting in one letter that "a single life . . . had always been my choice" (I, 177) and in a later one that it is "the single life . . . which I so much prefer" (I, 454; cf. III, 149-50). In a letter to her uncle John Harlowe, pleading to be released from all obligations to Solmes, Clarissa sees marriage with anyone as a condition of potential sacrifice in which what she will most lose, and most regret losing, is the untrammeled independence of her autonomous self. She is, as she points out to her uncle, "a free and open spirit" (I, 153), one that resists all imposition of external restraint on its free choice of activities. Of course Clarissa does not tell her uncle what she later tells Anna Howe, that marriage is a long road, which women tread "with tender feet, upon thorns, and sharper thorns, to the end of a painful journey" (I, 454). Told to her uncle that would have been a fruitless impropriety; told to Anna Howe it is an observation her witty but pliant correspondent will understand if not necessarily act upon (cf. I, 132); told to herself it is a pointed image of the progress of a martyred, subservient self. Clarissa characterizes her willingness to remain single as a token of obedience to her family: though she cannot marry Mr. Solmes she will not marry anyone else either, and thus will not run the risk of marriage with a partner whom her family considers unsuitable. Seen in the light of Clarissa's attitudes toward free will and the thorns of marriage this argument is certainly, though unconsciously, specious. Margaret Doody has shown convincingly that Clarissa's willingness to settle for the single life is a convention in the fiction of Richardson's time.[2] But there is far more to Richardson's handling of this position than a reiteration of contemporary cliché.

Lovelace, who shares many attitudes with Clarissa, including a distrust of marriage, speaks of his "aversion to the state of shackles" (I, 514). The image, of course, implies a rendering up of one's autonomy, and Clarissa would certainly agree with him on that aspect of marriage. Her preferred image, however, is that of the thorn, with a generalized reference to the sufferings of martyrs as well as the specific suffering of Christ. But Clarissa's ideas about the thorns of marriage include other dimensions as well as these, and those others, in their turn, go back to some different ideas, which are deeply imprinted in Richardson's text. In a long letter to Belford, Lovelace recalls the jilting that had caused him to seek revenge on all women, and he blames "those confounded poets" who had inspired him to write "sonnet, elegy, and madrigal" on Petrarchan themes, "darts, and flames, and the devil knows what" (I, 145). But Richardson's awareness of the stuff of convention opens up profounder affiliations with the same segment of the literary past. The intertextual life of his novel reaches in an extraordinary number of directions, and included in that life is an echo of some earlier kinds of rose-gathering, the thorns of which, in Richardson's rendering, are turned not upon the plucker but the plucked. Indeed, these are the same echoes Blake was to pick up in his *Sick Rose*, whose bed of joy has been invaded by a worm and whose life is being destroyed by that invasion. Clarissa undermines her assertions about her reason for staying single with the analogy of death and sexual activity, which surfaces stubbornly and persistently throughout the novel. Long before the rape she regards Lovelace as a potential murderer of her personality, if only in a bizarre, premonitory nightmare. Suspecting that her relatives had set out to destroy him, she dreamed that Lovelace seized her, carried her to a churchyard, stabbed her to the heart "and then tumbled me into a deep grave ready dug, among two or three half-dissolved carcasses; throwing in the dirt and earth upon me with his hands, and trampling it down with his feet" (I, 433). The novel broods over the old play on "death" and "dying" through which Renaissance wits had equated sexual climax and personal extinction but the play becomes grim and deadly, as it was to do in Blake. The thorns of marriage are something more, it seems, than a revision of the traditional instrument of the martyr's torture. Marriage, however legitimate its framework for the fulfillment of desire, promises a puncturing of the self as well as the body, an attack upon the inner life which could lead to the death of personality. Marriage and sexuality are therefore a threat not only to the autonomy of the free spirit but to its integrity, even its survival. Clarissa's offer to stay single becomes a solution to a complex series of related problems. Though she is certainly self-deluding about the full extent of her motivation, she knows what she ought never to lose, and she opts for a condition that is in fact no sacrifice at all.

The optimum situation for Clarissa is one that would allow her to accommodate herself to society without confronting it; that is, to adjust to a world that is necessarily other, a world with which she can be quite at ease, but to do so with a complete and self-sustaining order of self. The conditions, she argues, are already there. As she puts it to Mr. Solmes, she possesses "in her own right, sufficient to set her above all your offers, and a spirit that craves no more than what it *has,* to make itself easy and happy" (I, 379). She is financially and spiritually self-sufficient, independent of others both in what she owns and what she is, capable of an unusual but unimpeachable autonomy. It should be possible, then, to be both single and social, free within the confines of self and yet engaged with all the forms of bourgeois society. Lovelace was to say that Clarissa was a "lover of forms," as indeed she was (II, 245). She feels that she can find an order for herself within those forms, but that such an order would have to make room for a part of herself the forms could never touch. Thus, the ideal structure of consciousness for Clarissa is that of an independent, self-sufficient system which is not isolated from society but perfectly meshed with the social scheme that surrounds it. The desirable framework for consciousness is a contextual autonomy, one that would permit obeisance to external order as well as to the self's radical freedom.

A shape for this combination of autonomy and contact was already at hand in the organization of the well-to-do household. Ian Watt has shown how the establishment of separate rooms for each member of the bourgeois family, particularly the closet attached to a woman's room, helped to develop conditions favorable to the expression of private experience.[3] But there was a further potential to those conditions which could affect the essential forms of the self. In a letter to Miss

Westcomb, Richardson urges that a woman make out of her closet a personal Eden in which she could be comfortable, secluded, and at home:

> Retired, the modest lady, happy in herself; happy in the choice she makes of the dear correspondent of her own sex (for ours are too generally designers), uninterrupted, her closet her paradise, her company herself, and ideally the beloved Absent; there she can distinguish herself: by this means she can assert and vindicate her claim to sense and meaning.[4]

Women were offered paradisal enclosures, personal enclaves giving full due to every sort of civil demand upon the self, and from whatever quarter. The closet was a sort of sanctuary within which the woman was quite alone and self-sufficient, yet could reach out and contact others through her correspondence. A woman could be both social and subjective at once, as intimately self-revelatory as she chose to be, yet part of a larger system that enfolded her and offered acceptable forms for the self's actions. Further, the paradisal closet could slip naturally, perhaps inevitably, into a figure for the enclave of the self; that is, the closeted self, a private place within the encompassing familial framework. The conditions Clarissa wanted were no more than an extension of that interplay of sociality and seclusion available to most middle-class women. If such an arrangement was not only possible but expected within the substantial household, it would seem both reasonable and inevitable for that arrangement to shape the structure of one's life if one chose to avoid the various thorns of marriage. It was, after all, simply an enlargement of the field within which the sanctuary that was the paradisal enclosure found its place.[5]

Clarissa's urge for contextual autonomy has other ties to the moral framework of Richardson's time. Ian Watt, Christopher Hill, and others have argued that Clarissa's independence of spirit is firmly grounded in the history of Puritanism and bourgeois individualism, and that there are clear affinities between Clarissa and such images of Puritan self-sufficiency as Robinson Crusoe.[6] But what Clarissa wants is a good deal more tense and intricate than the conditions of Crusoe's independence and its insistence upon the individual's accountability to himself. Defoe's novel is a strongly positive book about the human potential for physical and spiritual survival. Put in the most relevant terms, it is a book about the economies of the inner and outer man, and how the two necessarily work together—up to a point. Crusoe has first of all to demonstrate his capacity for building a self-sufficient economic structure, one that does not reproduce the world from which he came but shows the same spirit that shaped the old, well-stocked system. Defoe's ironies are cool and incisive: as it turns out, Crusoe is an extraordinary exemplar of the energy, ingenuity, and self-sufficiency that built the social order he had once rejected. Still, Crusoe's introspection is not so subtle as to make him aware of those ironies. His self-analysis is severely moral, less capable of perceiving such intricate juxtapositions than of spelling out the causes and conditions of penance. He knows that his sins of rejection have brought him where he is, that he is not only alone but isolated, and that all the protective enclosures he has built on the island cannot supply him with a fully satisfying independence of the spirit. He is a paragon of economic man, not of the man for whom externals are no more than the dirt and grass that sustain the body. If he is a hermit, he did not choose to be one.

Indeed, the limitations of his subjective independence make for one of the central thrusts of Crusoe's punishment. His proven capacity to build an economy for the body, and his recognition of his sin and his dependence upon God, together gave him the impetus to survive in the spirit. He did not, after all, go mad or do himself in. But survival is not all that Crusoe needs. Brooding over the fate of some sailors whose wrecked ship he has seen, Crusoe is beset by "a strange longing or hankering of desires I felt in my soul upon this sight."[7] The hankering is for the cancellation of this solitude by the glimpse of another human face: " 'O that it had been but one!' I believe I repeated the words, 'O that it had been but one!' a thousand times" (193). Though he can get along alone, he is not nearly as self-sufficient in the soul as he is in the body: "I whose only affliction was, that I seemed banished from human society, that I was alone, circumscribed by the boundless ocean, cut off from mankind, and condemned to what I call silent life" (164). God has made his solitude tolerable but not delightful: " 'How canst thou be such a hypocrite,' said I, even audibly, 'to pretend to be thankful for a condition, which however thou may'st endeavor to be contented with, thou would'st rather pray heartily to be delivered from?' " (126). Crusoe may be as self-sustaining as Adam in Paradise but he has fallen *into* his insular Eden and he would be only too happy for the chance to tumble out of it again. Neither bread alone, nor even a combination of bread and penance, can give him everything the self requires or lighten the weight of his isolation. He is far more paradisal without than within.

But his isolation has still other dimensions, and it is because of them that Crusoe is compelled to reach for support outside himself. There is nothing in his capacities of self that could help him build a perfectly autonomous subjective order, one that would give him sustenance under any circumstances. Further, there is no evidence in the novel that he would have recognized the need or even the possibility of such an order. From what we see of Crusoe in England and South America he showed neither the interest nor the talent to create a well-stocked larder for the self, and it was therefore not possible for him to do so on the island. It seems that he had never felt the compulsion to put together a horde of subjective goods on which he could draw and feast in a period of isolation. Crusoe had been the perfection of economic individualism, so much so that he tended to treat others primarily as commodities, however grateful he may have been for their favors or loyalty. But the insufficiencies of that sort of individualism are startlingly evident when he is alone on the island. It is at this point that the analogy of Crusoe and Clarissa begins finally to break down, and the differences take on at least as much significance as any similarities. In fact, the analogy is both accurate and inadequate, as Richardson's suggestion for turning a closet into a paradise makes clear.

Whether Richardson had echoes of Milton in mind when he made the suggestion is irrelevant, although the prominence of Milton in the middle-class Puritan culture which Richardson knew with profound intuition makes the inference almost certainly safe. In any case, the model for a Puritan version of the paradisal enclosure, and the warrant for an extension of that enclosure into a figure for the self, had long been available in the Puritan tradition through its major piece of creative literature. Richardson was tapping a familiar mode with his kindly recommendation. There is more to the mode than its mythic substratum, since it opened the way to forms of subjective order that made possible a set of balanced, equitable responses to all the demands of contemporary life. The "paradise within thee, happier far" revealed to Adam at the point of expulsion promised the chance for an inner life that would be as rich and complete, as satisfying and self-sustaining, as all Edens are.[8] That, too, is an available mode for Clarissa to live by, and it is as necessary an analogy of her choices for being as is the more external, pragmatic orderliness of Robinson Crusoe. The possibility of a subjective paradise meant that there was a feasible home for the inner resources Clarissa said she possessed, those goods of the soul that made her inner life entirely her own. Her subjective wealth was seeking a kind of location that Crusoe, with all his self-sufficient insularity, could never want nor achieve. Clarissa needs to be both Adam and Crusoe, paradisal within and independent without, self-contained, dutiful, and free. Committed to the fulfillment of her obligations as daughter and paragon, as well as to the reverent protection of her selfhood, she wants a way of being in the world that gives all that is necessary to every value put forth by both self and society. She wants a delicate counterpoint of accommodation and sequestration, engagement and withdrawal. She prefers a mode for her personality that would be in society but not of it, that is, a self surrounded by the structure of the community, active and orderly within it, but free from it all the same. The self would be private but sociable, autonomous but interested, self-sufficient but cooperative with all those forms of civility Clarissa so loves.

Richardson is many things but he is, above all, a master ironist. The first letter in the novel had implied an essential tension between Clarissa's free will and her status as a paragon, and the rest of the novel sets itself to work out that suggestion. Quite late in the story, when Clarissa is out in the world, Lovelace ridicules her discomfiting sense of obligation to others, arguing that "she never was in a state of *independency*; nor is it fit a woman should, of any age, or in any state of life" (III, 24). That point had been made much earlier by her mother, when Clarissa was still part of the parental community. To Clarissa's insistence that she could never acquiesce to Solmes her mother says only, "Ah, girl, never say your *heart is free*! You deceive yourself if you think it is" (I, 103). There is no place for an autonomous system of self within the larger enclosure of the family, not to speak of the world as a whole, which Clarissa had once described as "one great family" (I, 34). When Lovelace tricks her into slipping out of the family garden Clarissa leaves a smaller community for a larger one, expecting that there will be room within it for the self to operate in flexible and open independence. But in fact the parental enclosure, her home in the world of the garden, prefigures a set of smaller enclosures, not larger ones: Clarissa moves from one incarceration to another, through a series of private and public prisons, until she ends in the smallest enclosure of all, her coffin. Lovelace's mockery of Clarissa's urge for "independency" was preceded by another sardonic comment whose irony, though surely unwitting, lends a grim tone to this interplay of desirable and deadly enclosures. Clarissa had just managed to flee from him: "She is *thrown upon the wide world*!—Now I own that Hampstead Heath affords very pretty and very *extensive* prospects; but 'tis not the *wide world* neither; and suppose *that* to be her grievance, I hope soon to restore her to a *narrower*" (III, 24). All of her incarcerations are dark travesties of Clarissa's drive for autonomy within the social order: she was separate from society, as she wanted to be, but in exactly the opposite mode from what she had planned, and with a totality of isolation she had never desired.

Given Clarissa's penchant for interweaving the order of self with the forms through which it engages the world, the result is predictable. The dream of contextual autonomy had offered her a framework within which she could find support for the wholeness of self. That is, the coherence of her selfhood depended on the coherence of an order honoring all that the self could want, an order that would satisfy her simultaneous desires for both seclusion and sociality. If that order were somehow rendered ineffective, the self, which was learning to function inside of it, would be without external support. Thus, when the order of contextual autonomy was caricatured in a series of incarcerations, that parody demonstrated the brittleness and vulnerability of the order; and when those weaknesses were revealed, Clarissa no longer had any guarantee that her selfhood would remain both whole and coherent. Its totality and stability were simply too closely involved with—indeed, reflective of—the totality and stability of the order by which she was trying to live. Both body and self, person and personality, became vulnerable at this point. Clarissa's earlier guess that a penetration of the one would be an invasion of the other was proven to be sound, verified when her paradise within became a hell of madness after the violation of her body. In her first intelligible letter to Lovelace after the rape she expressed her awareness of the defenselessness of her private enclosure with appropriate, if unconscious, grossness:

> O Lovelace! If you could be sorry for yourself, I would be sorry too—but when all my doors are fast, and nothing but the keyhole open, and the key of late put into that, to be where you are, in a manner without opening any of them—O wretched, wretched Clarissa Harlowe! (III, 210-11)

When Lovelace entered Clarissa's body he fractured her selfhood, just as his disrespect for the sanctity of her parental garden had ruptured the order on which she was planning to base a fully satisfying life.

An order divided against itself cannot offer coherence. It can offer no more than division. The result was seen in the magnificently imagined series of mad papers, particularly the tenth with its poem on "my divided Soul, / that wars within me" (III, 209). Clarissa had suspected occasionally that she was being, as she once put it, "cheated, as I may say, out of myself" (III, 153). She put it that way in her last reasonably peaceable interview with Lovelace—which, through Richardson's deftness of touch, took place in a garden. Her suspicions were verified almost exactly, though in reverse, for it was her self, or part of it, that was cheated out of her. In a discomposed letter to Anna Howe, shortly after the rape, she speaks both of a lost "*best self*" and also of "*self*, this vile, this hated *self*! I will shake it off, if possible" (III, 321). She ends her anguished brooding with a desire for a division of self that would ease the pain: "self, then be banished from *self* one moment (for I doubt it *will* for no longer)." Three days later, complaining again that "*self* would crowd into my letter," she wishes that this internecine division would be completed, that God would "give me a truly broken spirit, if it be not already broken enough," for then she would be "take[n] to His mercy" (III, 324).

Yet the final ironies belong to Clarissa. After the rape and her successful effort to rebuild her fragmented selfhood, Clarissa achieves a freedom of action she had never enjoyed before, a self-sufficiency so pure that she needs nothing except her newly established self and her expectations of apotheosis. But the difficult act of self-healing, which was accomplished only by Clarissa and her God, did not result in a simple reinstatement of the old order. Indeed it could not, because so much had happened to her, both within and without, so much had been taken away that she ought never to have lost, that she had no way of returning to her former system of self. There was no turning back into the garden once Lovelace had locked the door behind her. No longer paragon or virgin, admired only by Lovelace, Belford, and Anna Howe (a strange trio whose continued admiration tells much about Clarissa herself), Clarissa had to heal herself into an unconventional pattern of autonomous living. It was at this point that she became very different from Milton's Adam, who in other ways was an important predecessor. In Book Eight Milton contrasted God's self-sufficiency with a solitary man's lack of completion. As Adam said to God: "Thou in thyself art perfet, and in thee / Is no deficience found" (415-16). God, that is, is His own context. Man, on the other hand, has to mate and reproduce himself in order to find a context in which to function: "Man by number is to manifest / His single imperfection, and beget / Like of his like, his Image multipli'd, / In unity defective, which requires / Collateral love, and dearest amity" (422-26). Man and God together cannot make a society because man needs some of his own kind for self-completion. But Clarissa, alone with her God, has found that perfection in singleness Milton's doctrine would not acknowledge, but which Richardson had shown to be necessary to her from the beginning. There were, however, essential changes in the context of her situation. She was now both self-sustaining and dutiful, as she had wanted to be with her parents; but what she was independent from and what she was dutiful to had taken on a combination of characteristics that was peculiar to her new situation. The subjects from which she was independent had increased, while the subject to which she was dutiful had condensed into a pure absolute: "All I wished was pardon and blessing from my dear parents. Easy as my departure seems to promise to be, it would have been still easier had I had that pleasure. BUT GOD ALMIGHTY WOULD NOT LET ME DEPEND FOR COMFORT UPON ANY BUT HIMSELF" (IV, 339). No longer at war with the corporate authoritarianism of society, she transcends all contexts except the largest one, finding her autonomy within the divine order.

This was contextual autonomy of a sort that Clarissa had not planned on having, and that she was compelled to have only through adversity; yet its structure was both simple and perfect, a model of adequacy that made it possible for her to attach her autonomy to the most satisfying context of all. Here, as at almost every step in the novel, Clarissa and Lovelace are both doubles and foils, reflecting each other's ways and desires but nearly always as mirror images. Here, too, all the heavy-handed equations of Lovelace and Satan, which are studded throughout the novel, take on a most subtle point. Clarissa could never have desired a subjective independence so free-floating that it owed its primary allegiance only to itself. When she effectively dissolved all connections with her earthly context she was left with one final connection, the one that most mattered. Any step beyond that, into the dissolution of all connection, was never even conceivable for her. But that was a step Lovelace had long ago taken. He and Clarissa are among the major advocates of personal autonomy in the eighteenth-century novel, beginning with their mutual "aversion to the state of shackles" (I, 514) and extending into many of their relationships with others. Yet it is the differences in the quality of the desired autonomy that make Clarissa and Lovelace into mirror images of each other.

Lovelace is less like Clarissa in this matter than he is like his Satanic forebear in *Paradise Lost,* who found in himself the source of all value, the only fit object of obeisance. Lovelace, like Satan, seeks to be his own context, that is, to be as Adam describes God, perfect in his singleness. Lovelace's mind is its own place and almost the only place. He accepts from society only those values he finds compatible with the fulfillment of his extraordinarily complex bundle of desires. From his own social stratum he picks up a few elements, such as his snobbery about the bourgeois rich and some sanction for libertine ways. From Clarissa's stratum he seems to have taken nothing at all. His is the sort of freedom that exists only because its possessor sees himself as no longer accessible to claims other than those he chooses to make on himself. What Lovelace eventually finds is a somewhat ambiguous and incompletely acknowledged version of what Satan found: that is, a hell within, which is the bitter counterpart of the paradise within reserved for their victims. And hell comes about because Lovelace, like the romantic heroes who followed him, turns out to be attached, after all, to the same sources of value he had boasted of rejecting; and those values torment him just as they were to torment his romantic successors. The combination of pride and remorse which comes upon him appears again in many of the imitations of Byron as well as in the Byronic sources themselves, though neither the Byronic figures nor their imitations had anything like the complex ambivalence of Lovelace. Out of the mass of ironic situations that descend on everyone at the end of Richardson's novel, the case of Lovelace is outstanding. His autonomy was more contextual than he had suspected, and it made him most vulnerable in those very areas where he had thought himself to be freer than anyone.

Although she ends with an ambivalence as intense as that of Lovelace, Clarissa achieves the epitome of terrestrial freedom. At that point there is only one more prison to be released from, her violated body (cf. III, 321); and that release, in this very long novel, takes a good deal of drawn-out time. When she succeeds, and all society mourns, Richardson lingers over the details of Clarissa's funeral rites, savoring the ironies of her final participation in the social order. Clarissa, who has fled from her ultimate prison, leaves her spiritless body locked up in its final box as the center of the sociality of the requiem ceremonies. Here, finally, is the contextual autonomy that Clarissa had always desired, but only her shell is there to enjoy it. This is a last and bitter emblem of her urge for peace and independence within the encompassing community.

The lessons Richardson passed on to his most important successors had little to do with his claustrophobic moralism or even with the intricate texture of his epistolary mode, which no one ever used with better effect. His novel offers an image of a society at war with itself, unable to reconcile the species of individualism that saw worldly success as a sign of the elect and the equal and opposite individualism that saw the self's integrity as deserving of a context in which to do its work. Clarissa is the subject and victim of that conflict, a martyr to her inability to accommodate the demands of inner and outer forms. Some of the novels that followed Richardson's work focused less on his mode or his moralism than on his explorations of the relations of self to its own system and to the large system encompassing it. It is from that point of view in particular that Rousseau—on the surface a most unlikely successor to Richardson—sets up a link between the Puritans' uneasiness with social order and the romantics' profound ambivalence toward it.

Some of Rousseau's contemporaries felt that *La Nouvelle Héloïse* was little more than a transmigration of Richardson from London to Clarens. They pointed toward the preachiness of the respective heroines, the high moral tone, the comparable sets of two women in active correspondence, and the oppressive fathers, each of whom seeks to promote a marriage his daughter does not want.[9] But in our time there has been skepticism about the likeness between the novels, with scholars like Daniel Mornet wondering whether the similarities go beyond such superficial analogies, indeed whether the shift toward a more positive view of feeling and the grounding of passion in the spectacular Swiss landscape actually make for two very different modes of encountering experience.[10] It is possible to say that each of these positions is correct in part. Rousseau sought to carry further what Richardson was doing, but at the same time he set out to invert the character and qualities of the struggle for autonomy in *Clarissa*. Rousseau's novel is a profound and serious parody of the deepest elements in Richardson, in fact an ironic reversal of their import. Julie is something more than a countrified Clarissa, a rural sister under the skin. Rousseau made a world for her that turns the shapes of Clarissa's Hell into a paradigmatic but unsteady Eden.

Rousseau was as aware as Richardson was of the necessary separateness of the paragon. He knew that the beautiful soul is not only distinctive, a model to follow, but distinct as well,

singled out from all others because it has to be specially regarded. Richardson added some specific conditions to this,
and Rousseau was prompt to grasp and develop them: Clarissa
preferred to be separate as well as separated out, free in her
edifice of self as well as outstanding through her conspicuous
qualities. She felt that she could do this because she had within
herself all the sustenance that she needed, a qualification only
a paragon could have. It is, then, a condition that is possible
only to a specific figure, one of the elect. Rousseau, taking up
this counterpoint of distinct and distinctive and doing with
it what Richardson could never do, turns into practice all the
potential for autonomy Clarissa reached for but could never
realize.

La Nouvelle Héloïse is bound together by a series of shelters
or images of shelter, enclosures having all the richness and
self-sufficiency of traditional Edens. In the second part of the
novel, after Julie and Saint-Preux have become lovers but
before any resolution has been reached, Lord Bomston offers
them a home on one of his estates in England. At his place
in Yorkshire, "les environs sont solitaires, mais agréables et
variés,"[a11] the requisite Edenic river flows through the grounds,
and the yield of the land is so good that the resident has all
that he needs and more. But Bomston cannot resist pushing
his image of these pleasure-grounds toward the fabulous, turning his land into a peaceable kingdom in which lions, lambs,
and lovers shall all lie down together: "l'odieux préjugé n'a
point d'accés dans cette heureuse contrée. L'habitant paisible
y conserve encore les moeurs simples des premiers tems"
(199).[b] With an irony that needles more than it pierces, Rousseau has Bomston offer this Britannic paradise to the lovers
only after he points out how fine a refuge it would be for an
already fallen Julie: "mais si Julie pure et chaste a pourtant
succombé, comment se relevera-t-elle après sa chute?" (198).[c]
What he offers, then, is not an Eden of origin but a postlapsarian one, an end to the fall and not a beginning of it. The
meaning of Bomston's paradise establishes the meaning for
all the other comparable sites in the novel: they are all sought

after for their potential as exemplary shelters, places one comes to after a fall into experience, locales in which to rest and seek private peace. Julie picks up this point in her reply to Bomston. She acknowledges his offer but finds it insufficient since it promises legitimacy but not felicity: "Non, si vous voulez que je sois paisible et contente, donnez-moi quelque azile plus sûr encore, où l'on puisse échaper à la honte et au repentir" (208).[d] Bomston's world of gratified desire could not offer all the precise conditions necessary for Julie's self. She too needs Eden but its qualities have to be adapted to her self's own special history.

Rousseau rings other changes on the image of the autonomous refuge at several crucial points in his novel. Indeed, he carefully ensures that most of the major characters have something to say about an ideal enclosing shelter, and in each case the qualities of that shelter reveal the radical elements of desire driving and sustaining that personality. No two Edens are quite the same, though all the characters share in a compulsion for the richness and self-sufficiency of the paradisal enclosure. Rousseau builds on a kind of perspectivism, differing interpretations of the same basic figure, to open out the deeper layers of personality. In a letter to Lord Bomston in Part Four, Saint-Preux describes a place above Meillerie to which he and Julie had climbed while waiting for a boat to be repaired. Though they are surrounded by inaccessible crags, forests of black pine, and other forms of awesome natural immensities, the open spot where they stand has all the lineaments of a classical paradise. It is wooded and pleasant, with streams running among the rocks, with wild fruit trees, grass, and flowers. Saint-Preux reads the scene under the impetus of his own history and hungers: "En comparant un si doux séjour aux objects qui l'environnoient, il sembloit que ce lieu désert dut être l'azile de deux amans échappés seuls au bouleversement de la nature" (518).[e] This is not at all like that "azile plus sûr encore" that Julie wanted. There is nothing here of that deep felicity of the self she had to have. Rather, it is a place for lovers who, unlike Julie and Saint-Preux, had managed to keep themselves safe from the threats of nature—a word that, in this novel, has all sorts of interrelated meanings including, particularly, the various hungers of the body. Saint-Preux's imagined lovers are now alone in the one safe spot in the landscape. He reads the scene as he does because of all that has happened, and not happened, in the history of his life with Julie.

The most striking of all the shelters in the novel is Julie's private garden, which Saint-Preux describes to Lord Bomston in Part Four. The garden, which she calls Elysium, is close to the house but hidden from it by a covered walk.[12] Even when one is nearby the eye still cannot penetrate it because of its dense foliage; and an unwelcome intruder cannot get inside it because it is carefully locked. The world within this clandestine Eden has all that anyone needs in the way of natural surroundings, including thick shrubbery, flowers, a brook, and a variety of birds who are there only because they are content with the place. Lord Bomston's Britannic paradise was not nearly as sumptuous as this. Yet, though her Elysium is in nature it is not entirely of it. Nature has made this refuge, Julie says, but under her direction: "il n'y a rien là que je n'aye ordonné" (472).[f] Wolmar later terms her attitude *friponnerie* ("roguery") and reveals some of the secrets of Julie's guidance (479). Her exemplary refuge, it seems, has to be teased out of nature, neither imposing on it nor giving it entire freedom. Of course this is perfectly consonant with contemporary ideas about gardens and the art that conceals art; but it also shows that a full and various content is so necessary to Julie's idea of a private enclosure that she will step in to make certain that it appears. The garden is a complete and integrated whole, as replete with diversity as Eden is supposed to be. Thus, when Saint-Preux says of Julie that "la paix regne au fond de son coeur comme dans l'azile qu'elle a nommé" (487)[g] the reader can pass by the surface sentimentality because underlying it is a profound image of the beautiful soul as a paradisal enclosure, well stocked, willingly cut off and thoroughly self-sustaining.[13] Still, it is Julie as Mme. de Wol-

mar who has created this Elysium. It has become possible for
her only with her marriage, and is identifiable with herself
only at that stage in its history. Saint-Preux shows his awareness of that distinction in a letter to Julie toward the end of
the novel. Responding to her suggestion that he think seriously
of Claire as a wife, Saint-Preux replies that he is still in love
with a woman who no longer exists, the old Julie, and that
Mme. de Wolmar is his best refuge against their old selves:
"Quand cette redoutable Julie me poursuit, je me réfugie
auprès de Madame de Wolmar et je suis tranquille; où fuirai-
je si cet azile m'est ôté?" (677).[h] It is only when Julie owns
an *azile* that she can become one for others. The seclusion
Elysium affords her sustains her position as a paragon.

Yet her garden, however autonomous its order, is a paradise
in a community. The situation of Julie's Elysium of the self
is much like that of the closet paradise Richardson had proposed for middle-class ladies. In each case the home for the
self is a private enclosure within a larger one, the latter not
a visible but a social shelter.[14] In Rousseau's novel the enclosure is part of the ménage created by Julie's husband to accommodate his interests and in particular to give shape to the
only passion of which he is capable, a love of order and
balance (cf. 490-91). Lord Bomston, a friendly outsider, describes it as a society of privileged souls. It is, in effect, an
Eden of the elect, those elegant selves who need only each
other to arrive at a stability and completeness unobtainable
in any ordinary form of communal order. A just combination
of the right people will make it completely autonomous. Here
is Saint-Preux inviting Bomston there to spend the winter:

> O quel hiver nous alons passer tous ensemble, si l'espoir de
> notre réunion ne m'abuse pas! Chaque jour la prépare en
> ramenant ici quelqu'une de ces ames privilégiées qui sont
> si cheres l'une à l'autre, qui sont si dignes de s'aimer, et qui
> semblent n'attendre que vous pour se passer du reste de
> l'univers. (597)[i]

Separated from the great world though not antagonistic to it,

Wolmar's ménage is neither social nor antisocial but para-social. It is a surrogate structure, competitive with society but only as models of differing possibilities are competitive. The ménage is a private, self-occupied prescription for the ills of society that is not part of society but parallel to it, a condition that permits Wolmar his favorite status of the dispassionate but well-disposed observer. His perfect community searches within itself for symmetry and moderation, a self-sustaining harmony of needs and capabilities. The community derives its tone from that level of intensity of experience compatible with "une ame saine, un coeur libre du trouble des passions"(470).ʲ Obviously, only individuals possessing those qualities will be invited inside.

And indeed it is the presence of those qualities that makes Wolmar's ménage homologous with Julie's Elysium, an echo not only in form but in the desired mode. In Elysium natural energy is brought together with the human impulse for order, and this is done in such a way that those energies are subordinated to the desires of mind. Elysium is a compromise in which nature, though it never ceases being itself, is eased into satisfying the needs of man as well as its own. The garden, which offers an image of natural freedom, has in fact been carefully structured to give nature a liberty compatible with a system benefiting all its participants. Elysium is not, however, merely a fiction of freedom. It does not restrict all of nature but only its fullest license, the sort which could threaten that equilibrium of forces and interests that gives harmony to the whole. It is a perfect, self-sustaining marriage of mind and nature. It does not signal a capitulation but an adjustment. The ménage, too, is a marriage of the orderliness of mind with the energies of nature. "Nature" in this novel covers a broad spectrum of meanings, one of the most potent being, as I have indicated, sexual passion.[15] In fact, though, the term enfolds all those impulses that urge the self toward free and individual expression, that openness of gesture that reveals the self's compulsion to externalize its desires. Some of those desires are compatible with an order of the sort that Wolmar wants:

the free-flowing sociability of the participants is described in a number of letters, the landscape is there to be encountered by sensibility, children are loved, work (not too laborious) is undertaken as much for its joy as for its results. Other passions, those that trouble the heart and make the soul unhealthy, are not so cooperative. These are weeded out of the system. Their potential for the destruction of familial order is too well known to all the inhabitants, both to those who had participated in Julie's earlier life and those who had heard about it later. It is only with the subjugation of those disordering passions that Julie could be certain to have the "azile plus sûr encore" she had spoken of to Lord Bomston when she refused his offer of a haven in England. Thus, nature in the ménage is not required to capitulate but to adjust, a compromise of precisely the kind Julie achieved in Elysium. It seems that autonomy, a full and self-sustaining freedom, is possible only when the mind sublimates the energies of nature into sane and productive channels. Both Wolmar and Julie have succeeded in accommodating consciousness to the necessarily other, and the result is a set of enclosures that come as close to the paradisal as postlapsarian bourgeois can make them. Of course there is a sense in which this need to compromise is not Wolmar's problem but that of the other inhabitants. He is, after all, the man of no passion, and therefore those unhealthy impulses are no challenge to him. This means that the ménage is as much an image of Wolmar's self as Julie's Elysium is of her own. Saint-Preux had commented on the analogy of Julie's soul to her garden. She makes the same point about her husband and his household with equal specificity. "L'ordre qu'il a mis dans sa maison est l'image de celui qui regne au fond de son ame, et semble imiter dans un petit ménage l'ordre établi dans le gouvernement du monde" (371).[k] Wolmar's *azile* is the objectification of the autonomy he wants for himself, with all the appropriate content. As Julie puts it, the ménage is Wolmar's paradise in this world, and they ought to do all that they can to make him happy within it (594).

As for Julie herself, it seems as though she has achieved that contextual autonomy, the accommodation of consciousness and the other, which Clarissa looked for but could never bring about. Julie's Elysium, like the self it images, is a fine and private place. Saint-Preux compares it to newly discovered South Sea islands (471). It is a sanctuary within a shelter and therefore a kind of cynosure: in this paradise of the elect one inhabitant is more elect than the others, for only Julie has that special, privileged insularity that permits a retreat within a refuge. The conditions of her Elysium allow for both distinction and privacy. She, as all other paragons, must be visibly differentiated from everyone else, if it can be so arranged. It is as though those who surround a paragon of whatever sort need a visual metaphor for the paragon's distinctiveness, a graphic acknowledgment of his or her separateness from others as a perfect representative of desired values. And of course such separateness implies that the paragon is autonomous as well as exemplary: the very act of circumscription not only sets the paragon off but builds a world for this model figure that is necessarily self-contained. Julie's *hortus conclusus* draws not only from the tradition of enclosed gardens but also from the variety of special locations that figures of distinction, from kings to hermits, so often inhabit.

One of the tenser threads Rousseau weaves into this intricate web has to do with Saint-Preux's own uniqueness. At several points Lord Bomston indicates that it is both Julie and Saint-Preux who are the exemplary figures, "ames d'une certaine trempe" (204).[1] But as both Richardson and Rousseau came to recognize, there can be a cost to such perceptible centrality. Lovelace is provoked to violence in part because an attack upon a paragon would violate the best in women. Nothing less than such a revenge would make up for the slight one woman had given him. As for Saint-Preux, he learned early what it means to be among the elect of sensibility, distinguished, as Julie asserts, for his ability to sustain grand passions (209). Few others can feel what he does, an ambiguous gift that can lead to both pain and—in his and subsequent cases—occasional bathos: "O Julie, que c'est un fatal présent du ciel qu'une ame sensible!" (89).[m] The difference between Saint-Preux and Julie in the latter half of the novel is that she has found a new mode of exemplariness, which draws admiration from all, while he remains pretty much in his old ways, though greatly tamed. Saint-Preux's separateness is like that of the poet at the end of *Kubla Khan,* who has to be put inside a magic circle to render him harmless. The special values represented by such figures are as unnerving as they are distinctive. In Saint-Preux one finds the seed of all those ambivalent romantic pariahs whose autonomy was both willed and enforced, self-generated and compelled by a system that found them beyond absorption—though neither the system nor the elect could quite leave the other alone.

It appears, however, that Julie's *locus amoenus* has enabled her to evade the cost. Doubly ensconced, tucked (when she wills) into an insular enclave whose access she controls, Julie has guided the shaping of a *hortus conclusus* that offers all she asks of it. It is different from the traditional enclosed garden because it is not only an image of the sequestered self but also an acknowledgment that, with the world as it is, a self such as hers may well need sequestration. Her Elysium is therefore both a sign of her distinctiveness and a recognition that her own kind of eminence needs protection as well as display. Here, precisely, is the beginning of a major romantic version of the paradisal enclosure, one that has ambivalence as its radical tone because of the varying causes for the separateness, the varying desires for which it seeks satisfaction.

Thus, Julie has worked out a version of what Clarissa sought, but she did so with a combination of ancient tropes and natural shapes that neither Clarissa nor her creator would have chosen to imagine.[16] Julie's *azile* has many of the properties of traditional Edens. The Miltonic model, itself an invention from classical tropes and forebears, is an "enclosed green" to which "access [is] deni'd," a sort of fortress-paradise that has "in narrow room Nature's whole wealth" (IV, 133, 137, 207). These are also characteristics of the Elysium near

Clarens. But the immediate context of Julie's enclave involves contemporary aristocratic gardens and, most of all, an essentially new meaning given to the impulses generated by topography.

Yet there is more here than even these variations of source and tone. Julie's Elysium has far more autonomy about it than Clarissa would have wanted, because it is further out of society than her love of social forms could have tolerated. The difference is in the structure of the encompassing context: for Clarissa it is society itself, for Julie it is a tangential order parallel to society. Rousseau has continued Richardson's anatomy of contextuality but he has so different a view of the situation that he reverses Richardson's conclusion. He keeps up the paragon's urge for self-sufficiency within an enlightened framework, but changes the framework just enough to make the mode of that self-sufficiency something new in the world. Each of these novels is a fable of mind seeking to accommodate itself to the givens of bourgeois society; yet they put very different constructions on the relations among self, society, and value because they offer differing contexts within which to find a place for the sequestered self. That place, the enclosure of consciousness and private value, is far more discrete in Rousseau, protected from confrontation by a layer of insulation that is itself free from the necessity of perpetual engagement with society's order. Julie's enclosure is at several removes from the great world, Clarissa's only one; a slight difference with momentous implications.

This, finally, is Rousseau's antidote to Richardson's tragedy of the paragon. It is also the reason why the enclosure of consciousness becomes the subject of one of Rousseau's ultimate ironies, a revealing twist to the consequences of the Richardsonian world. All of the shelters that image the autonomous consciousness in Rousseau's novel are counterparts, but as mirror images, of Clarissa's various confinements. The series of incarcerations in Richardson's novel become a series of asylums in Rousseau's, enclosures that are Edens rather than prisons. Rousseau continues Richardson but inverts him, echoing the inner structures of Richardson's novel but in a mode that is parodic rather than reverent. Wolmar's paradise may be only in this world but it is a paradise all the same, and a home for Julie's private Elysium. The order of Richardson's novel offered only a private system of Hell.

Still, Rousseau cannot leave this situation alone. If he is careful to map out the conditions that make possible an autonomy for the elect—that is, for *his* kind of elect—he leaves behind some signals of hesitancy, gestures that serve to qualify his model for Eden though they do not quite undercut it. If he is ironic toward Richardson he is more surreptitiously ironic toward himself, because he remembers not only how Richardson failed to make a paradise for his elect but also why that taste for paradise turned sour. Echoes of Richardson's shrill claustrophobia appear quietly but precisely at several points in Rousseau's novel, disclosing a subliminal uneasiness with all those enclosures that spell out a self-sustaining perfection. Julie's Elysium, the most graphic of these Edens, offers the most visible instance: when Saint-Preux first goes inside her garden for a visit, the door disappears, and the way out is as invisible as the entrance had been; but then he has Julie to show him how to get back to the world she shares with others. Yet she cannot so easily help herself out of the shelter that encompasses her Eden, that is, her husband's ménage. It is Wolmar's paradise but not quite her own, though she says that it contains all she will ever need in this world (689). She has her husband, a legitimate lover who is responsive to social symmetry but not to religion, the landscape, or any of the potential disharmonies of active passion (see 591-92). His ménage is set up to keep their souls free from such irregularities. Julie also has her former lover, who cannot touch her but is there to remind her of what had once been, and is still so elsewhere. In a pattern that is echoed in Goethe's Lotte, she shares her family life with the one and her sensibility with the other, a compromise that would appear to promise completeness if not bliss.

The ménage, then, has still another function to fulfill. It

emphasizes consonance, a system of harmonious relationships within the self, and between the self and the social order. For Julie and the others it offers a condition in which all the various roles that one wants to take can be taken, since even roles that are very different from each other could not—within Wolmar's system—come into unsettling conflict. In her earlier life there had been no consistent accord among roles. Julie as daughter had found easy compatibility between the different values of self and society. Julie as lover had brought into the household a countervailing system of values which could in no way be reconciled with her earlier function. The result was a fracturing of the self. Neither role could be played out without a deadly cost to the other; yet her need, simply, was to choose between those costs. The consequence was a division of the self so similar in kind (if not in extent) to that of Clarissa that their situations tell a good deal about the ambiguities in the bourgeois attitude toward the paragon. As it turns out, the exemplary figure is subject to a severely limited freedom, simply because she is exemplary. The paragon in society is more restricted than her audience, less able to move easily among roles, subordinate to more insistent demands upon herself than she makes—through her exemplariness—upon the social order. When that enforced conformity is violated (Clarissa's escape from home, Julie's affair), the cost is immediately evident, and it is always to the paragon's autonomy. (Clarissa's various imprisonments take on an especially complex import at this point.) A transgression of the givens of a role threatened to shatter the self's earned order, jeopardizing the independent system of the self.

The result, if there is to be survival at all, is a requisite shift in roles. In Clarissa's case her flight from the familial enclosure led to the collapse of her role as paragon, and that change led inevitably, if not inexorably, to the change in her status as virgin and the role that went with it. As has often been pointed out, she became damaged goods in a society where the values of commerce determined the commerce among values. In effect the internal and external revolution, which came close to destroying Clarissa, did away with many of the faces with which she greeted the world. She was led into a different pattern of roles by her own stubborn will and the help of her Heavenly Father. The counterpart who helped Julie shape a new system of values was also a father figure. Wolmar, who is presented throughout as a paternal surrogate, had put her together again, a point of which she is fully aware: "ce lien si redouté me delivre d'une servitude beaucoup plus redoutable, et mon époux m'en devient plus cher pour m'avoir rendue à moi-même" (364-65; cf. 665).[n] In giving her back to herself Wolmar also gives a self back to her. In his ménage she can safely assume an assortment of roles—mother, lover, friendly exlover—because her surroundings offer a calculated antidote to every form of divisiveness. Since it is self-contained and self-sustaining, and a spiritually, if not literally, fully enclosed structure, the ménage is an image of perfect wholeness, and that wholeness will be reflected in its inhabitants. It consciously selects passions so as to leave no opportunity for fractures within or without. Thus, Julie can be both free and exemplary because the flexibility and totality of her selfhood are guaranteed by the peculiar order of Wolmar's world. This is one of the essential modes through which the ménage offers an antidote to the pressures of society. It is designed, in great part, to be less ambivalent than society is about the likes of Julie.

But that is not, it seems, nearly enough. If Wolmar's paradise is only of this world, Julie makes clear to Saint-Preux that her own paradise is yet to come, that Wolmar's cold secularity frees her from the destructiveness of sentiment but not from a wish that he would share in its warmth. Saint-Preux makes that point indirectly to Lord Bomston: "On diroit que rien de terrestre ne pouvant suffire au besoin d'aimer dont elle est dévorée, cet excès de sensibilité soit forcé de remonter à sa source" (589-90).[o] Julie's ambivalence is controlled but clear. The more she lives in Wolmar's perfect society the more otherworldly she becomes.

Yet that is still not the final tale that Rousseau tells of his

Eden. He will not let us rest but toys continually with our complacency, compelling us to keep adjusting our views of Julie and her situation. In her last letter to Saint-Preux Julie confesses that the proximity of her former lover had unsettled her stability, that perhaps one day more would have put Wolmar's harmony into permanent disrepair (740 ff.). Her death, she implies, is not robbery but preservation, a fixing into permanence of the honor she now values above all else. Julie had once been among the elect of sensibility, so extraordinary that, as Lord Bomston put it, neither she nor Saint-Preux could be judged by ordinary standards (165). She is now, for those around her, a paragon of spirituality. But that final letter shows that the early paragon is still there inside the later one, and her Eden is not flexible enough to harmonize such conflicting achievements. Julie's selfhood was more unified than she had suspected. The later additions to her personality were accretions, not substitutions. All that she had ever been was still within her as part of a complex that extended further back into her history than she wanted or believed. Her final letter is therefore an ironic rebuttal to Saint-Preux's insistence on the pastness of their old selves as well as his remark that he uses Mme. de Wolmar as his shelter from the old Julie. Here Julie's enclave establishes an essential dilemma for the romantics who were to follow: one may well bring inside the paradisal enclosure some illusions about the self which can turn the enclosure into a trap.

At this point some basic differences between Richardson and Rousseau begin to emerge, and they reveal how, though Clarissa was a necessary step toward Julie, she could not show the way toward subsequent romantic developments. In Rousseau there is nothing like the Manichaean dichotomy of angel and devil, which gives the substance of fable to Richardson's novel. Lovelace, it seems, is most aware of the dichotomy and its attendant imagery: he plays often with the idea of Clarissa as an angel of light and himself as a prince of darkness. But there is more, because Lovelace is also a power-figure, the agent of the profound feeling in Richardson that sexuality is associated with sadism, violence, and a potential for ultimate destruction. The novel shows that Clarissa's fears are not only her own, that Richardson's notorious prurience is interwoven with his deep uneasiness about what he has seen of a capacity for savagery within the self. When this uneasiness is combined with the Manichaeanism and the types who embody it, Richardson takes his place at the head of a line that culminates in Sade and the Gothic novelists. That combination is also the essential element that ties Richardson's bourgeois realism into traditional forms of the romance.

In *La Nouvelle Héloïse* there is no Manichaean myth, no opposing power-figure who threatens the exemplary female, no sense anywhere of a field for variegated cruelty. Further—and in perfect correlation—there is no fear that sexuality can extinguish the self, or that there are all sorts of thorns in the marriage bed. The major threat to the self in Rousseau's novel comes from within, which makes for a very different myth and a very different reading of the order and energies of the self. Lovelace is the serpent who entices Clarissa from the parental garden; but the serpent in Julie's world is her own refusal to admit what the novel makes eminently clear, that sensuality and sensuousness are too close to permit even the most guarded association. Her enclosure of the self cannot protect Julie from herself. Clarissa never faced such dangers. Indeed, from the time of her rape she knows that the only place where she is beyond attack is the subjective enclave she retains and strengthens in preparation for her death. Julie is not nearly so secure: though she may serve as an *azile* for Saint-Preux, she has carried a wily snake into her paradise within, and the pierce of its bite is inescapable.

The potential for a disorder of the self was always there in Saint-Preux, but it was brought under relative control, mainly through Wolmar's direction. Julie shares this same potential, though only she knows that. The intensity that made Julie and Saint-Preux a breed of the elect also made them more vulnerable to imbalance. The opposite was true for Clarissa. Julie found that no forms for the inner life could contain the war among her various modes of excellence. The result was a radical ambivalence, which became the dominant tone in most romantic versions of the paradisal enclosure. Together with her former lover Julie shows how the struggle for the self was fully internalized, how the threats were deprived of their viciousness but not their danger, how the paradisal enclosure could be too rich and fertile, with more in it than one would willingly have. Internalization bred joy and uneasiness, and together they bred figures as diverse as Werther and Julien Sorel, a distinctive and disturbing progeny. These two and Rousseau's pair of lovers shared in the same unpromising delusion: they were convinced that, however different they felt themselves to be, they were still insiders, capable of participating without hindrance in the order of values that gave society its legitimacy and moral efficacy. Their delusion is an essential part of the literary and moral history of their time.

At the end of his novel, with an ironic sense of the insufficiency of all Edens, Rousseau returns to Richardson, aware that in these terminal acts the heroines share in an ultimate gesture. There is only one possible relief from Julie's ambivalence, and she accepts it with melancholy and comfort. Like Clarissa, she finds her way out of all the inadequate enclosures only with death. Here, finally, the movements of both books can be seen as a whole, and their relationship is revealed as an elaborate interplay. Claire's words in speaking of Julie's tomb—they are nearly the last words of the book—put the point with sufficient, if sentimental, irony: "beauté, c'est donc là ton dernier azile" (745).[p] Richardson and Rousseau built on the same elemental narrative, a quest for forms of shelter for the self which would acknowledge the self's contextual autonomy. The quest ended with a shelter found but with the self no longer there.

TWO

Places for the Mind

Lovelace's references to himself as Satanic are a complex bit of self-examination; that is, though they are sometimes blunt, they are more than facile allusions designed to draw simple responses. He is aware of his position as society's grand antagonist (he could never be a little one), of his role as Clarissa's mirror image, and, finally, of himself as self-sufficient arbiter of contrary moral laws. We have seen that Lovelace, like Milton's God, chooses to be his own context. Though he would never say of himself, as Adam did of God, that he is perfect in himself, he would not admit, as Adam did, that singleness is a human deficiency "which requires / Collateral love, and dearest amity" (VIII, 425-26). Of course, as we have seen, Clarissa herself could not accept that argument, but in her case she was single in company with her God while Lovelace (like God *and* Satan) wants no other support than what he can draw from within. He is most like the Satanic predecessor in this intricate pairing of autonomy and antagonism, a combination whose influence was to be as massive as it was self-destructive. Satan had been there before him, and with an equal degree of ambivalence.

Milton isolated and identified what came to be seen as a predominant form of autonomous selfhood. But the history of Satanic autonomy in *Paradise Lost* is itself so tense and complex, with Satan asserting and recanting in rapid sequence, that the main result which emerges from that history is an understanding of Satan's great pain. Still, we can see stages in Satan's arguments for independence, and if the arguments are inconclusive the stages show what most matters to him.

Satan's meditations on what the mind can do never go into detail on how it brings about its achievements. He is so busy asserting his power that he never shows his capacity for autonomy in action; and of course he could never really show it because the freedom he claims is actually quite inadequate, unable to change the Hell within or to help him flee from it. That insufficiency becomes evident during the progress of his meditations. His arguments for the mind's self-generated morality had been prefigured by an impudent, outrageous assertion that he threw out to Abdiel during the early stages of the war in Heaven. Standing before the third of Heaven that chose to follow him, Satan contends that they are all autogenetic: in his words, "self-begot, self-rais'd / By our own quick'ning power" (V, 860-61). This assertion of autogeny is obviously about as far as a claim for autonomy can go, and Satan toys with it for a while. But the enforced self-examination he went through on the burning lake seems to have weakened his claim of literal self-generation, though the result is not apparent until he first comes into sight of Eden. There he recants the assertion of autogeny: "he deserv'd no such return / From me, whom he created what I was / In that bright eminence" (IV, 42-44). Yet that acknowledgment of God's supreme creativity is still not Satan's final position on the matter. When he returns to Eden in Book Nine (the symmetry is neat and nasty) Satan takes back his recantation just enough to leave it ambiguous. That is the point in the text where he reveals the hateful war of contraries within himself. Clearly this admission of agony is a bad time for Satan, yet he has to pull himself out of it at once in order to accomplish his serpentine business. As he works his way through the despair of this bitter declaration Satan envisions the triumphs in store for him, lies to himself about the number of angels he had "freed from servitude inglorious" (140-41), and then speaks of God's creation of angels, "if they at least / Are his created" (146-47). That last remark is a bit of self-serving bravado, a necessary, self-induced boost for his courage as he prepares to undertake the temptation of Eve. Of course this is brazen and deceptive but it is self-deceptive; it is the language of public rhetoric but it is entirely self-directed. Satan's turn for support to a hazy, hesitant version of his former claim of autogeny reveals its radical importance for him. Now more than ever, after a climactic moment when he stared into the darkness within himself, Satan needs at least the possibility that they are all, in fact, self-created, independent from their very beginnings. Autonomy had always been, for Satan, a crucial factor in the process of self-support and self-definition.

That is why his meditations on autonomy turn up regularly at points of crisis. Immediately after his fall, Satan experimented with a line of argument about the indestructibility of angelic essence, and his thoughts there may well have been the basis for his grandest claim for autonomy, the argument about the mind as its own place, made just two hundred lines later. With Beëlzebub as his audience he states that, though the fallen angels are now cast down, their divine strength and empyreal substance cannot be destroyed and will therefore quicken again shortly. As Beëlzebub puts it, "the mind and spirit remains / Invincible, and vigor soon returns" (I, 139-40). From that point about the invulnerability of mind it is only a step, in Satanic logic, to the position that the indestructible mind is not only too potent to be subject to place and time but that it can control the felt qualities of the inner life; and Satan takes that step in the argument almost immediately. But if his case for the permanence of angelic substance is the first step in his claim for moral freedom, then the shape of his argument for autonomy is radically faulty: he turns a technical statement about the immortal vigor of empyreal substance into a declaration of the mind's moral strength and absolute independence, and that is an intolerable leap in logic.[1] The inadequacy of his assertions was soon apparent, for it took only one distant glimpse of Eden to collapse Satan's claim for moral sovereignty into a recognition of the subjective Hell that he has to live. His essence is surely indestructible but his Hell is equally unavoidable. It faces him whether he is staring within or without: "Which way I fly is

Hell; myself am Hell" (IV, 75). Satan's boast about the strength of his subjective life is not only proven to be accurate but it is turned in upon himself with bitter confirmation. His inner world is shown to be as commanding and effective as he had claimed, and he is the object of its effectiveness. Indeed, the superiority of the mind to place, one of the most telling points in his assertion of autonomy, is demonstrated upon himself: "for within him Hell / He brings, and round about him, nor from Hell / One step no more than from himself can fly / By change of place" (IV, 20-23). Satan becomes the victim of his fierce inner life, which has the power to make him miserable about what he is lacking and what he has become. During the debate preceding the war in Heaven Abdiel said scornfully to Satan that the rebel Angel was "thyself not free but to thyself enthralled" (VI, 181). It is not long after his fall that Satan realizes the truth of that sneer, though his awareness is sometimes submerged in bursts of bitter vanity. His state is not characterized by self-sufficiency but by self-servitude. If his boast is ironically correct about the potency of his subjectivity, it is painfully wrong about his ability to control that potency in grim and aggressive independence. That was true even in Heaven, which his vanity had made a place of intolerable discomfort for him. In the second half of his central assertion Satan claimed that the mind can make a Hell out of Heaven. In arguing for subjective independence Satan pits the literal against the psychological, subordination and service against the mind's self-subsistence, the realities of the external world against the tone of the inner life. All that would seem to make sense when he speaks of turning Hell into Heaven; but why should he want to choose the opposite and make Heaven hellish? In fact such a decision would have been mindless, had he been led to make it. Satan chose evil to be his moral mode for what seemed to him to be very good reasons, but he would never have chosen to be miserable. When Heaven became hellish for him that was not an instance of the power of mind over place but of the inexorable effects of place upon mind.

His selection of evil has an equally complex motivation, and his view of it is equally self-deceptive. Satan's assertion that the mind is its own place occurs while he is down on the burning lake, just after the fall recorded in Book One. It follows his acknowledgment of God's superiority in power and precedes his choice of evil (in Book Four) as the moral mode through which he will work. Thus, the sequence takes in, in order, the recognition of compulsion, the assertion of autonomy, the moral choice; i.e., I am pushed; but I am free; therefore I shall choose evil. If there is illogic here too (there is an enormous gap between steps two and three), we can be helped by Hazlitt's recognition of the dominance of power in Satan's personality, dominant even over "the abstract love of evil."[2] Just after his fall, when he begins to examine the conditions of his new state, Satan is concerned primarily with opposition, with his stance as Adversary: "To do aught good never will be our task, / But ever to do ill our sole delight, / As being the contrary to his high will / Whom we resist" (I, 159-62). As he works over the problems of his role the attitude of contrariety takes on a great deal of significance in itself, simply as an act of resistance. A similar pattern occurs in Book Four. Satan's despair, which is both an instigator and a product of his opposition, leads him to recognize that "all Good to [him] is lost" (109). Since submission is unthinkable he can embrace either lethargy or evil. In the great council in Book Two, when the fallen angels went over the various schemes for their future, Belial argued smoothly for "ignoble ease, and peaceful sloth" (227); but Satan, ambitious and driven, rejected lassitude. His will to independence would permit no luxurious isolation in the mind's own places. As it turns out, however, his options for action are decidedly limited. When he finally chooses evil, in Book Four, he makes clear that he does so, first, because that is all that is left and, second, because the choice will give him some ascendancy in the universe of things: "Evil be thou my Good; by thee at least / Divided Empire with Heav'n's King I hold / By thee, and more than half perhaps will reign" (110-12). Thus, his choice of evil is in great part a matter of power and stance, having to do with his compulsion to oppose and with the given moral qualities of God's creation. Contrariety is a primary good for Satan, one which exists prior to the choice of any other good. Satan's value system has to be the opposite of God's, all that God's is not. In effect this means that his values are inseparable from those of his opponent, that they do not express his freedom but his subservience. His autonomy is compromised because it is his Rival who sets the conditions, determining the rules of the game. Satan is finally only a follower, dependent for his values upon those of his Predecessor. Once he chooses to be the Adversary there are no other choices to be made.

The result of all these paradoxes and flimsy self-deceptions is a buildup of subjective pressures, and they become so intense that they, and not his mind, take over the guidance of crucial actions. When he returns to Eden in Book Nine, the sight of good is odious to him, not only because he cannot have what has been granted to inferior creatures, but also because what he sees intensifies, by contrast, all the misery he is going through. His attempts to destroy good are now not only willed acts of war, the product of opposition, but the compulsive gestures of one who is under intolerable tension: "For only in destroying I find ease / To my relentless thoughts" (129-30). His antagonism to good has become, in part, a matter of relief. In his previous attacks upon good he had been subservient to God's moral universe without knowing it. Now he is equally beholden to the war of contraries within himself, the special agonies that had grown up as he saw the nature of God's Nature. In seeking to subordinate good, Satan has made himself his own prisoner.

Milton had already touched briefly on the possibility of the prison of consciousness in *Comus*: "He that has light within his own clear breast / May sit i'th' center, and enjoy bright day, / But he that hides a dark soul and foul thoughts / Benighted walks under the midday Sun; / Himself is his own dungeon" (381-85).[3] The image appears again, with other kinds of darkness around it, in the words of the Chorus looking on at the hero in *Samson Agonistes*: "Thou art become (O worst imprisonment!) / The Dungeon of thyself; thy Soul / (Which Men enjoying sight oft without cause complain) / Imprison'd now indeed" (155-58).[4] Satan's case is a bitter double of these situations, and he shows paradigmatically the most ironic way they can come about. When he insisted that the locus of reward and punishment was to be found only within the confines of one's being, he opened the possibility that those confines could turn into a prison, that the self would become captive to its own self-hatred. This prison house of the self would then be a precise and cruel counterpart of the paradisal enclosure whose sight so sickened him, the enclosure which, after the Fall and the promise of a Paradise within, also became part of the self's potential. Later, for the romantics and their successors, the chance of subjective entrapment and the opportunity for a Paradise within would not be the fate of separate beings, as they were in Milton, but would be equally potential within the same enclosure of self. The history of subsequent quests for autonomy is, in an important sense, the working out of those warring possibilities. For Satan, though, there was only the chance of a self-induced incarceration.

The example of Satan ought to have suggested to his imitators that autonomy and the urge for combat cannot live comfortably together. Others seemed to be aware of that possibility, Rousseau most prominently so. In the *Confessions* and the *Rêveries* he established a mode of the autonomous consciousness that was as definitive of a kind as the one Satan promoted, but with the considerable difference that Rousseau's kind frequently worked, for himself and others, and Satan's generally did not. Such success may have been the result of fortuitous circumstances or of the conditions Rousseau demanded. In any case, the order of autonomy exemplified by Rousseau is in many ways the mirror image and necessary complement of the one established by his Satanic forebear. Certainly it was equally as compulsive, resulting in far more than the ambiguous instance of Julie's *azile*. There are explorations of self-sufficiency running through Rousseau's work from beginning to end, from his arguments about the independence of primitives in the second *Discourse* to the imagery of the self-contained consciousness at the end of the *Confessions* and in several of the *Rêveries*.[5] Every example has the same set of characteristics: limited desires in a small space. The mind can build beautifully and with perfect success if it learns to eject and cut off, to bring within a tiny, circumscribed area all of the things that it needs.

Rousseau guessed that principle immediately. The stupid and peaceful savage he established as an ambiguous paragon is peaceful precisely because his wants are easily satisfied, if not from one tree then from the next. Still, this is not an earned self-sufficiency but a found one, and the ease with which it operates dovetails only too neatly with the savage's minuscule capacities of consciousness. One cannot speak of the adequacy of the savage's imagination or of the dangerous teasings of his self-awareness because, as Rousseau describes the most primitive man, there is no imagination and little consciousness at play in him: "Ses modiques besoins se trouvent si aisément sous sa main, et il est si loin du degré de connoissances nécessaire pour désirer d'en acquérir de plus grandes, qu'il ne peut avoir ni prévoyance, ni curiosité."[a] [6] He is capable of compassion, perhaps his only positive response to experience aside from the usual hungers; but that is so far prior to reflection that he shares the capacity with horses and cattle.[7] If he has no thought of the future it is not because he prefers, as Rousseau finally did, to live in a timeless moment but because all he has ever needed is available in the immediate present. His is the fortuitous autonomy of a lucky animal, not that of a compulsive loner who has earned his independence from place and time by cultivating the processes of his subjectivity. There is self-subsistence in both, and there is no question that the savage state reflects some of Rousseau's most profound desires for himself; but the qualities of self-subsistence in each could not be precisely the same.

These difficulties in regard to the savage model stem in part from Rousseau's odd but extraordinarily influential blending of self-consciousness and didacticism. Amiel's statement that Rousseau's views are "la généralisation de son moi" holds a considerable measure of truth.[b][8] Rousseau argued frequently that self-understanding was human understanding, that the contemplation of his own selfhood could tell him a great deal about the nature of man. This proponent of the idiosyncratic personality felt that he could comprehend others and show them what they themselves were like by examining the most secluded intricacies of his own being. He makes that last point specifically in a draft of the introductory pages of the *Confessions*: "je veux tâcher que pour apprendre à s'apprecier, on puisse avoir du moins une piéce de comparaison; que chacun puisse connoitre soi et un autre, et cet autre ce sera moi."[c][9] Further, in his third *Dialogue* he insists that the model for the savage described in the second *Discourse* came out of his intuition of the contours of his own subjective life: "Il l'a décrite comme il se sentoit lui-même."[d][10] In these and similar cases Rousseau offers his own self as the ultimate source of knowledge, sometimes because a man needs to show others what one of their fellows can be like, sometimes because he feels that he is himself a particularly good example of what elemental man must have been like. In one way or another, then, he projects out of the recesses of his own being the paradigms he sets up throughout his work. That identity of source should give them at least a family likeness; and in fact it does give them that, but no more. The primitive self-sufficiency Rousseau delineates in the second *Discourse* is very different in mode and possibility from the forms of autonomy described in *La Nouvelle Héloïse* or in the series of intensely private events in the *Confessions* and the *Rêveries*. His views on the primitive come out of the same general area as these others, covering the same pervasive obsession with self-sufficiency; but the worlds of the *Discourses, La Nouvelle Héloïse,* and the autobiographical writings examine the self from so broad an assortment of perspectives that they cannot possibly make precisely the same demands upon it. There are different kinds of complexity at play in the jungles and in Julie's Elysium. And in the case of the savage referred to in the third *Dialogue* there is an element of transparent duplicity involved. When Rousseau speaks of the sources of his savage model, he is in fact arguing cannily for his own radical innocence, stressing his own unspoiled purity underneath all the layers of the civilized ego. His attempts at self-justification ought not to tempt us into sentimental equations. Rousseau's primitive could not possibly have experienced what Rousseau himself did on the island of Saint-Pierre.

Rousseau was far more subtle with himself than he was with the savage, aware not only that his finely honed capacity for soul making was the prime mover of his own autonomy, but that his mind found its most complete satisfaction in watching itself at work. He was both a student of subjective processes and a contemplator of Being (his own segment of it in particular, but the world's as well). This combination meant that he was often a witness of the processes of his own contemplation, observing himself as he led himself into the recesses of Being. Much of Rousseau's work, even the studies of politics and education, has to do with a compulsion for the inspection of self that seems to have possessed him at least from his thirties, when he began his most significant writing. His various statements about the need to generalize self-understanding into the understanding of man are a sufficient signal that it is not only his overtly autobiographical writing that is concerned with the examination of self. Yet there is nothing in his work more lucid and vivid about these matters than the exploration of subjective processes that he wrote up, near the end of his life, in the *Rêveries du Promeneur Solitaire*. These autobiographical essays are his final instruments of self-analysis, continuing and raising to its purest state the anatomy of self-awareness he had carried on through the *Confessions* and the *Dialogues*. The earlier works had already set down some of the qualities of tone and even several of the incidents taken up in the *Rêveries*. But the special contribution of these last lyrical pieces lies in their exploration of the possibilities for an autonomous consciousness within the circumstances of contemporary life.[11]

At the exact center of the essays as we now have them, that is, in the middle of the *Cinquième Promenade*, there is an extraordinary delineation of one of the purest modes of the autonomous consciousness. In the essays that precede it Rousseau builds carefully toward his analysis of that state, establishing the conditions that help to shape it, showing what was not quite like the experience as well as what the experience itself was like. The most startling of these steps toward the understanding of the purest state is the product of a misstep, described in the *Deuxième Promenade*. Rousseau had been out on one of his walks when he was struck down by a Great Dane who had been running in front of a carriage. He hit his jaw on a rough paving stone and knocked himself unconscious. His awakening was Adamic. He was new and just barely there: "J'apperçus le ciel, quelques étoiles, et un peu de verdure. Cette prémiére sensation fut un moment délicieux. Je ne me sentois encor que par là. Je naissois dans cet instant à la vie."[e 12] That which ties him to the world is the slimmest of contacts, a primary moment of perception, which—because it is pristine and pure, without context or history—is fully delicious. Further, there is no distinction of self and other for this newly emergent consciousness. The small world he inhabits is not only the object of consciousness but its locale as well. This is a place where consciousness takes over, and which is infused so thoroughly by it that what he sees is, finally, only more of himself: "il me sembloit que je remplissois de ma legere existence tous les objets que j'appercevois."[f] It is not, then, a matter of establishing continuities between self and other but of finding a precise and discriminating awareness of self: "je n'avois nulle notion distincte de mon individu."[g] Indeed, his own bleeding appears to be happening elsewhere and he watches it distantly, as though it were a brook. He feels no discomfort, no pain or fear or uneasiness. Quite the reverse, he experiences a ravishing calm, which gives him an extraordinary, incomparable pleasure. The result of all this is a sense of absolute immediacy in place and time ("tout entier au moment présent"). It is a moment of selfless consciousness.

In his description of the tumble and the awakening Rousseau turns the Adamic myth inside out, making his private renaissance into pure origin a postlapsarian affair—much as it is in Blake, where the world as palpable place comes into being as a result of Urizen's fall. Rousseau's curious and costly Eden is taken up in the *Rêveries* because of their commitment to experimentalism and to exploring the possibilities of autonomous Paradises within. There is no doubt of his self-sufficiency in this Adamic moment (since he obviously needs no more than the little he has) nor of his pleasure in the state (which he is careful to stress). Nor is there any question about the adequacy of consciousness to achieve the state, because consciousness has no active part in it at all. Nothing is asked of consciousness other than it be itself after a severe accident to the body. Rousseau has no more control than a child would have over the reproduction of this condition of being; in fact, the analogy of the condition he describes to that of a child's earliest sense of the world is quite precise. Wordsworth had spoken of similar states in the *Immortality* ode, with the child's "obstinate questionings / Of sense and outward things, / Fallings from us, vanishings; / Blank misgivings of a Creature / Moving about in worlds not realised." For the child whom Wordsworth describes these events were glorious and dazzling; but they are the exclusive property of that early stage of self. Wordsworth regarded such moments as the origins of our seeing, master lights that determine it but are no longer recoverable to the adult.

As Rousseau describes his version of the state in the *Deuxième Promenade*, it is far more blissful than anything he spoke of in regard to the savage. Yet this experience of Adamic originality has its own peculiar limitations, touchstone though it may be. How can one achieve it under ordinary circumstances, that is, without a willed mutilation of the body?

Moreover, the refinements of this state are not the result of condensation but of violation, of a rude ripping-away (analogous, surely, to the birth trauma), rather than a careful reduction of self and its needs to their purest condition. Finally, with all his eagerness to find the point of origin within, there is no evidence that Rousseau preferred or even desired infantile solipsism of this delightful but extremely limited kind. When he awakens from the fall into the life of a newborn, Rousseau cannot identify either self or place: "je ne savois ni qui j'étois ni où j'étois."[h] In Book One of *Emile,* speaking of the newborn's modes of perception, Rousseau is quite specific about their insufficiency: "Nous naissons capable d'apprendre, mais ne sachant rien, ne connoissant rien. L'ame enchaînée dans des organes imparfaits et demi-formés n'a pas même le sentiment de sa propre existence."[i] [13] But in the most cherished state of self-sufficiency, described briefly in the *Confessions* and more extensively in the *Cinquième Promenade,* Rousseau does not want such an unwitting consciousness, with no sense of personality or location. Rather, the conditions he describes as best come into being only with the most extensive knowledge of the process of getting the self there and with the most profound sense of the self's "propre existence." If consciousness is to put away both history and context, it should do so only with the fullest understanding of what it is doing, because only then can it have a thorough awareness of itself, of what it irreducibly is when everything else is taken away. The moment of accidental infancy described in the *Deuxième Promenade* is like the self-sufficiency of the savage: it is unconscious and unlearned, and it therefore knows nothing of the achieved bliss of the best possible state.

That state is the central concern of the *Cinquième Promenade.* There, Rousseau is more careful than he is anywhere else to make certain that our understanding of the ultimately incommunicable is as clear as he can make it. To do so he puts together a set of steps designed to guide us to the core of his consciousness through our apprehension and absorption of the same materials, images, and landscape he had himself taken in. A clear if subtly ordered path goes from the beginning of the essay to the experience at its center, and Rousseau leads us along it with consummate skill.

No other place had made him so happy as the island of Saint-Pierre, a tiny place in the middle of the lake of Bienne. It is, he says, especially well placed for one who, like himself, likes to circumscribe himself ("se circonscrire"), to draw a boundary around himself so that there is a clear demarcation between where and what he is and where and what he is not (1040). One leg of the implied compass is at the exact center of the circumscribed area, the other out at the edge, where what he is meets what he is not. Thus, the center of self is exactly correspondent to the island of Saint-Pierre, placed, as Rousseau describes it, "au milieu du lac de Bienne,"ʲ that is, at the innermost point of the circumscribed area surrounding it. To confirm the parallelism, Rousseau points out that the lake has "une forme presque ronde,"ᵏ corresponding to what would have to be the roundedness of the area he has outlined for himself. The self and the island image one another, each echoing and replicating the other's position within the scheme of things. Put another way, the shape of the island and its relation to its surroundings are precisely the shape and relation that he wants for his selfhood. He is one of those who "*aime à se circonscrire*" (my italics).ˡ This does not mean that he is always able to do so.[14]

Despite its size the island is unusually well stocked, with a variety of landscapes, places for poultry, pigeons, and fish, vineyards, meadows, and the like. It has the sort of dense, compact completeness that is always associated with Eden, and that Rousseau had already laid out in his description of Julie's Elysium. Both are paradisal enclosures, both are images of the self in its circumscribed plenitude. And if Julie's pleasure garden was a parody of all the incarcerating structures in *Clarissa,* Rousseau's island has about it something of both. He had been forced to go to the island after having been stoned by the villagers at Motiers. In a sense (one he quickly grasps) he is trapped on the island: "il m'étoit impossible de sortir sans assistance et sans être bien apperçu, et . . . je ne pouvois avoir ni communication ni correspondance que par le concours des gens qui m'entouroient" (1042).[m] And there is nothing he enjoys more. If his enemies have driven him to this place, he could wish for nothing better than a continuation of this felicitous incarceration: "j'aurois voulu qu'on m'eut fait de cet azile une prison perpétuelle, qu'on m'y eut confiné pour toute ma vie" (1041).[n] In the *Confessions*, referring to the same episode, he made use of the same image of the paradisal prison: "Ah que je changerois volontiers, me disois-je la liberté de sortir d'ici dont je ne me soucie point avec l'assurance d'y pouvoir rester toujours."[o] [15] A few lines after that he offers a more extensive version of the comment in the *Cinquième Promenade* on the "prison perpétuelle." Finally, when Rousseau was ordered to leave the island, he wrote a letter asking for a similar mode of captivity, but his request was never passed on.[16] He refers to the affair and that request once again in the first *Dialogue*, complaining about his having been chased "successivement de tous les azyles les plus reculés, les plus solitaires où il s'étoit de lui-même emprisonné."[p] [17] All he wanted, he says there, was to finish his days in "une paisible captivité."[q] When Rousseau first arrived at the island of Saint Pierre, such a paradisal imprisonment not only seemed possible but—an additional boon—it would have offered a clear if indirect triumph over the plotters who had been chasing him everywhere. His intuition that his self-sufficiency could find its most perfect and satisfying flowering in a state of captivity was, as it turned out, one of Rousseau's most significant legacies (see chapter eight). Rousseau, like many of his successors, wins by losing. In taking away nearly everything from him, his enemies have given him all that he needs.

Indeed, Rousseau points out in the *Cinquième Promenade* that he came to the island stripped of everything, "seul et nud."[r] But that sort of total reductiveness clearly was not satisfactory, because he sent for his housekeeper, his books, and his small set of possessions. In the most desirable circumstances he would require very little, but that little would be necessary. It would also have to be visible. He seemed to feel a compulsion to see the boxes containing his goods, partly because he could then take pleasure in not unpacking them, and partly because he could not be perfectly content unless they were obviously there. By leaving them in their boxes he gained a freedom even from that which was his; in effect he is saying that they are his but not him. Yet in having them sent for after all, he acknowledged that he needed them near him as a basis, a prop on which to lean and from which to do his business. We shall look at the reasons for that shortly.

The first part of his business was also calculatedly visible. To take the place of his books and papers Rousseau ostentatiously filled his room with flowers and hay, the result of his newly revived interest in botanizing. He set about his botanical work with an unusual passion for procedure and an immense appetite for an infinity of detail. He wanted to describe the flora of the island with so much precision and specificity that he could never, in fact, finish the job; and to accomplish that happy impossibility he divided a section of the island into little squares, each of which he could go over at every season. This was not simply a question of giving himself something to do but of doing it in a certain way. Mode was more significant than result; or, from another perspective, the most desirable result of the mode had less to do with flora than with the reality that contained them and the consciousness that perceived them. A reality composed of such an extraordinary mass of detail required, as its opposite, a consciousness functioning at the fullest possible stretch. No halfhearted measures for Jean-Jacques when it came to the pleasures available to the self. The absolute delight of projecting the energies of consciousness onto the world was sui generis and needed no justification. Since consciousness loves botanical details, it should be bombarded with them in an unending supply; and since it delights in its own skill in handling such details, it should so organize reality that the skill will always have material through which to evidence itself.

But there is more, and it goes beyond the principle of pleasure. Each square he maps out on the island is a link between himself and the world, each offering a point of contact for the self as it seeks to engage itself with external reality. When he is out botanizing, peeking and poking into nature's most private activities (note his delight over the discovery of the flowers' ways of reproduction), Rousseau is connecting himself most intimately with the world that surrounds him. Such linkage is, in itself, a pleasure. But it is also the most efficient way of confirming that the autonomous self is surrounded by a context, that it is not floating freely in a vacuum. His elaborate botanical plans gave him a great deal of world with which to work. So much specificity meant that there would forever be continuities between himself and nature, that it would never cease to have places for him to look at and touch as he sent his attention out over the world.

But this is only one side of the story, one sort of exercise of the independent self. It was only the first step in a carefully structured dialectic of self and nature. Rousseau followed his depiction of the pleasures of botanizing with the analysis of a very different sort of situation. Botanizing was a morning exercise, followed by a good dinner in pleasant company. In the afternoon he would often set out in a boat to the middle of the lake and simply let go:

> et là, m'étendant tout de mon long dans le bateau les yeux tournés vers le ciel, je me laissois aller et dériver lentement au gré de l'eau quelquefois pendant plusieurs heures, plongé dans mille reveries confuses mais délicieuses, et qui sans avoir aucun objet bien déterminé ni constant ne laissoient pas d'être à mon gré cent fois préférables à tout ce que j'avois trouvé de plus doux dans ce qu'on appelle les plaisirs de la vie (1044).ˢ [18]

The contrast with botanizing is marked and precise: each is, in form and mode, everything that the other is not. Consciousness engaged in botanizing is extrospective, directed outward with considerable intensity upon the elaborate content of the external world. Consciousness set adrift is introspective, focused within on the intricate universe of its own content. Extrospection is framed and rigorously guided by a complicated system of squares. Introspection, like the boat, floats in total passivity, with no foreseen direction, no constant or determined objective. Extrospection is linear and temporal, concerned with what happens to the flora down the passage of the seasons. Introspection is nonlinear, and it is so unconcerned with temporality that Rousseau needs the setting of the sun to warn him that it is time to go back.

What follows this dialectical interplay is, in certain ways, a synthesis of several aspects of the two modes, though it is clearly an extension of the experience in the boat. As evening approached, Rousseau would go down to the edge of the lake to look for a hidden retreat, "quelque azyle caché" (1045). Surrounded by this shelter, separated from the rest of his minuscule world by this act of self-circumscription, he entered a subjective condition of unparalleled reductiveness. The sound of the waves and the agitation of the water arresting *(fixant)* his senses, his soul was emptied of its agitation, its restlessness, by the very slight restlessness of the sound of the waters. In fact, those sounds had taken the place of everything else sensuous within himself. The only other content in consciousness, aside from this slight but firm hold on exteriority, was the pure minimum of self, the "sentiment de l'existence" (1047), beyond which there is only nullity. This total content—the wave sounds and the sense of one's being—is the absolutely irreducible. Yet for Rousseau it is also absolute plenitude since it offers all that he needs for thorough, incomparable satisfaction. Though he cannot do with less than he has, the world within the self is complete, "d'un bonheur suffisant, parfait et plein, qui ne laisse dans l'ame aucun vuide qu'elle sent le besoin de remplir" (1046).ᵗ

Rousseau is as careful to point out conditions and limits as he is to describe the qualities of his reverie. There must be peace and no passion within the self, and a moderate, regular movement outside of it. A strong or uneven movement would recall the self to the world of surrounding objects, and from

there to the yoke of its troubles.[19] Rousseau has come as close
as he can to making the self its own context; yet, though the
state is perfect, the self is not, in these ideal conditions, perfectly self-sufficient. At one point he seems to say that the self
needs nothing else but itself: "De quoi jouit-on dans une par-
eille situation? De rien d'extérieur à soi, de rien sinon de soi-
même et de sa propre existence, tant que cet état dure on se
suffit à soi-même comme Dieu" (1047).[u] Yet he also says that
a full immersion in the soundless world within would have
made him uneasy and could not sustain the most satisfactory
form of reverie. To achieve that perfection he had to have the
noise of the waves entering the recesses of his subjective enclosure because without that minimum of contact there is the
effect of nothingness, of extinction: "sans mouvement la vie
n'est qu'une letargie"; but even more, "un silence absolue . . .
offre une image de la mort" (1047).[v] These comments, it should
be noted, occur immediately after those on his godlike self-
sufficiency; but the conflict may only be apparent. It seems
likely that we should take the statement "on se suffit à soi-
même comme Dieu" as referring to the sources of pleasure:
we need no other sources than those we can offer to ourselves.
That does not mean that a full cutoff from outside is necessary
or even desirable for the most satisfactory experience. In the
Cinquième Promenade Rousseau went up to the edge of total
interiority but he did not go into it completely. The sound of
the waves made up, in its regular movement, for all the shift-
ings of everyday consciousness Rousseau had eased out of
himself. That sound was the only other presence in the self,
the tiny but requisite continuity with the world outside. Without that sound he risked the death-in-life of solipsism, and
that would have seemed too much like an entrapment within
the walls of personality. The most perfect reduction still required the condition of insularity: it had to be a point surrounded by waters. The noise of the waves gave him contact
and context. This is another version of contextual autonomy,
in structure the same as Julie's but with as little content inside
of it as consciousness would allow.

There is, Rousseau points out, a somewhat inferior state one can settle for when conditions are less than ideal. Should there be complete silence outside, with no regular movement available to help consciousness with its process of reduction, he can turn within and call on his cheerful *(riante)* imagination. This aspect of self can produce "légéres et douces idées," which are sufficient to ruffle the surface of consciousness without causing any serious disturbance.ʷ In this way "le mouvement qui ne vient pas du dehors se fait alors au dedans de nous" (1048).ˣ Here the mind is obviously both triumphant and self-sufficient, supplying what place cannot give, demonstrating its independence from circumstance. Rousseau felt that he could bring about this sort of reverie even in a genuine prison, where there would be no pleasurable external reality on which to fasten his attention. In that case all presence would be drawn from within himself, so that all awareness would be self-awareness; but that, with its aura of solipsism, clearly unnerves him, as we have seen. It could only be second-best. He prefers the less-than-complete autonomy that ties him to the fewest things outside. He wants to lean, however lightly, on place.

Rousseau is far more thorough in his independence from time. In fact, he demonstrates this independence by spatializing time, turning that which is beyond seeing into the stuff of the visual imagination. His life, he says, is a line. Along it he can see widely scattered points representing rare, brief moments of the most intense delirium and passion. Fine as these moments are, they are not the best situation he can imagine for himself. He would like less delirium and more continuity, a reduction in the intensity of the passion but with a more enduring presence of such pleasures. Put another way, he wants a state in which point and line (the moving point) become identical, where there is no before and after but, rather, the sense of a permanent present. His ideal of temporality would be composed of continuance without sequence:

S'il est un état . . . où le tems ne soit rien pour elle [l'âme], ou le présent dure toujours sans neanmoins marquer sa durée et sans aucune trace de succession, sans aucun autre sentiment de privation ni de jouissance, de plaisir ni de peine, de desir ni de crainte que celui seul de notre existence (1046)[y]

then he would be perfectly content. In effect he is doing with temporality what he wants to do with his selfhood. In the perfect state his soul would find "une assiette assez solide pour s'y reposer tout entiére et rassembler là tout son être" (1046).[z] That would be the most thorough sort of self-circumscription, with his whole being drawn together there at the pure center. Time, too, would be perfectly circumscribed because it is in an eternal present: past and future, once on either side of this immediate moment, would now be entirely contained within it. Consciousness and duration would both be enfolded within the same sort of enclosure, both at the still center of being.[20] This is the fullest mastery the mind can exercise over time and over itself. Rousseau's ideal is the absolute condensation of consciousness into a state of lucid self-awareness. That state is, at once, both the epitome of the adequacy of consciousness and the condition in which consciousness is most free.

By now we can see the point of Rousseau's love for the lush diversity of a well-stocked Edenic landscape, and also for his insistence that his few goods had to be present and visible though unpacked. When he speaks of the possibility of reveries in prison he admits that they are better and more agreeably achieved "dans une Isle fertile et solitaire, naturellement cir-conscritte et séparée du reste du monde" (1048).[aa] He wants not only the separateness implied in the insular structure but also a condition of fertility, and he wants that condition for several reasons. First, such richness is an identifying property of Eden, and he needs the form and meaning of a paradisal enclosure around him as the basic mode of landscape. Further, he wants that lushness as a contrasting state to the one he is trying to achieve within himself. Edenic repletion is a necessary precondition, a requisite leading-in; but when he starts to go within he has to put that world behind him, abandoning the landscape and his few visible goods. That is why the starkness and depletion of a prison cell would not be nearly as satisfactory as the qualities of a fruitful island, though the cell certainly fulfills the requirement of a circumscribed form. The cell is not only silent but empty. It offers nothing to give up, no contrasting conditions, no possibility for demonstrating the process of putting the world away. The activity of internalization takes its meaning as much from its point of departure as from its place of arrival.

In effect Rousseau makes that meaning perceptible through its antitheses, a tactic he had been employing not only among the various essays as a group but in the *Cinquième Promenade* in particular. As I have indicated, we are led through a series of steps toward the center of his most striking experience. The series begins with a collocation of images of self and landscape. It then goes into the description of several states that are not like that of the contracted consciousness though, in retrospect, they are seen to hint at it insistently. The conditions of botanizing (extrospection) have to do with an intense probing of exteriority, a probing that contacts nature at innumerable points. It is the epitome of continuity, the most elaborate system of connections Rousseau could concoct. The next step, the reverie in the boat, is a move within, designed to contrast at nearly every point with the mode of botanizing. We are working toward the center of self, having taken the requisite turn, but we are not quite there yet. The introspection in the boat mentions nothing about establishing continuities with his external surroundings, though his recognition that the sun is setting means that a minimal continuity, however subliminal, must be there. Most important is the plethora of activities within, "mille reveries confuses mais délicieuses,"[bb] a burgeoning inner life which is as swarming with content as the botanical world outside. Though the various swarmings occur in different areas of being, and are themselves very different orders of being, they are alike in their incessant activity. His contact with areas of his inner life is as varied and complex as his contact with the flora on the island.

The final step is furthest within. As he goes deeper into the self, the swarming disappears. The myriad of delicious reveries has to be put away so that he can concentrate on a single subject, the purest feeling of existence, and can balance that with a single thread of continuity, the sound of the waves. Rousseau combines the continuity of extrospection with the self-absorption of introspection, but he has reduced the masses of inner and outer details to a balanced pair of opposites, one for each direction of the self. Once again he not only tells us where he has been but how he got there, and in particular how getting there is not the same as getting to any other place.

It is in such precise demarcations among the states of the self that we find some of Rousseau's essential contributions to the analysis of autonomy. He had an exceptional awareness of the ways in which the mind searches out all the places it wants to get to, how it goes about extending itself over the world as well as moving inward upon itself. His skill had as much to do with the understanding of extrospection as of introspection, and his highest skill was in the differentiation of the two. But he was able to show variations even in the forms of subjective exploration. He knew enough about reveries and how they are achieved (no one seems to have known more) to show, as he did in the *Cinquième Promenade,* that they are not all of a piece. Though it might be exaggerated to say that each reverie is identical only with itself, his elucidations throughout the *Rêveries* lead mainly to a series of subtle differentiations among them. In the *Septième Promenade,* for example, he refers to conditions of reverie, which, though they have an obvious familial relationship with those in the fifth, are remarkable mainly for their idiosyncrasies. He also points out in that essay that there are variations in extrospection as well, in modes of seeking to possess the world beyond the self. He sneers with only minimal politeness at those who think of the plants he inspects as the source of medicinal potions. Part of his attitude comes from his distrust of doctors and a vague faith in the body's own powers of healing. (He had already attacked professional medicine in *Emile*.) But Rousseau's assaults in the *Septième Promenade* are directed primarily toward the view of nature as instrumentality, as a series of tools designed for man and his mind to better themselves. Those attacks are sufficiently Keatsian to prefigure most later Romantic assaults on the self's temptation to arrogance, that is, the egotistical sublime. The point is not in the assertion of the autonomy of consciousness, a stance he shares with some of the instrumentalists, but in the extrospective modes through which that autonomy is exercised. For it is only when consciousness acknowledges the independence and self-sufficiency of that which it seeks to possess—when the world is taken for what it is and not for what it can do, when the necessary appropriation of the external is for the sake of both sides of the transaction—that the best sort of encounter between nature and the mind can occur. The proper relationship is not that of a rape, as it is in Wordsworth's "Nutting." Rather, prefiguring Coleridge and the Wordsworth of *Home at Grasmere,* the possession of the other should be achieved through a wedding of the world and the mind. All those fruits of the earth Rousseau examines are "la parure et le vétement de la terre . . . sa robe de noces" (1062).[cc] The botanist is a ceremonial sort, his extrospection the work of a husbandman of the mind.

Rousseau's perfect confidence in his handling of these matters explains why he would subject himself to a sardonic self-parody at the end of the *Septième Promenade*. He describes how, on one of his botanical excursions, he went through some difficult terrain and came to "un réduit si caché que je n'ai vu de ma vie un aspect plus sauvage" (1070).[dd] Intertwined trees closed off this retreat with impenetrable barriers, except for a few gaps through which he could see a broken, frightening landscape. Inside the enclosure *(enceinte)* Rousseau found various flora, which drew his attention. But under the pressure of all those objects he went, eventually, into a reverie, "en pensant que j'étois là dans un réfuge ignoré de tout l'univers" (1071).ᶜᶜ The place was an encompassing shelter of the sort he had prescribed for Julie and, in a variety of texts, for himself as well. It had the usual sort of vegetation, a few birds, the requisite thick wall to keep out the world—all that he needed to get a reverie going. In such a situation, placed at the center of such an image, it was only natural for him to indulge his predilection for insularity: "Je me comparois à ces grands voyageurs qui découvrent une Ile déserte, et je me disois avec complaisance: sans doute je suis le prémier mortel qui ait pénétré jusqu'ici; je me regardois presque comme un autre Colomb" (1071).ᶠᶠ This echoes Saint-Preux's exclamation over the quasi-virginal insularity of Julie's Elysium, where he likens her enclosed garden to undiscovered islands he had encountered during his travels in the South Seas. In Rousseau's case the analogy was prompted by "un mouvement d'orgeuil,"ᵍᵍ and that bit of detached self-observation offers the clue to his tone and prefigures the conclusion. A familiar clicking noise came in upon him, and in order to trace it he pushed his way through some heavy underbrush. There, twenty steps from his island, was a stocking factory.

This scene should be viewed as the second of two framing events, the first of which is the tumble into infantile solipsism described in the *Deuxième Promenade*. At the center between these events is the stark profundity of self-contemplation in the *Cinquième Promenade*. The first scene led into the center by describing a related but essentially different affair, the second leads out by showing the requisite conditions in a comic light. Both sides offer perspective on the center. Together they present a spectrum of tonal possibilities ranging from infantile bliss to subdued, self-directed mockery. Rousseau's confidence and skill permit him to be both in his material and above it, a performer in and commentator on all these probes toward the nucleus of self.

Rousseau's obsession with process is the distinguishing principle in his quest for an autarchic mode of living. The discussion and demonstration of process, and particularly of the qualities and conditions that define it, make up the central activity of the *Rêveries*. All of the expected gestures of self-justification, the delineation of the complot, even the examination of truth, seem to function most of all as a background, a list of causes for his decision to place himself, whenever possible, at the deep center of a paradisal situation. The cool skill he shows in the *Rêveries* reveals his profound understanding of what is involved in the attainment of subjective autonomy, at least of the sort he wants. He is fully aware of what he knows and what he can accomplish with that knowledge. Indeed, Rousseau was so familiar with the emptying of consciousness, as well as all that led up to it, that he could spell out the requirements precisely and with care—something that Satan could never do with his own assertions of autonomy because his arguments for it were essentially fallacious. When all the difficult conditions are met—and the *Cinquième Promenade* shows exactly how he could meet them—Rousseau exhibits an absolute mastery over place and time. With him the mind is indeed its own place, showing a success that no Satanic bid for independence could ever achieve.

This matter of comparative accomplishment is hardly tangential because Milton's Satan and the Rousseau of the *Confessions* and *Rêveries* were among the most influential models of autonomy sent down to their Romantic successors. The nature of their influence has so much to do with how and why their quests for autonomy took place that the outlines of a radical narrative need to be sketched out. The quest, in both cases, comes about because of a fall. In Satan's case the plunge is precise, literal, and classic. In Rousseau's it is a far more subtle and multileveled affair. His reading of his life finds falls, separations, and expulsions in a variety of circumstances, from childhood to maturity. He begins the first *Promenade* with the imagery of what turns out to be an ambiguous, fortunate fall out of society into insularity, and that institutes the curious ambivalence about his disconnection from the social order that is perceptible all through the *Rêveries*. Indeed, the Rousseauistic model established the difficulty of separating the desired from the enforced in the tumble into isolation. There is no such difficulty with Satan. The quest for autonomy, then, takes its origin in a rebuff, a rejection that, in Rousseau's case, may well have been sought out and welcomed. After the fall the past is recollected in whatever sort of tranquillity is available to one who has been ejected from what once seemed a most desirable place. The next step is a pulling-together of one's strength, a regrouping which, in practice, is often both literal and psychological. In Satan's case it takes the outward form of an assembly of his troops, but, more intricately and significantly, of an insistence that the source of all the values by which he will act is to be found only within himself. With Rousseau the pulling-together surfaces in all the imagery and statements about objective and subjective circumscription, which, it has long been recognized, point to defining stuctures in his work. After the marshalling of forces, the hunt for autonomy begins. Its success is, to say the least, uncertain: the narrative, with its uneasy blend of the willed and the compelled, turns up in as diverse a set of figures as Goethe's Werther, Byron's Cain, and Huysmans's Des Esseintes. As for prelapsarian autonomy—the sort that exists, for example, with Byron's Don Juan and Haidée on Lambro's island—it is nearly always unselfconscious and (perhaps therefore) it nearly always has no future.

The forms of autonomy attempted by Satan and Jean-Jacques are instances of the same basic desire, and they follow the same narrative line. Toward the beginning of the *Deuxième Promenade*, Rousseau had argued that "j'appris ainsi par ma propre expérience que la source du vrai bonheur est en nous, et qu'il ne dépend pas des hommes de rendre vraiment misérable celui qui sait vouloir être heureux" (1003).hh Of course this is the mind as its own place, at least for turning Hells into Heavens. Yet the forms that Satan and Jean-Jacques separately propose are clearly very different in mode (not to speak of achievement), and therefore those forms present a spectrum of approaches rather than a single one. As such, they make available a considerable flexibility in the practice of autonomy, with progeny as diverse in kind and concern as Obermann and Manfred. Satan, as we have seen, has to be concerned with the moral dimensions and ramifications of autonomy as well as its relation to power. His position as Antagonist, as God's opposite, means moral opposition, and that requires an examination of the categories of valuation as well as the sources of value. As the immediate postlapsarian events indicate, Satan discovers these matters in the very process of setting himself up in opposition. There had not, after all, been any need for a prior ordering of value, a prelapsarian pondering on whatever it is that an ejected angel would need most. There had never been such beings before. Further, he never questions or even examines his ability to handle the sort of autonomy that he claims he now has. This is not entirely a question of his massive vanity, or even of evasion: with a consciousness geared for battle Satan's interests are elsewhere, not in the possibilities and processes of self-sufficiency but in the immediacies of engagement. Satan's autonomy is the modal antithesis of the Rousseauistic sort. Rousseau had sketched out the major contours of his value system long before his enemies drove him (with his own active help) out of society. He spends much of his time considering how to get at those states he had already decided were the ultimately desirable ones. Further, the field of action for his values, the place where he puts them into practice, is as remote as possible from any state of engagement. What he does best is best done alone. His is the line of autonomy that goes down through Obermann, Satan's is that which goes through Manfred. But of course (as we shall notice frequently in the following chapters) the modes are as often combined as they are seen in pure separation. In fact, this combination is one of the principal factors in the ambivalence of the Romantic hero.

Rousseau, unlike the ignoble savage of the *Discourses,* went through what Jean Starobinski has called the perils of reflection.[21] Any self-subsistence he came to was therefore post-reflective, earned after encountering those perils. The effort was well worth it. Rousseau aimed toward Eden, a Paradise within him far happier than any state Satan's aggressiveness could attain, or that Rousseau himself could find in the fullness of social activity. The point is most evident in a comparison of his and Satan's incarcerations. With Satan there is an exact correlation between inner and outer prisons, in his case all the landscapes of Hell. With Rousseau, under the most favorable conditions, there is a most satisfying opposition between the compulsions from outside and the freedoms within. His inner world is thus very much like the pristine internal wholeness that Michael promised to Adam, a more felicitous Eden, which was the bright opposite of the Hell within that Satan had built for himself out of disobedience. By his internalization of these mythical regions of reward and punishment Milton prefigured the romantic subjectivization of value. Rousseau, along with Richardson and Sterne, continued that process and gave considerable impetus to it. But the differences between Milton and Rousseau are as instructive as any similarities, and they point to some basic facts about the various kinds of autonomy that were to appeal to the romantics. For if Rousseau follows Adam in cherishing the order of the Paradise within, he shares with Satan what Adam could never put forth, an absolute insistence upon the autonomy of consciousness. At its best, when his imagination was perfectly adequate to all his needs, Rousseau's subjective world was both autonomous and Edenic, and that ordering of the patterns of the inner life was, for many of his successors, the most desirable of all. He owed obedience only to his most transient desires and to his persistent longing for that state of the purest self-sufficiency that is the *sentiment de l'existence*. Neither supine nor aggressive, Rousseau wanted nothing more than the opportunity to find the conditions outside of himself that helped to activate his inner Eden. That private Paradise was stark and nearly stationary, withdrawn, self-conscious, and fleeting. At the end of his life it was all that he needed. His skill in achieving it made Rousseau's mode the model of its kind.

ᵔᵕᵔ THREE ᵔᵕᵔ

The Internalization of Energy

Sterne's Uncle Toby is an instance of another kind of adequacy. He is not only one of the great equestrians of eighteenth-century fiction, a grand master of the hobbyhorse; he is a superior craftsman as well, an expert at artifice. Toby and his assistant Corporal Trim are continually building, destroying, and rebuilding models of cities and fortifications. They follow the real wars in Europe with play wars of their own, exact replicas of the dangerous world across the channel from the surroundings of Shandy Hall. Toby had once been directly involved with those hazardous actualities, and that encounter had cost him a wound that was probably, though not certainly, unfortunate for his generative organs. As a result he had been divorced from effective action and forced to build, at Shandy Hall, a reproduction of the world of experience. At one point, when his brother questioned the expense of his military operations, Toby argued that his activities were ultimately "for the good of the nation," though he never explained how or why.[1] Yet if the national import of his maneuvers is never quite clear, it is certain that Toby's miniaturizations had their own self-generated, self-sufficient pleasures. Every year, "and sometimes every month," he and Trim added "some new conceit or quirk of improvement to their operations, which always opened fresh springs of delight in carrying them on" (446). The energies Toby had once expended in literal combat became energies of a mind engaged in superior play. He made mortars out of boots, and escarpments out of the dirt in his kitchen garden. When it rained he would retreat into a sentry box from which he could direct the simulated attacks upon the town he and Trim had built. "The town," Sterne says, "was a perfect *Proteus*" taking every shape that Toby's mind chose to give to it. Whatever the harm done to his generative energies, Toby's actions indicate that his mind is able to make do with a self-contained and coherent system of its own devising. He shares that ability with some of the other strange inhabitants of Shandy Hall, not least with Tristram himself.

Toby's passion for the techniques of war is supported by a considerable library of books on military architecture, a collection Sterne compares to the equally elaborate stock of books on chivalry in Don Quixote's library. Quixote, himself a bookish equestrian, is clearly a prototype for some of the hobby-horsical inhabitants of Shandy Hall, particularly those whose quirky obsessions set them apart from the general run of things. The influence of Cervantes on Sterne, one of the most important continuities in literary history, results in more than some oddities of personality. Sterne's acknowledgment of Cervantes as a predecessor extends from echoes in the tone of his characters' speech (e.g. the "*Cervantick* gravity" of a remark by Tristram's father [169]) through an invocation to the "gentle spirit of sweetest humour" whom he would have for a muse just as Cervantes did (628). In a letter written after the first two volumes of *Tristram Shandy* had been published, Sterne spoke of "the Cervantic humour" of the book, which arises from "describing silly and trifling Events, with the Circumstantial Pomp of great Ones."[2] Yet Sterne's reading of Cervantes affects much more than matters of tone or temperament. Quixote is close to Toby not only because of their specialized libraries or even their passion for combat but (more important for Sterne's basic concerns) in ways that reflect the hold each of these characters has on life, his modes of comprehending and organizing experience.

The protean order and inner coherence of Toby's game of war comes from the diligent energies of his mind; and those energies, in turn, are servants of an idiosyncratic system of values, which not only controls his game but determines the odd responses he sometimes makes to innocent remarks. Quixote had begun the same sort of activity from a far more advanced position. All that he does is directed by a consciousness that has put together, out of bits and pieces of the past, an independent and fiercely held order of values. Sometimes Quixote acknowledges that those values have only an internal existence, that he is alone in his age; but for the most part he acts as though he were one among others, that his standards for living have a counterpart and a life somewhere else outside of his own frantically energized imagination.[3] He is a better argument for the mind as its own place than Milton's Satan ever was. But Quixote does not see that his readings are self-generated. A dupe of literary artifice, he is deluded, above all, about the singularity of his own experience. Only he holds these standards now, and therefore they take their being only from within himself. Unwittingly hermetic, he cannot know that the energies of his mind are such that, being itself independent of experience, it has created an independent order of reality that the world cannot touch. Quixote's mind has an autonomous life of its own, necessarily separate from the world that surrounds him, protective of its presuppositions, unassailable by all ordinary attempts at contradiction. Whatever the effects of external reality upon his body, Quixote has a mind so fine that it cannot be violated by a fact. That combination of aloofness and intense, internalized energies was to have a considerable effect on literary history, particularly on various interests that went into romanticism and extended at least as far as Thomas Mann.[4] Quixote's activities are a mad prefiguration of the decadent impulse to live life as though it were art—though Quixote, of course, does not know that it is art he is imitating, that the values derived from old fictions are now at several removes from the reality with which he seeks to engage them. If those values ever had any relevance to reality they now have none, their life contained only within their narrative existence and Quixote's disordered brain. Their order is relevant only to itself. For Sterne the "peerless knight of *La Mancha*" (22) was a model of quirky obsessiveness, his travels the paradigm of all hobby-horsical activities; but above all Quixote represented the ability of the mind to fashion a world for its own private use, however mad its preconceptions and conclusions. Quixote showed Sterne how the energies of the imagination can establish an internal order on which reality can gain no hold.

Sterne turned this model to advantage, not only in the figures of Toby and Tristram's father but particularly in the narrator himself and in the order of the book he is writing. As we are continually reminded by modern critics of Sterne, the action of *Tristram Shandy* takes place within the writer's consciousness; or, as some would have it, Sterne reminds us that the action of all novels takes place, essentially, in the mind of the author.[5] Cervantes had hinted at that way of reading fiction, particularly in the second part of his novel, and Sterne took up the suggestion. The adventures Don Quixote went through under the impetus of his autonomous imagination are turned within and become the adventures of a consciousness that claims the fullest self-sufficiency. The actions that are imitated in *Tristram Shandy* are not those of a hero smashing his way to fame and disaster but, instead, the activities of the faculty that does all the imitating. The energies of the imagination are so fully internalized that they turn in upon themselves, use themselves as characters, and shape the narrative out of their own capacity for shaping. All of the conflicts between clock time and the time of the mind serve mainly to define precisely the true location of the action. We look out on clock time from the perspective of the time within. We can watch clock time being manipulated because we are locked into a very different mode of temporal awareness. Subjective energies have conquered, for the moment, the rigors of that inexorable progress of temporality that led Don Quixote (and will lead the ailing Tristram) to his inevitable end. The lessons Cervantes offered about the autonomous inner life were carried out by Sterne with a vengeance, though not entirely in the spirit of his predecessor.

Sterne's own version of autonomy so shapes the world that

the reality of consciousness is the only coherent and entire reality offered in the novel. He has been called a solipsist but it is more accurate to speak of him as, preeminently, a realist of the order and processes of consciousness. Though he shows how the self-sufficient energies within are perfectly adequate to the demands made upon them, Sterne does not argue that the world out there owes its being to him alone or that the life inside is the only true life. Consciousness becomes the primary reality of which we are aware because, in contrast to its intensity and wholeness, everything else in the novel is fragmented and incomplete, rendered in bits and pieces but never as a totality with a complex and coherent meaning. In a letter to Robert Dodsley, Sterne pointed out that "all locality is taken out of the book—the satire general."[6] The effect of this disembodiment is to give the Shandean world a curious free-floating quality, making it a microcosm but with no precise acknowledgment of any substantial macrocosmic orders outside itself. The Shandean world is characterized by its discontinuities and by the insubstantiality it lends to most kinds of reality. Personal relations are odd and disoriented, dominated by quirks of personality. Social reality has even less substance: the tiny world of Shandy Hall seems to float in a vast space in which palpable entities such as London or France only occasionally come into view. The record of Tristram's trip to France is an opening out of air and perspective but the shutters close up again very quickly. Metaphysical reality is there mainly as a background, though it sometimes comes forth as a dark, inexplicable causality whose major effect on us is to frustrate our desires and expectations. Its principal function at those points in the novel is to verify that the world outside the mind is not really amenable to man. Other than that we know very little about the greater patterns of reality: Sterne tells us less about the content of our external experience than about our inability to control it. In this universe of accidents and fragments consciousness stands alone, unattached to any unifying principle except itself. The only substantial order is that which is supplied to itself by the ordering consciousness. Again, this is not to say that Sterne sees value only in consciousness and its operations. Aside from the genial warmth, which makes this a comic and not a tragic novel (it is, after all, written against the spleen, not in favor of it), there is the value of sympathy, embodied in this novel most eloquently during those moments in which the Shandy brothers reach out through their idiosyncrasies to touch each other's souls.[7] Such moments of unverbalized affiliation are a haven in this world of intense and compressed inwardness; but they appear only sporadically in *Tristram Shandy*, and the life within remains the only complete life.

Indeed, the sense of an impaired wholeness of experience informs Sterne's world at nearly every level, and it helps to define his precise relationship to another acknowledged predecessor, Rabelais. At one point in the novel the narrator speaks of "my dear *Rabelais*, and dearer *Cervantes*" (191) and Diderot referred to "ce livre si fou, si sage et si gai," which is "le rabelais des anglois."[a] [8] Sterne found in Rabelais a number of usable elements of wit, among them his parodies of scholarly effusiveness and his pervasive fascination with rhetoric.[9] Rabelais's appetite for language and its order is a major mode through which his extraordinary energies find release, but Rabelaisian gusto cannot be satisfied only with words. It spreads in a myriad of directions through his book, ingesting and releasing ideas, linguistic phenomena and the things of this world in a perpetual scrutiny of the limits of human experience. His is a universe of multiplicity, both in the kinds of energy that are always in search and in the captives that energy snatches up and releases in every sort of emission.

Diderot's comment on Rabelais and Sterne turns on their general modal likeness, what he calls their mad and exuberant wisdom, but the sources and objects of Sterne's gusto are only partly like those of his predecessor. Where Rabelais reached out, Sterne reaches within. The hungry expansiveness of his predecessor turns into the centripetal concentration of *Tristram Shandy*. Where Rabelais added on, Sterne cuts off— sometimes, as in Tristram's case, quite literally. The novel says little about food or drink or any other bodily pleasures except sex, on which it dwells continually; yet, despite all the allusions and sniggering, sex in Sterne's novel is far more a problem of performance than a clear and present joy. A long series of events and comments touches on failed or insufficient sexuality, suggesting the deepest threats to the body's capacities. Sterne is, however, shrewd enough to leave many questions unanswered. What we never quite know about the wounds of Toby or Tristram, or even about the effectiveness of the Shandy's bull, is ironically opposed to what we are regularly shown about the potency of the autonomous consciousness. If the extent of Tristram's chance circumcision is never fully clear, his ability to turn the accidents of consciousness into the conquests of art is less subject to suspicion because it is given such frequent substantiation. Of course he complains perpetually about the digressions into which he is accidentally led; but at the same time he points with pardonable pride to the facility with which his work contrives to be, simultaneously, digressive and progressive. Every detour of his peripatetic consciousness is, he insists, "a masterstroke of digressive skill" (72), and though we may balk at the sweepingness of his boast there is plenty of truth in it. If his wanderings are impulsive and accidental, subject to the random spurts of internal energy, Tristram is able to so contrive the machinery of his work that "two contrary motions are introduced into it, and reconciled, which were thought to be at variance with each other" (73). That is, he can cooperate with his impulses, giving them free play but at the same time making them profitable to the overall movement of his memoirs. In fact, if we follow through Tristram's references to the pattern of digression and progression in his work, it becomes plain that he is pointing out how the rhythms of his creative imagination are modeled on the rhythms of sexuality. He makes that point clear himself. In volume five, chapter twenty-five Tristram gives his opinion that "provided [an author] keeps along the line of his story,—he may go backwards and forwards as he will,—'tis still held to be no digression" (382).

In volume six, chapter five his father points out that St. Ambrose had had to "turn his *Amanuensis* out of doors, because of an indecent motion of his head, which went backwards and forwards like a flail" (414). The scattered allusions to the rhythms of digression and indecency come into full blossom in the thirty-third chapter of volume six. There, Tristram argues that "in good truth, when a man is telling a story in the strange way I do mine, he is obliged continually to be going backwards and forwards to keep all tight together in the reader's fancy" (462); and he goes on to develop this collusion of images in one of the most intricately obscene passages in a book that is noted for them.[10]

But Sterne's salaciousness, whatever its level of fun, is thoroughly functional, and it is put to the service of his profound concern with the possibilities of the mind. Each of the Shandy males is more successful with the conquests of the mind than with those of the body, and each is apt to turn the failures of the one into the triumphs of the other. Toby, we are told, does not know the right end of a woman from the wrong (100-102), and his potential for bodily performance is one of the persistent puzzles of the book; but when he goes down to the bowling green that was to be the home of his fortifications "never did lover post down to a belov'd mistress with more heat and expectation, than my uncle *Toby* did, to enjoy this self-same thing in private" (98). Walter Shandy turns his monthly conjugal service into a lugubrious melodrama; but when he finally discovers a copy of Bruscambille's treatise upon long noses "he solaced himself with *Bruscambille* after the manner, in which, 'tis ten to one, your worship solaced yourself with your first mistress,—that is, from morning even unto night" (225). And though Walter finds distaste and confusion in the engendering of children, he begets ideas with exuberant joy. Tristram knows how to treat his father's intellectual pleasures with all the appropriate ironies:

It is the nature of an hypothesis, when once a man has conceived it, that it assimilates every thing to itself as proper nourishment; and, from the first moment of your begetting it, it generally grows the stronger by every thing you see, hear, read, or understand. (151)

Our bodies, it seems are part of the world and therefore subject to various disasters and indignities; but our minds, however absurd their obsessions, are seen to be inviolable—indeed, impervious. All of the references to physical impotence or indifference in Sterne's novel serve mainly to emphasize the demonstrable areas of the mind's fertility and power. The energies of the body are transformed into the energies of consciousness, which take over the bulk of the Shandean environment. Of course Tristram is far more efficacious than his father in making contingency serve his purposes. Walter Shandy's plans are continually shredded by the accidents of the world but Tristram is able to shape his narrative by turning fortuitous impulses into the energies that organize his memoirs. Tristram's giggles and complaints are part of what he calls the "fanciful guise of careless disport" (301) with which he masks his abilities. If his world has been carefully circumscribed, its contours defined by the reach of his subjective energies, Sterne's narrator knows how to map that landscape of the mind with admirable felicity.

Thus, however significant the influence of Rabelaisian and Cervantean modes on *Tristram Shandy* the shape of reality that is imagined in Sterne's novel is very different from the configurations of experience bodied forth by his predecessors. These differences are crucial, not only for our precise understanding of Sterne's achievement but, in particular, for the effect each of these figures had on literary history. Taken as a whole, the evolution from Rabelais to Cervantes to Sterne, especially from the point of view of romantic developments, shows a pronounced shift in the field in which energy does its work.[11] The probings of the order and activities of the imagination undertaken by Cervantes, his curiosity about the effects of private value on the exigencies of experience, stand midway between Rabelais's exuberant openness and Sterne's dense interiority. Quixote's wide and chaotic wanderings, impelled by his need to enact what he thinks, are at several removes from the tight, self-centered world of Shandy Hall. For Quixote there could be no question of elaborate playing at war within the confines of an ancestral manor. All the broken teeth and smashed limbs he causes and receives show that his mad values, however autonomous, demand a grim and costly engagement with an exceedingly hostile reality. Quixote's values have a curious existential status; they find their present being solely within himself but they are not fulfilled until they are acted on in the presence of their opposite. Cervantes' novel is a parody of the quest-romance, which means not only that it must have elements of the quest and the romance in it but—since it is a parody—it must be an antiromance as well. Quixote cannot complete his business and Cervantes cannot complete his parody until the antitheses are engaged, that is, until the values engendered in subjectivity are actualized in experience. At the same time, the context in which Quixote performs his affairs is radically and inevitably alien to the values of his self-sufficient consciousness, which remains safely locked up and impregnable to experience. Thus, his relation to the world outside the self is both continuous and discontinuous, and he is, simultaneously, both engaged and detached. Still, though Quixote's mind is necessarily isolated from its context, it is not willfully so. The world outside the self demands his attention, and he does all that he can to attend to it.

Toby's war games have no such problems. They are continuous with reality only to the extent that they mimic it. They have no more connection with experience than a mirror does with the world it reflects; that is, they offer simulation and not involvement. The games are acknowledged counterfeits of the truth, mere semblances of external fact, and Toby finds them perfectly satisfactory just as they are. He knows that what he has created is an abstraction, a self-sufficient echo. As if to confirm his awareness of discontinuity, Toby locates

his performances in an enclosed garden cut off from the surrounding world of the Shandeans:

> it was sheltered from a house, as I told you, by a tall yew
> hedge, and was covered on the other three sides, from mor-
> tal sight, by rough holly and thickset flowering shrubs;—
> so that the idea of not being seen, did not a little contribute
> to the idea of pleasure pre-conceived in my uncle *Toby's*
> mind. (98-99)

Quixote's quests are public and publicized, but Toby hopes
to keep his own inexorably private, disconnected from everything that does not concern his hobby-horsical values.

The qualities Toby seeks for the universe of his games are
characteristic of the Shandean landscape, and they serve not
only to distinguish Sterne from Cervantes but to lead us into
the deep center of Sterne's reading of the world. His novel is
composed of centripetal movements, not a going-out to external experience—as quests always had been—but a going-
in, away from outside involvement. Toby's withdrawal into
his garden is typical of those movements. The garden itself is
representative of some of the essential forms that populate
and structure Sterne's fictional universe.

Most of the events in the novel take place in a set of dissociated enclosed shapes, all homologous with Toby's garden.
The world of Shandy Hall is the largest of those shapes. It
has no more magnitude than the midwife's world to which
Tristram twice refers at the beginning of the novel, indicating
precisely the extent of landscape with which he will be dealing:

> by which word *world*, need I in this place inform your
> worship, that I would be understood to mean no more of
> it, than a small circle described upon the circle of the great
> world, of four *English* miles diameter, or thereabouts, of
> which the cottage where the good old woman lived, is sup-
> posed to be the centre. (11)

Later Sterne calls this "that circle of importance, of which
kind every soul living, whether he has a shirt to his back or

no,—has one surrounding him" (35). Shandy Hall is at the center of its own small circle inscribed on the circle of the great world. Within the circumference of its space it holds a series of smaller enclosures, each of which is characterized by its isolation and discontinuities. For example, most of the action of the novel occurs in separate rooms of the Shandy house. Each of those rooms, when it is the locale of the main action, is treated as though it were an entire and self-contained cosmos, one that is aware of the life outside its walls but is most deeply involved with its own internal activities.

The smallest shape in the set is also the most potent. It is that enclosure surrounding the individual selves of each of the inhabitants of the Shandean landscape. Every one of those insular selves is dissociated and self-contained, independent of its counterparts except at rare and touching moments, and concerned mainly with its own internal energies. Like the world of Shandy Hall each mind in this novel is separate, self-obsessed, private and discontinuous, as autonomous as any such entity can be. Sterne had learned more from Locke than the dangers of associative thought. He appears to have been most deeply moved, most affected in his own organization of experience, by Locke's assertion that we can know only our own constructs of reality and not reality itself. We are prisoners in the enclosure of consciousness, able to come close only to those ideas of experience that are inside the enclosure with us. The reality of things is forever unavailable to us. We know of them only through representations, much as Toby is able to comprehend unseen wars only by newspaper reports. It seems that our autonomy is forced upon us, and we must make of it what we can. For Sterne's characters this means that, when external reality impinges upon consciousness, the latter is far more likely to keep its energies within than impel them without. Though these people are all part of the world of Shandy Hall, they are each separate and discontinuous to a degree unmatched by anything in Richardson or Rousseau, where contextual autonomy—the striking of a mutually beneficial balance between the self and its context—was a compelling desire it seemed possible to satisfy.

If Clarissa and Julie finally failed, the characters in *Tristram Shandy* never had a chance to begin. Witness, for example, the effect of the news of Bobby's death. Most of the characters, when they hear about the disaster, are unable to reach out and touch the self of any other: each self is caught up with its own reading of the event, obsessed with the content of its own interiority. Each is the creator of a private cosmos, communication from the midst of which is forever hampered by the insufficiencies of language and the idiosyncrasies of individual response. Only Trim manages to break through, dissolving the kitchen crew into tears with the simple gesture of dropping his hat on the ground and thus showing how quickly and easily we are gone (361). But that is one of those fleeting, sporadic moments of contact in this world of enforced discontinuity and passionate interiority. Of course we learn something about some of the private quirks of Tristram's mind; he is not an impersonal narrator though he is frequently an omniscient one. Yet, though we are closer to him than we are to anyone else at Shandy Hall, we do not share as much of the intimacies of his consciousness as we do of Clarissa's. Sterne's novel tells us relatively little about the radical levels of Tristram's soul, those areas that were opened up by Joyce in the monologues of Leopold or Molly Bloom. We are never deep within the stream of Tristram's consciousness. He too is forever locked inside his unassailable individuality.

Shandy Hall is a microcosm peopled by monads. Sterne's characters, unlike Cervantes' equestrian hero, do not need to complete their values by confronting them with contrary opinions. Their passions find sufficient fulfillment within the self. Sterne's novel, unlike that of Cervantes, is built almost exclusively upon multiple discontinuities. The book he made out of those conditions shows the mind in thorough control of the potential of its material. His decision to cleave the mind together with itself, to leave wholeness and power primarily within consciousness, offered an image of perfect adequacy achieved within a severely limited cosmos. However much Sterne echoed Rabelais and Cervantes he in fact offered a clear alternative to them. Sterne and his predecessors gave to those who succeeded them a broad spectrum of modes in the mind's engagement with reality.

The romantics who followed Sterne looked upon him with considerable admiration, but their respect and affection were sometimes tinged with a degree of ambiguity. Sterne, and Cervantes before him, stood at decisive stages in the development toward romanticism's concern with the autonomy of the self. From the perspective of literary history they were seen to represent an internalization of energy and value that was a necessary precondition for an independent and efficacious imagination. The exhortation of Edward Young to "dive deep into thy bosom [and] contract full intimacy with the stranger within thee" meant that Sterne, who dove deeper and stayed longer than most, would have something to offer to romanticism.[12] *Tristram Shandy* was unmistakably an event for those romantics who affirmed the value of interiority and the interiority of value. Their persistent investigation of the possibilities and effects of the energy within, and their stress upon the privacy of individual judgments of experience, led them to rummage through history for models and predecessors. Quixote charmed them, Rousseau attracted and appalled them, Milton's Satan stirred up their iconoclasm, and Sterne presented a striking instance of the mind at play with its private energies. He had obviously thought some of their thoughts well beforehand.

Consider, for example, Tristram's father. None of the characters in the novel has done more pondering about the way the world ought to be ordered than Walter Shandy. He is, of course, the only philosopher in town, the self-appointed resident thinker, and he takes the responsibilities of that position very seriously. It is his business to speculate upon the conditions in which one has to live in this threatening world, and to find ways of controlling those conditions for the benefit of the inhabitants of Shandy Hall, in particular for the child whom he has carefully, if routinely, engendered. Walter grounds his speculations upon his sense of the efficacy of intellectual systems, and his investigations into the history of ideas have shown him that other thinkers have had equal faith in the capacity of their systems to give order to experience. As he puts it to his brother: "Learned men, brother *Toby*, don't write dialogues upon long noses for nothing" (229). But as Sterne's novel shows they have indeed written their treatises upon names and noses to no purpose; or, to be most precise, they have written them primarily to bolster their confidence in the mind's ability to articulate the world systematically. They have looked for fixities, points of stability in the chaos of experience, but they have come up only with untenable fictions, images of order that have no effective relationship to the world where they are supposed to be applied.

The differences between Walter's and Toby's constructions are particularly instructive. Toby's fortifications, as we have seen, are not an attempt to engage experience but to mimic it, simply for his own pleasure. Walter's ideas, whatever their qualities in themselves, are attempts not only to engage but to manipulate experience. Toby creates another kind of reality, the sort that exists in models and pantomime. It is a counterpart reality, not only dependent on its source of inspiration, but also, as all imitations, claiming a coherent and satisfying life of its own; and that life is its primary area of interest. Walter reveled in the pleasure of thinking but his pleasure was far secondary to the purposiveness of his thoughts. Toby's world is inner-directed, Walter's (like Quixote's) is outer-directed. Toby shifts his little world as the outer shifts; that is, it rides with the flux of experience. Walter wants fixities, which is precisely what the world out there will not tolerate—that is, if the mysterious world out there can be said to do anything so specific as be tolerant or intolerant. Walter is a prime example of the arrogance of consciousness, Toby, not surprisingly, of its humility. Walter's confidence in his private constructions is complete, unshakable even by poorly hung

windows and muddle-headed chambermaids who cannot keep
a name straight while running up the stairs. He continues to
insist that closed systems of thought, impregnable in their
inner coherence, can enclose the world and make it safe and
profitable for his surviving offspring. Even though he loses
out on names and noses Walter still feels that he can guarantee
the successful education of his child through a skillful use of
auxiliary verbs (405-07). But it is Sterne's business to show
how misplaced Walter's confidence has been, how sterile are
these and all systems that insist on unshakable fixities.

Sterne's uneasiness with closed systems comes from more
causes than Walter Shandy's touching absurdities. All the parodies of learned foolishness in the novel show how ideas of
order that were complete and self-contained, claiming to sys-
tematize and control important segments of experience,
seemed often to collapse when they confronted the sly resistance of the world outside the mind. Walter's ways of thinking
had no give to them, no means of opening up their tightly
closed order to admit accident and the unforeseen. And that
is precisely where they became both useless and comic, ridiculous in their attempts to capture a world that was always
slipping away from them in its infinite fluidity. Tristram's
head was not quite where it should have been when Doctor
Slop's forceps closed around it, and Walter's attempts to coordinate passion with the clock came to grief with his wife's
passionless reminder of that clock. No intellectual system can
close itself off against those kinds of contingencies. No idea
of order that claims it can contain the world can afford to
ignore the world's fondness for surprises.

In fact, there is discernible in *Tristram Shandy* only a vast
and radical tentativeness. Sterne is not only suspicious of fictions and fixities but of closure as well, of saying that this is
so and it is now all finished. Closure is claustrophobic and
limiting, an assertion of finality that is perpetually belied by
the world of Shandean experience. No wonder that Tristram
said he would like to write two volumes a year indefinitely,
with no end in mind except the end of his life (37). Endings

were too much like the clicking shut of the lock with which Walter and his fellow speculators closed up their intricate systems. The real world of *Tristram Shandy* resisted endings because they gave a false sense of ease and conclusiveness. How many events in Sterne's novel ever really finish? If they are not broken up into fragments of narrative, which reappear at irregular intervals, they seem, for the most part, to melt into other scenes, which then take up their own odd positions in the novel. Sterne, it appears, was suspicious of all sorts of stopping places, which he considered conditional at best, delusive at the worst. That uneasiness extends, finally, to our usual conceptions of narrative sequence, with their neat packages of beginnings, middles, and endings. Those bundles of completed narrative are the precise equivalent of Walter's fully enclosed systems, and they are equally stiff and fallacious. Our images of order are irrelevant, our traditions of shaping them are pernicious. In the arrogance of our consciousness, we give to our intellectual and narrative structures a privileged status they cannot sustain under the pressures of reality. We are far more Quixotean than we realize. Sterne's shaking-up of the traditional forms of the novel was long considered scandalous; but, given his preconceptions about systems and his antipathy to closure, the true scandal would have been for him to do otherwise.

There were, of course, a number of theorists and practitioners for whom Sterne's dislocations of narrative were the best news out of England since the work of the late Shakespeare. For Friedrich Schlegel, for Tieck, Hoffmann and Jean Paul, for Byron and the other romantic ironists, Sterne became an exemplary instance. He was a paradigmatic experimentalist who had sensed the implications for narrative form of the issues Cervantes broached, and he turned his understanding of those issues into the web of artifice and irony that was *Tristram Shandy*. Schlegel put the case for the Sternean mode most cogently in several pages of his *Gespräch über die Poesie*. There, he extols the structure of Sterne's arabesque, the witty interplay of contradictions, the "künstlich geordnete Verwirrung,"[b][13] which for Schlegel and many of his contemporaries was the most potent mode available for the conducting of narratives.

But there is probably something more to the ironists' adulation of Sterne than the matter of the arabesque mode. Two fragments from Schlegel can help us here. The first is from the *Athenaeum*: "Es ist gleich tödlich für den Geist, ein System zu haben, und keins zu haben. Er wird sich also wohl entschliessen müssen, beides zu verbinden."[c][14] The second fragment is from the *Ideen*: "Zur Vielseitigkeit gehört nicht allein ein weitumfassendes System, sondern auch Sinn für das Chaos ausserhalb desselben, wie zur Menschheit der Sinn für ein Jenseits der Menschheit."[d][15] Schlegel clearly shares Sterne's suspicion of closed systems, or at least of those that are so fixed that they cannot cope with threats and contradictions. All systems, Schlegel argues, are surrounded by chaos, the enemy of systems, and only the most flexible versatility will permit the system maker to cope with both. One way to cope, apparently, is to build into each system a vision of its opposite, so that the mind will simultaneously have a system and not have one. In that way the ironist gives himself an ultimate elasticity, a freedom of movement all those arrogant artificers, the Walter Shandies and the makers of traditional narrative, can never have. But there is still more: Schlegel also shares with Sterne a suspicion of that privileged attitude of the mind driven by an impulse to round off and close up an experience. Schlegel's uneasiness with stopping places is nowhere more apparent than in these lines from the familiar 116th fragment from the *Athenaeum*:

> Die romantische Dichtart ist noch im Werden; ja das ist ihr eigentliches Wesen, dass sie ewig nur werden, nie vollendet sein kann . . . Sie allein ist unendlich, wie sie allein frei ist, und das als ihr erstes Gesetz anerkennt, dass die Willkür des Dichters kein Gesetz über sich leide.[e][16]

Those lines make plain the essential point of departure Sterne shared with the ironists who followed him. All those neat forms parceling off pieces of the life and action of the world are fictions of freedom that actually make the mind a prisoner of its own delusions. One cannot have a viable autonomy unless one recognizes this. Sterne had posed the issue with the projects of Doctor Slop and Walter Shandy, the learned treatises of a host of intellectuals, and the contrasting practices of Tristram himself. His arabesques were the outward manifestation of a profound uneasiness with any confinement of the mind, any attempt to limit its adaptability to the pressures of experience. The mind must be free to create an order that asserts the provisional. That freedom is under attack in a world of closures and fixities because such a world is a confining one, with no room for free play. It is the mind's self-created straitjacket. All the romantic ironists, from Schlegel to Byron, began with that observation.

The question, then, is how to make art in the face of these pressures; or, more productively, how to make art out of these pressures. How can one so order the products of the imagination that they are, simultaneously, systematic and unsystematic? Consider the needs of the romantic ironist. He had, above all, to preserve the freedom and autonomy of consciousness because the will of the poet, as Schlegel puts it, can tolerate no law over itself. The difficulty was in being autonomous but not arrogant, in insisting on the primacy of the free consciousness while avoiding that smugness of the intellect Sterne found in learned doctors, Tieck found in the theatrical audience, and Byron found in Don Juan's mother. The romantic ironist prides himself on his lucidity, on the clarity of his awareness that fixities and hobbyhorses tie chains around the mind. He has, or wants to have, a lucid, privileged, free consciousness that is distrustful of inflexible fictions. Yet that lucidity makes him aware of what Sterne had already shown, that there is a danger in the uncritical exaltation of the autonomous consciousness. (Compare Milton on his Satan.) Both Tristram and his father are proud of the independent capacities of the mind. But the difference between the ironic consciousness and the arrogant one lies in the ironist's awareness of contingency, of the need to embrace multiplicity while acknowledging both the tentativeness that pervades experience and the noisy proximity of chaos. The ironist knows that he needs to say yes and no at once. That is a large order indeed, particularly when it comes to shaping imaginative structures that can take all these different pressures into account. As it turns out, Sterne had thought about these problems, too, and had put his thought into magnificent practice.

Sterne's approach to a solution takes a curious form in which aloofness and involvement, artifice and accident, container and contained, are set off against each other. We have to begin by recognizing that there are two books called *The Life and Opinions of Tristram Shandy*. One of these is an abortive memoir, an autobiographical sketch undertaken by Tristram Shandy; the other is a novel by Laurence Sterne. One of these books—Tristram's memoir—exists only in a work of fiction; the other—Sterne's novel—exists as a work of fiction. One of these authors, Tristram Shandy, claims that he is not always in full control of his material, that he is subject to the whims and capricious energies of his associative faculties. Sterne, the author of the novel, has created that world in which Tristram, the pawn of his own irresistible impulses, bounces about from one memory to another. Tristram's memoir seems forever subject to the anarchy always threatening to swallow up the fixities of human experience. Sterne's novel impersonates that anarchy, offering an artful semblance of chaos, a mimicry of the forces that challenge the constructs of the mind. Thus, on Tristram's level there is that perpetual alternation of self-creation and self-destruction, that permanent parekbasis, or digression, which Schlegel saw as the basic rhythm of the ironic mode.[17] On Sterne's level there is only creation, carried on with a cool detachment and passionate skill, which are the antithesis of Tristram's frantic, self-disparaging search for order. Sterne has created a flexible system of artifice that not only acknowledges its opposite but contains within itself an image of that opposite, granting chaos its right to exist but asserting the power of the mind to create an accurate semblance of experience. The authorial consciousness in *Tristram Shandy* is free and autonomous, subject to no power over itself; but it takes the world as the world is, not as one would like it to be. That combination of detachment and engagement was ingenious and exemplary, giving equal due to both consciousness and contingency. Sterne's imitation of the mind's disorder was, in fact, a fruitful instance of the mind's capacity to shape alternatives to chaos.

The dichotomy of the inner and outer versions of *The Life and Opinions*, that is, of memoir and novel, should not be taken to mean that Tristram is no more than a victim of chaos. As we have seen, he has learned (or claims to have learned) to cooperate with chaos, turning the randomness he cannot avoid into productive digression. Sterne would never accept a dichotomy, even the one that orders his book, without such a finely nuanced qualification.

The major romantic ironists who followed Sterne worked out their own versions of such gestures, some under Sterne's direct influence, others in his spirit or in the spirit of Schlegel's cryptic pointers. The requirements were always the same: an assertion of the autonomy of consciousness and an acknowledgment of the proximity of chaos. Tieck's *Gestiefelte Kater*, for example, puts on the stage a set of fictive spectators who are the precise counterparts of Sterne's fictive readers. They are there, as characters in Tieck's play, to watch the performance of a play called *Der Gestiefelte Kater*. Of course this is homologous with Sterne's work within a work: Tieck turns to the ironist's use the old tradition of the play within a play. But where Sterne's fictive readers had appeared at irregular intervals throughout his novel, Tieck puts his fictive spectators on stage both before and after the performance of the inner play, and this gives him an opportunity for a close examination of these spectators' expectations. In fact, when they file onto the stage they carry along with them the baggage of stubborn, unexamined preconceptions about dramatic illusion and the meaning of fictionality. Tieck's attacks upon these privileged absurdities lay open not only the spectators' craving for conventional order but their imperious attitude toward the relations of drama and audience. They quibble about improbabilities and offenses to rational illusion, refusing to acknowledge that the apparent irrationalities in the play should not seek their justification from the real world but from the order of the play itself. That is, they insist upon their own autonomy of judgment but refuse to grant to the text that independence and self-sufficiency, that self-sustaining and self-justifying status, which defines the autonomy of the work of art. Of course, in attempting to make the play subservient they are doing the same to the author as well; and Tieck's fictional playwright, crushed and aggressive at the same time, is forced to come out and plead for understanding from the spokesmen of rational illusion, asking them to suspend judgment until they have seen the full reach of his (rather tame) imagination. It is ultimately in regard to this matter of the imagination's prerogatives that Tieck leads his most concerted attack, offering up a dazzling pyrotechnics of illusion-breaking and interplay among various levels of fiction. As he shakes up the fictive spectators he shows the real ones that he can create a most skillful imitation of disorder, subjecting all the spectators to a chaos over which he has total control. The demands and presuppositions of the critical observer cannot dictate the acts of the artificer, because he and his work will tolerate no law over themselves. Tieck shatters illusion because his fictive spectators refuse to give in to illusion, because they will not permit that willing suspension of disbelief constituting not only poetic faith but an acknowledgment of the autonomy of the imagination. He breaks open their closed systems, countering their smugness and inflexibility with an example of the artist's freedom and with a mocking warning of the need to recognize the chaos that surrounds us all. He has, like Sterne, built an order that contains its opposite within itself. That, it seems, is the only way for the ironist to say no and yes at once.

Here, then, is a theater of the mind, a performance in which the actors and the action are surrogates for the encounter of consciousness with contingency. What Tieck does with the encounter is only the most graphic instance of the practices generally followed by the romantic ironists, who were aware that we are all spectators and necessarily prey to the same imperiousness and ignorance as the fictive audience in Tieck's drama. The lucidity of the ironist creates an imaginative order in which the mind acts out contingency, watching itself at work in a paradoxical structure in which consciousness is both actor and spectator at once. Sometimes the roles are fused in the same figure, for example in the narrator of Byron's *Don Juan*. He is a clear-eyed performer who sees all the temptations his mind is heir to, and, with a confidence born of that lucidity, permits himself a repeated submission to the temptation of chaos. He knows the necessity for impulse and the equal and opposite necessity for system, and he has found a dialectical mode of the imagination, which gives free play to each of those inimical opposites. Whenever the form of *Don Juan* crumbles into a mass of digressions and ridiculous rhymes the narrator acknowledges his fall, grins, and returns to the narrative sequence again. *Don Juan* is another theater of the autonomous mind, another instance of the ironist's recognition that only the imagination that acknowledges contingency can match its massive power.

What Sterne could offer to the romantics, they took up, oftentimes zealously. Yet there were equivocations and demurrals, not only among those who were less than sympathetic but even among some who took Sterne as a significant model. The reasons for hesitation were diverse and variously expressed, but all appeared to point toward a single conclusion. Sterne's self-consciousness about the techniques of fiction presented a set of tactics that could be fruitfully used to attack all sorts of conventionalities about literature. His awareness of chaos and the mind's need for a lucid autonomy to cope with chaos appealed to a number of romantics. But there was a sense that the qualities of the world he depicted could carry one only so far; that his insights and innovations could be made to do marvelous things but that the reach of his spirit was far less than the romantics needed for their greater purposes. Schlegel made the point quite clearly in his *Gespräch über die Poesie*. In the "Brief über den Roman" he praised Sterne for his originality as a writer of arabesques, what Schlegel calls in another part of the *Gespräch* a "künstlich geordnete Verwirrung, diese reizende Symmetrie von Widersprüchen, dieser wunderbare ewige Wechsel von Enthusiasmus und Ironie."[f][18] Schlegel is clearly taken with the ebullient energies of Sterne's imagination and his ability to so shape the world of his novel that he produces a skilled semblance of chaos, a mockery of order that is, in fact, a prodigious instance of the mind's ordering capacities. According to Schlegel the arabesque is "eine ganz bestimmte und wesentliche Form oder Äusserungsart der Poesie";[g][19] yet he goes on to say that the humor of a writer like Sterne, though it is the natural poetry of the higher classes of the age, is still somewhat distant from the greatest art. Diderot, Jean Paul, and Sterne are especially useful for understanding the greatest because, once we have developed a sense for the special qualities of their work, we are well on the way to appreciating what Schlegel calls "den göttlichen Witz, die Fantasie eines Ariost, Cervantes, Shakespeare."[h][20] Sterne helps us to understand the greatest though he is not among the greatest himself. He controls a lesser range, admirable in its kind but not sufficiently encompassing to enfold the full scope of romantic potential.

Coleridge had similar points to make. He found Sterne's teasing sexuality embarrassing and, in his Course of Lectures delivered in 1818, he chided Sterne for mixing "the best dispositions of our nature" with the basest, therefore running the risk of turning the humorous into the abhorrent.[21] Still, in the ninth lecture of the series Coleridge uses a sentence from Sterne as a concise illustration of his definition of humor (a definition that was paraphrased from Jean Paul, one of Sterne's great romantic admirers). In humor, Coleridge argues, "the little is made great, and the great little in order to destroy both; because all is equal in contrast with the infinite"; and he goes on to exemplify this with a dictum of Walter Shandy's:

"It is not without reason, brother Toby, that learned men write dialogues on long noses."[22] But in a section of the lecture devoted specifically to Sterne, Coleridge gives a more precise reading of Sterne's characteristic excellencies, and in so doing he places Sterne, as Schlegel did, in a category separate from the greatest. Coleridge admired Sterne's ability to reproduce the most exquisite energies of the inner life, "bringing forward into distinct consciousness those minutiae of thought and feeling which appear trifles, yet have an importance for the moment."[23] But, Coleridge argues, Sterne is a humorist, not a man of humor, and this distinction in kind is also a distinction in quality. With a humorist like Sterne "the effect of [his] works does very much depend on the sense of his own oddity,"[24] that is, on an obtrusive and idiosyncratic consciousness, which pushes itself forward into the work. The man of humor—Cervantes, for example, or Shakespeare—remains objective and aloof because "the effect of [his] portraits does not depend on the felt presence of himself" in what he writes. The humorist, it appears, uses himself as an instance but the man of humor has the "superadded power" of presenting these peculiarities of character on a more universal level, "to men in general."[25] In the previous lecture Coleridge had approached Cervantes' universality from another direction. Quixote, he asserted, is a personification of "the reason and the moral sense, divested of the judgment and the understanding," while Sancho stands for "the common sense without reason or imagination."[26] Taken separately each is limited and variously ineffective. Joined together, however, they "form a perfect intellect," an image of the total human mind, which is a creation of genius so high that it "has been achieved by Cervantes and Shakespeare, almost alone."[27] Sterne's mastery of "the minutiae of thought and feeling," his delicacy in handling the subtlest gradations of consciousness as well as the characters who embody them, opens up profound areas of the human mind. Yet the man of humor has a reach and sweep this analyst of the enclosed consciousness, with all his exuberant mockery of the great and little, could never match.

Sterne, it seemed, did not have the metaphysical resonance the romantics found in Cervantes or Milton or Shakespeare. Quixote was generally honored as an aristocrat of the imagination, struggling to bring together the ideal and the real in the face of a hostile environment.[28] If he was the dupe of fictions, to which he allied himself with an alarming energy, Quixote's madness was read by the romantics as a compulsive search for a better way to live. Though his body was subject to battering, his mind and values were unshakable, and what they touched upon was of the most profound human concern. For the romantics Sterne was not only more terrestrial than Cervantes but, because of the centripetal nature of Sterne's world, he could not share in what they saw as Cervantes' interest in ideality. Further, there is no possibility of a Quixote-Panza contrast in *Tristram Shandy*. There is no measurable standard of ordinary reality, no concrete, hard and fast, common-sensical voice of the belly in Sterne's novel. Toby and Yorick were widely praised by the romantics but as heroes of sensibility, tender, fanciful, and sympathetic, attuned less to the patterns of the universe than to the movements of their own souls.

As the comments from Schlegel and Coleridge imply, Sterne's overriding concern with accident and contingency did not build a literary cosmos that was sufficiently far-reaching to serve as a model for the totality of romantic experience. The dense and frequently impenetrable texture of romantic reality supported a multilayered, symbolic, and correspondential scheme that was both familiar and forever strange, unified, aloof, and alive all at once. For many romantics the resistance of this kind of external experience was equal and opposite to the correspondingly intense energies of consciousness. It was a warfare of peers, expressed in the appropriate image of a marriage. For others, the pressures of externality on the self were finally triumphant, though not until the self and externality had met and measured each other's capacities. Clearly there was a variety of potential responses to this meeting, but the responses occurred only after it was shown that there had been some kind of encounter. For this reason the most serviceable models for the romantics were those who had been forced to confront a similar kind of difficult reality at some stage in their experience. Rousseau, Quixote, and Milton's Satan, each in very different ways, were seen as having learned to function in the face of an aggressive and frequently threatening external order. Each had established a form of the autonomous consciousness that could meet with that most difficult order and acknowledge its stubborn and intricate facticity as well as his own private desires. Each kind of autonomy, however tenuous and tentative, was won only after a costly series of struggles. As a result, the battles both Quixote and Satan went through became paradigmatic for those romantic figures who felt compelled to meet the world in active confrontation. Romantic Quixotism and romantic Satanism (figures like Schiller's Karl Moor have something of both) were at one in at least this regard. Yet even the most passive romantic heroes—René, Obermann, Childe Harold— became passive only after they had experienced the puzzling, intransigent otherness of the world outside the self. Each had disengaged himself because of massive and unacceptable pressures, which made it impossible for him to come to terms with anything other than his own most intimate order. His withdrawal was, in effect, a negative engagement with the world, a passive rebuttal to the indignities with which he was threatened. However vague those threats—and sometimes, as in *René*, they are very difficult to specify—the meeting with resistance always, at some point, took place. Though we may come late into the story of one of these abstracted figures, as we do in Byron's *Manfred*, some form of justification for the desire to withdraw is given, even though the justification can be calculatedly mysterious. Withdrawal alone was never sufficient. Autonomy was never sought without a recognition that it was the most desirable alternative in a set of difficult choices. There was always a tension between the conflicting desires for autonomy and engagement, and that was so whether those desires were experienced sequentially or simultaneously. Even the most lyric instances of the craving for autonomy, as in Rousseau's *Cinquième Promenade,* implied a narrative about past or present tensions. There was no such implicit narrative in Sterne, who offered an autonomy floating genially in a vacuum, smiling broadly and with immense satisfaction upon its own considerable skill. Quixote and Satan seemed far more adaptable. The Don could be transformed into an image of the tough, independent consciousness that seeks to engage the world for the sake of ideality, while Satan became a grand instance of the self-sufficient mind in conflict with aggressive tyranny. But Tristram himself never achieved such a position, although the novel that bears his name contains an internalization of energy so thorough and so masterly that it has remained a prototype of subjective independence. The romantics wanted something more in their models of the self-sustaining consciousness. Whether it battled the world or embraced it, whether it was superior to experience or submissive to it, the romantic mind needed a context in which to do its work.

Some remarks from Friederich Schlegel can help us to round out these issues. In the "Rede über die Mythologie," which forms a central part of the *Gespräch,* Schlegel argues that the modern poets, in their attempts to give name and form to the most sacred things, have had to work in a spiritual vacuum. They have lacked not only a maternal ground but also a sky, a living air—that is, a series of images that, taken together, create a total and encompassing context.[29] Each poet has been separate and alone, each work a new creation *ex nihilo.* Creative substance, indeed the order of poetry itself, has been drawn solely from the private world of each one's subjective energies.[30] That situation, Schlegel insists, needs to be changed: the poets must work in harmony with a scheme that is more encompassing than the order any one person can give. Modern poetry needs a mythology, a system outside the individual, which is, nevertheless, a *Mittelpunkt* ("central point") to which each belongs and from which each can draw his spiritual sustenance. Such a mythology is the most artful of art works, a new container for the ancient sources of poetry; and it creates a system of symbols in which all aspects of the modern imagination can share.

At one point in his discussion of mythology Schlegel asserts that myth and the arabesque are similar in form, that the artful confusion and asymmetrical contradictions of the latter are, in themselves, an indirect mythology. That would seem, at least, to promote Sterne to a higher position than Schlegel had given him in the "Brief über den Roman"; but in fact this does not happen, and—given the essential conditions of both Sterne's and Schlegel's worlds—it could not. A call for myth is a call for a community of individualities, a society of the spirit in which each person shares in a whole and draws on its order and imagery while affirming his own special place within it. But there is very little sharing in Sterne's world. Myth offers a collective center, but there could be no such *Mittelpunkt* in that group of idiosyncratic separatists who populate the grounds of Shandy Hall. They are necessarily and forever isolated from each other because the nature of consciousness makes them so. Their autonomy is enforced by their epistemology, which even under the best conditions makes agreement on the meaning of symbols very difficult to achieve. Since they can hardly get out of themselves, they could not be expected to share similar ideas about the imagery of transcendence or the meaning of the ideal toward which the romanticized Quixote courageously struggled. Tristram's autonomy was a magnificent achievement, a tribute to the possibilities of the creative consciousness in a confusing and disorderly world. But from the point of view of the most exalted romantic needs, as well as the conditions of romantic autonomy, Tristram's self-sufficiency had a poignancy about it as well as a somewhat chilling potential for entrapment. It stood alone, powerful, claustrophobic, and disembodied. How ironic it is that this comedy of the enclosed consciousness should be so profoundly concerned with closure, so suspicious of it. Sterne's novel did not offer an expansive, articulated and systematic image of reality, the sort on which the romantics could build a meaningful autonomy as well as a myth that would clarify the relations of mind and metaphysics. He was a hero of the feelings and a master of antitraditional modes; but the independence his work exemplified could never give full and adequate answers to the questions the romantics posed about the mind's demanding freedom.

ᥫᩣ FOUR ᥫᩣ

Egotism, Empathy, Irony

The romantics, it is clear, needed more flexibility than Sterne could give them. This is not to say that any one model could give them all the flexibility that they needed, but that every model had to have useable points to make about dealing with externality. A hampering of flexibility is a hampering of freedom; in effect, the mind's freedom in *Tristram Shandy* is hampered by the limited space in which it has to work, and the romantics did not want to be so cramped. The romantic mind, as I have noted, needs an adequate context because it has a considerable territory to cover in its exploration of its freedom. Its relation to externality ranged from superiority to submissiveness, from an arrogance of consciousness which makes Walter Shandy look like a yokel, to a humility that is far more yielding of the privileges of the self than the utmost docility of Uncle Toby. With such a spectrum to cover, the romantic mind could not afford to seek out limitations. It is one of the busiest minds on record, as diligent in testing the possibilities of its reach as it was in shaping images of that test.

The romantics were constantly occupied in examining the degree to which the mind and the world were commensurate with each other. The possibilities of such commensuration were broad and flexible; they saw a myriad of ways in which consciousness and nature could learn to come together in fruitful struggle. Wordsworth's metaphor of a marriage, with its attendant consummation and creation, is perhaps the best-known image for this exquisite fitting. But Wordsworth's was a middle way, giving equivalent weight to each partner in the relationship. The high argument in the Preface to *The Excursion* is an exercise in parity, its main point the creative efficiency that comes from interlocking the powers of mind and world. Blake, Wordsworth's most active antagonist in these matters, insisted in his marginalia to *The Excursion* that the outward creation was a hindrance to the mind as it ascended to its encompassing vision of eternity: "You shall not bring me down to believe such fitting & fitted I know better & Please your Lordship."[1] Yet the earlier Blake, on his way to a fourfold vision, could still look at a thistle and see it both as a thistle and a grey old man, finding analogies in the minutely natural.[2] In his marginalia to Lavater's *Aphorisms on Man* he remarked that "it is impossible to think without images of somewhat on earth."[3] Thus, there were times when even Blake thought of using the world in order to transcend it, beginning with a wild flower and ending with heaven. "Auguries of Innocence," for example, is a horde of correspondences in which nature is repeatedly transformed into the matter of the imagination.

Other writers did the same in different ways, drawing on nature's infinite capacity to supply images men could use to understand other modes of being as well as their own. At the beginning of Novalis's *Die Lehrlinge zu Sais* nature is presented as a *Chiffernschrift,* a cipher-writing or hieroglyphics, whose meaning can be read in stones, eggshells, the lights of heaven, and even iron filings *(Feilspäne)* around magnets. This is, of course, the book of nature, and the components of nature are characters men learn to read for supernatural meaning. As in Blake's "Auguries," nature is seen primarily as source material for figures and symbols. But Novalis is more in awe of nature than Blake is, and the key to this wonder-writing (*Wunderschrift,* a wonderful writing about wonders) yields itself to most men only occasionally and then merely in transitory intuitions. The nature described at this point in Novalis's book is stubborn and resistant. Though it is there to be used by the mind, only the rare man of extraordinary insight can join its individual parts into a sentence of universal meaning. Still, Novalis's fragmentary book is designed to present not just this one mode of relation to nature, favored though it may be, but a myriad of alternatives. Other possibilities offer themselves almost immediately. At the opposite extreme from Blake—that is, at the other end of the spectrum of commensuration—is the speaker in Novalis's book who proposes that the most perfect encounter with nature occurs when one blends oneself with all natural beings, feeling one's way, so to speak, into the center of their natural selves.[4] In such modes consciousness is empathic, obsessed with *Einfühlung* ("empathy"). The result, as Novalis's speaker argues, is an unparalleled awareness from within of the multiplicity of things as well as their palpable, individual particularity.

The variety of these instances of the engagement of the romantic self with experience shows that the available modes of engagement are not single and simple but manifold and complex. Consciousness and nature, it appears, can be antagonists as well as partners, and sometimes both at once. There is no definitive mode but a spectrum of them, going from a contest in which nature is used primarily to illustrate the affairs of the mind to a convergence in which consciousness may choose to blend with the universe or with another being. In a single passage in *Die Lehrlinge zu Sais* Novalis runs over the entire spectrum from one end to the other, beginning with the humanizing of nature by the mind, moving to a balanced I-Thou relationship, and ending with a thorough submission of the self to the world that it faces:

> Drückt nicht die ganze Natur so gut, wie das Gesicht, und die Gebärden, der Puls und die Farben, den Zustand eines jeden der höheren, wunderbaren Wesen aus, die wir Menschen nennen? Wird nicht der Fels ein eigentümliches Du, eben wenn ich ihn anrede? Und was bin ich anders als der Strom, wenn ich wehmütig in seine Wellen hinabschaue, und die Gedanken in seinem Gleiten verliere?[a][5]

The speaker at this point in the book does not seem to recognize that these are very different versions of the contract of mind with nature, and that the versions are never fully compatible. Other romantics were more sensitive to the differences and what they implied. Indeed, some of the most skilled practitioners of romantic consciousness (Coleridge, for example) could range over the entire spectrum, experimenting with a variety of ways of fitting together the mind and the world. Others looked for modes of accommodation between the extreme ends of the spectrum.

From one point of view, the order of relationships can be seen as adaptable and not fixed. It could be as flexible as one chose to make it. From another point of view, the relationships can be used to reveal typologies, so that ways of meeting with nature tell us something about forms of the romantic personality as well as diverse attitudes toward society, the ideal, and the uses of poetry. The poet who considers the submission of the self's autonomy to be a primary form of imaginative experience will most likely prefer a kind of poetry that plays down the doings of the authorial consciousness. He would not be an imitator of Sterne's ways or an admirer of the intrusive ironist. His opposite number, at the other end of the spectrum, is obsessed by the self's capacity to resist incursion and by the need to protect its independence. He would choose an epic of the self, most likely of the self's encounter with itself as well as with the solidities of natural and social experience. The epics of Blake, Wordsworth, and Byron come out of those obsessions. Such a poet could, like Coleridge, find Sterne morally obnoxious and yet admire the intensity of his concern with subjective patternings. But Keats, speaking of Hunt and Wordsworth, wrote that he preferred grandeur and merit that are "uncontaminated & unobtrusive."[6] The practitioners of romantic consciousness offered no single solution to the question of what they deemed best within themselves, what they wanted most of all to honor and protect. They agreed only on the importance of the fact of consciousness itself. After that there was only divergence.

Of course the emphasis upon the importance of consciousness can come about for a variety of reasons. Blake is an extreme example. By the time of his larger prophetic books and later works such as *A Vision of the Last Judgment* and the marginalia to Wordsworth, Blake had fully established the lineaments of his personal myth. Nature was the condition of "stony materialism," the place of physical generation and all sorts of enticements to corruption. This world of Generation is one phase up from Ulro, which is simply inert matter, the ultimate sluggishness of fallen being. Ulro had been formed as an act of self-engendered grace because the mind, in its tumble from the unities of Eternity, had to stop somewhere in order to recover itself. Generation is closer than Ulro is to Eternity, but not by much. It offers somewhat less of an impediment to seeing, though it is still far below the ultimate. "In Eternity All is Vision"; so Blake put it in the *Laocoön* engraving.[7] In *A Vision of the Last Judgment* he argued, in a Neoplatonic vein, that "There Exist in that Eternal World the Permanent Realities of Every Thing which we see reflected in this Vegetable Glass of Nature."[8] In *Jerusalem* he had put it more conventionally: "Imagination the real & eternal World of which this Vegetable Universe is but a faint shadow."[9] In *Milton* he points out the deceptiveness of materiality:

And every Natural Effect has a Spiritual Cause, and Not
A Natural: for a Natural Cause only seems, it is a
    Delusion
Of Ulro: & a ratio of the perishing Vegetable Memory.[10]

Baudelaire would have cherished these passages for Blake's adjectival "Vegetable," which has the proper combination of descriptive accuracy and contempt.

For Blake the imagination's autonomy is absolute and unconditional, more so than for anyone else of his time. Man is his own enemy because the world is as he sees it, and if he sees it materially, he will never know how free he can be. Put another way, the unfallen imagination, the imagination of and in Eternity, is fully conversant with all of its own capacities. It is at the absolute maximum of efficiency. In Eternity the imagination is all that it can ever be, and, since it is the highest property of the human, it is also all that man can ever be. Thus, Eternity offers not only the undiluted presence of God but also the fullest possible presence of man and his imagination. This comes to mean, finally, that Jesus (the ultimate of the human state), God, man, and the imagination are one and the same: "Jesus as also Abraham & David considerd God as a Man in the Spiritual or Imaginative Vision . . . Man is all Imagination God is Man & exists in us & we in him."[11] Given these circumstances, the mind has to remain aloof from nature, treating it as translucent matter that should be used only as a way through to the one state that really counts. Blake's identification of Jesus and the imagination is the definitive rebuff to nature, the unimpeachable proof of the mind's independence and qualitative superiority. Nature, it is clear, can be meaningful only insofar as it is perceived humanly, by a human and in human terms; that is, as it is transformed into its opposite. Indeed, nature matters only when it is recognized as the declined state of its opposite; and even then such recognition could result in a vituperative dismissal. At the end of the *Songs of Experience,* in the late poem "To Tirzah," Blake's bitter contempt for the "senseless clay" of the flesh crupted onto Tirzah, a nasty version of maternal Nature. In a neatly ironic shift the mother later turns into a temptress, whorish and befittingly wedded: in *The Laocoön* (about 1820) the material world was also known as Lilith, "Satans Wife The Goddess Nature."[12] Among other things, that marriage was an emphatic and unmistakable rebuttal to Wordsworth's spousal verse celebrating the wedding, in *The Recluse,* of "this goodly universe" and "the discerning intellect of Man." At no stage in Blake could there be any question of the fully aware mind giving itself to nature in that or any other way. To do so would be an unholy act and—what amounts to the same thing—a denial of the freedom of the imagination. There was certainly no possibility of succumbing to *Einfühlung,* that dissolution of the imagination's autonomy which is nature's ultimate enticement as well as its most drastic device. The mind's persistent guardedness is therefore not only a necessary condition for imaginative vision but also an acknowledgment that it is always in prey to the delusive and claustrophobic seductiveness of its mortal opposite.

For someone like the Emerson of the essay *Nature* the physical is an inferior order of being, much as it is in Blake; yet it is not a threat but an instrument, which it rarely is in Blake. In *Nature* Emerson affirms the priority and primacy of mind as well as its unconditional autonomy vis-à-vis nature; but nature is to be employed, not condemned. He argues that the primary purpose of the mind's encounter with nature is to convert natural details into analogues that can tell men something about themselves. That is, the mind's business with nature is ultimately self-reflective and self-referential. Emerson's *Nature* is a late, ripe instance of one romantic mode of the relation of mind and world, a mode in which consciousness and nature are perfectly commensurate and, in the most basic sense, made for each other. They are able to cooperate so effectively because nature is there, elementally passive, to be used by the self-imaging mind. Emerson shares with Blake the view that nature in itself has no meaningful existence outside of its relation to man. Blake had insisted in the *Proverbs of Hell* that "where man is not nature is barren."[13] Emerson's phrasing in his essay goes spiritedly to the same point: "All the facts in natural history taken by themselves, have no value, but are barren like a single sex. But marry it to human history, and it is full of life."[14] Once we grow aware that "there seems to be a necessity in spirit to manifest itself in material forms" and that "the visible creation is the terminus or the circumference of the invisible world" then the patterns of potential relationship between man and nature become evident (22). Nature is there as a set of utterances, to be understood not simply for their own inherent qualities, their tones, and rhythms, but as the language of God; and that language, like all divine modes of speech, is radically figurative. As Emerson expressed it in a journal entry, "every natural fact is trivial until it becomes symbolical or moral."[15] Nature's speech, in Emerson as in Novalis and occasionally in Blake, is an elaborate and coherent system of links among all the worlds to which man has access.

To put it differently, the laws of God are objectified in one way in the laws of nature and in another in the laws of nature's superior, the order of man's intellect. In "The Method of Nature," a lecture Emerson delivered on 11 August 1841, nature "is the memory of the mind. That which once existed in intellect as pure law, has now taken body as Nature. It existed already in the mind in solution; now, it has been precipitated, and the bright sediment is the world."[16] This curious sediment has mirroring qualities, as he pointed out in *Nature* five years before. The active consciousness determines very quickly that it can learn something about itself through nature because "the laws of moral nature answer to those of matter as face to face in a glass. . . . The axioms of physics translate the laws of ethics" (21). When man learns that "the smallest weight may be made to lift the greatest" he has achieved a spiritual insight as well as a physical one (21). This doctrine of nature as tool and the mind as technician is basic to Emersonian transcendentalism, and versions of that relationship appear everywhere in his work. Both man and nature are at their best in such orderly encounters, their roles carefully defined, their relative strengths always in view. "The world," he says in *Nature*, "is a remoter and inferior incarnation of God, a projection of God in the unconscious" (38). The mind, on the other hand, is the imitation and imitator of God, the most complete expression of the invisible world's perfection available on earth. It is subservient only to its source. Since the task of the mind is to turn the elements of nature into anthropocentric illustrations, it follows that the purpose, indeed the destiny, of unconscious nature is to be transformed into consciousness. The highest use of nature is as material through which consciousness can seek to fulfill itself: "Nature is made to conspire with spirit to emancipate us" (30). But obviously nature too is emancipated in the process because if it is transformed into consciousness it becomes something higher than itself, rising (so to speak) on the chain of being. It goes through a metamorphosis of kind and quality, becoming what Blake calls "Mental Reality." An artifact of the mind is always superior to a fact of nature. Nature benefits in this process, then, because—and insofar as—it is useful. In this essay and through most of his works Emerson sketches a conspiratorial, anthropocentric universe in which every element contributes to the proper business of mankind, the recognition of spirit in the world. Of course, since the mind is itself spirit, a fragment answering to the overall spirit that is at the center and everywhere, what the mind recognizes in nature is actually an aspect of itself. Ultimately, then, nature serves man as a relatively unsubtle instrument through which he can reach the highest forms of self-recognition.

These acts and attitudes take their origin, of course, in the poetry and speculations of English and German romanticism.[17] If Emerson could not have known *The Prelude* when he published *Nature* on September 9, 1836, he certainly knew and meditated on the materials in *Tintern Abbey* about the transformation of nature into consciousness. The passage on the "transparent eyeball" at the beginning of *Nature* is obviously linked to the lines on seeing into the life of things in *Tintern Abbey;* but that is the only point of linkage between Emerson's ecstatic passage and the rest of Wordsworth's poem. Wordsworth's comment on the experience of becoming "a living soul" is the culmination of an intricate account in which he carefully and precisely details the processes (insofar as he can describe them) by which nature turns into its opposite, mind, and, in effect, leads us out of itself. There is nothing about those or any similar processes in the material on the transparent eyeball. Further, Emerson's description of his ecstasy ("I am nothing") is, in fact, unique in his essay: his statement about radical passivity is essentially different in mode from all other statements about the relationship of consciousness and nature he makes elsewhere in *Nature*. In the rest of the essay, which is obsessed with the empire of the independent mind, the transformation of nature into forms for the inner life is the central and compulsive point. That, in particular, is where Emerson's *Nature* as a whole owes most to the Wordsworthian model. His essay is mainly about the espousal of mind and world, not the denial of self for the sake of a pellucid vision.

But Wordsworth's treatment of the natural hierogamy in his poem is at once more subtle, more tentative, and less hierarchical than Emerson's in *Nature*. Indeed, the two treatments actually involve nature in two very different kinds of service. The divergence has to do mainly with their different readings of the meaning, for man, of these elemental transformations. Wordsworth's passage begins with a recollection of how the "beauteous forms," which he now sees outside himself, had once, after a previous viewing, been internalized. He moves carefully through a development that goes from the restorative recollection of sensations of feeling and pleasure to the moral influence of those memories upon man's relation with other men, reaching eventually to that lifting of the world's burden that is a necessary prelude to his vision of universal life. This development is a kind of spiritual ascension (*askesis*), which appears to transform the impulses of bodily sense into the insights of bodiless vision. In fact, it is essentially parallel to his description of the various stages of his relationship to nature in this poem and *The Prelude,* where he begins with an early situation devoted entirely to pleasurable sensations, moves on to a more mature understanding of man and his place in the natural context, and arrives ultimately at those stages where nature, like Virgil for Dante, is left behind after it has gone as far with him as its powers can take it. (Of course the development is not nearly as neat, systematic, and unambiguous as this sketch makes it.) Here, as with Emerson, nature has to become its contrary in order to have its fullest effect on man. But Wordsworth is very cautious in *Tintern Abbey,* uncertain not of what he experienced but of the assertion that nature had helped him along to his highest states. He opens up the possibility that nature might not have had all that much (or anything at all) to do with those more exalted moments. The passage is studded with qualifiers: "perhaps

... I trust ... If this / Be but a vain belief"; all of which is part of a practice of hedging, a holding back from unequivocal commitment, which had become habitual both for himself and Coleridge.[18] That he had these moral and mystical experiences is unquestionable. That nature raised them up in him is, at the least, worth questioning.

Emerson was far less uncertain about the contract of mind and nature. In *Nature* the world can offer an ecstatic openness of seeing but its primary virtue for man—a task it has no trouble in fulfilling—is its service as a treasure house of illustrations. There is nothing like that obsession with the illustrative in Wordsworth, in part, surely, because of his sense of the ultimate density of nature, in part also because the compartmentalization into ecstasy and apothegm could not fit comfortably with his own experience. Emerson is as different from Wordsworth as he is from Thoreau, and for much the same reasons. Wordsworth's opposite out there in the experienced world did not yield itself so easily and so graciously. It certainly did not lend itself to unqualified moralism. Thus, whatever the effect on *Nature* of Emerson's reading of the English romantics, his point, tone, and set of mind in that essay are not those of Wordsworth and Coleridge. The attitudes of the English poets toward the results of the mind's redemption of nature—indeed, their basic perceptions of the process and the components—were clearly and irrevocably unlike his own. In fact, in the light of Wordsworth's tentativeness and caution, Emerson's ease and certainty seem positively eerie.

Emersonian transcendentalism, as it is seen in *Nature,* is as remarkable for its faith in the mind as it is for its lack of palpable contact with the materials that the mind turns into consciousness. The nature that he loves and uses is ordinarily abstract and nebulous, its features generalized, with no sense of fine detail. This combination of confidence and imprecision raises at least the suspicion that those two elements are inseparable in Emerson's work, that he might have been more unsettled if he were able to feel and render the physical world with all the finesse and incisiveness of Thoreau. Had he done so he might have arrived at the same awareness that Thoreau eventually reached, with some surprise and discomfort: nature is resistant to the degree that it is specific and concrete. The more precisely it is grasped, the more difficult it is to hold on to and know. Diversity is a product of detail, and it is problematical, to say the least, to legislate for such variety. One could apply to Emerson the strictures of Coleridge on some poems by Bowles:

> There reigns thro' all the blank verse poems such a perpetual trick of *moralizing* every thing—which is very well, occasionally—but never to see or describe any interesting appearance in nature, without connecting it by dim analogies with the moral world, proves faintness of Impression.[19]

There is little awareness in Emerson's essay that nature could be stubborn, that there might be room for ambivalence, that some of the analogies one drew out of nature might be darker and less gratifying than one would like. The mode he preaches assumes a serenely imposing consciousness, its desires clear, its ability to attain them dependent only on the will to use the mind. There is never any question that the mind might not be adequate for this job.

The Emersonian way is obviously an extreme, one of the most precarious positions that can be taken on the spectrum in which the autonomy and efficacy of the mind are measured against the facticity of nature. For each mode on the spectrum there were different desires and varying dangers, even though the exponents of any one mode were more likely to be aware of the hazards in the other modes than those in their own. Romanticism was nothing if not risky, but the chances Keats took were not at all like the gambles undertaken by, say, Rousseau. The dangers varied because, for each mode, there was a different conception of the relative strengths of mind and nature. On one side there was the possibility that mind, in its creative intensity, would submerge and even scorn the nature on which it worked. On the other was the possibility that nature, in its overwhelming particularity, would swallow up consciousness, at least for a while. Whatever the emphasis the balance was always tenuous and difficult to sustain. Blake feared nature so much that he rarely used it, knowing that the world that furnished him wild flowers and grains of sand for analogy was also the unholy Tirzah, "Mother of [his] Mortal part" who closed his "Tongue in senseless clay." Instances of such dilemmas are everywhere, and they run the gamut from the hybris of Hölderlin's Empedokles to Wordsworth's uneasiness over giving himself completely to the nature that he loved.

Empedokles' hybris is classical in name and in occasional references to the gods, but the components of his hybris are contemporary to Hölderlin's time. His arrogance was directed toward nature, and the powers that he wielded were derived from the mind's ability to find words for a nature that remains inarticulate unless human consciousness gives it speech: "ihr ehret mich . . . und thuet recht daran; / Denn stum ist die Natur."[b] [20] He named the unknown, as he says, giving life and youth to the hesitant world. In some ways his closest counterpart is not classical Greek but romantic English: his actions prefigure by several years the assertion in Coleridge's *Dejection* ode that nature lives only insofar as the mind chooses to give it life: "O Lady! we receive but what we give. / And in our life alone does Nature live." As Empedokles puts it: "und todt / Erschiene der Boden wenn Einer nicht / Dess wartete, lebenerwekend, / Und mein ist das Feld" (95).[c] Empedokles is a mythicized version of this form of enlivening consciousness. And it is no coincidence that he comes to have the same problem as the speaker in *Dejection*, that is, the need to link up once again with the life in nature he had previously attempted to dominate, the life that is still out there but no longer available to him. Like Schiller's sentimental poet, he is separated from that which he loves most, but in Empedokles' case the fault is entirely his own. In a magnificent passage of oblique self-analysis Empedokles parodies his disciple's admiration of the powers of the mind by showing what an

unregenerated mind thinks it can do when it is unchecked by
any respect for the materials on which it is working:

> Was wäre denn der Himmel und das Meer
> Und Inseln und Gestirn, und was vor Augen
> Den Menschen alles liegt, was wär es,
> Diss todte Saitenspiel, gäb' ich ihm Ton
> Und Sprach' und Seele nicht? was sind
> Die Götter und ihr Geist, wenn ich sie nicht
> Verkündige? nun! sage, wer bin ich? (109)[d]

By this time Empedokles had been shattered by his separation
from nature, and by the resultant deathlike speechlessness of
his spirit ("Allein zu seyn / Und ohne Götter, ist der Tod"
[108]).[e] Thus, his mockery of his disciple Pausanias is actually
a melancholy acknowledgment of the arrogance of consciousness that had caused his own moral isolation. Once he had
been heedless and thought he was self-sufficient, beholden to
no one and nothing outside himself. He performed as though
he were superior to nature rather than its necessary partner.
Now the fruitfulness of their relationship has turned into an
ashy wasteland; and only he can experience that spiritual
desert because the arrogance of consciousness is a failing that
only the strong in mind can possess. Pausanias, who sees the
power but not the hazards, calls Empedokles the "Hoch-
genügsame," he who is fully sufficient (114). Panthea, another
admirer, speaks of Empedokles' mind as a law unto itself
("nur sein Geist ihm Gesez" [112]). His mind, clearly, is its
own place; and Hölderlin was as unhappy about that sort of
condition as was Coleridge, who saw "the growing alienation
and self sufficiency of the understanding" as a sign of the
antichrist.[21] The condition was not just the bane of Milton's
Satan: it was also the enticing and sticky labyrinth that his
romantic descendants had to go through in their search for
the fullest self-consciousness.

Keats's awareness of that special peril in the romantic quest
came out in his uneasy, contemptuous comment on "the

wordsworthian or egotistical sublime."²² Such sublimity is an imposition of the poet's self upon the reader; or, in another perspective, an interposition of the self between the reader and the material. Egotistical sublimity is so fascinated with the content and contours of the mind that it presents the reader with more of the consciousness that works on nature than it does of nature itself. This kind of poet knows too much and displays all of his knowledge, filling his poems with all manner of dazzling private speculations about matters he ought to treat with more objectivity and modesty. As Keats puts it, poetry should not startle or amaze with itself but with its subject.²³ The sublimity Keats describes is dramatized in Hölderlin's *Der Tod des Empedokles*. The prophet who found names for the inarticulate succumbs to the temptations of the imperious intellect: in his pride over the powers of mind he renounces the necessary respect for his materials. Like the self-obsessed poet whom Keats set up as a foil to both Shakespeare and himself, Empedokles did not permit nature to share in his independence of being but demanded that it exist largely to serve his own interests, primarily the gratification of the ar-rogance of consciousness. In fact, that haughtiness is what makes this hero contemporary, a fit partner for the Words-worth described in Keats's letters as well as for other modern egotists. After all, these were current dangers, peculiar to the prevailing understanding of the contract between conscious-ness and nature. And they were dangers less apparent to those who were prone to them than to those, such as Keats, who were on the other side of the spectrum and saw the likes of Hölderlin's Empedokles or the persona in Wordsworth's poems as symptomatic of contemporary smugness. If the Wordsworth of Keats's letters was largely a straw man, that matters less than Keats's success in building up a viable myth. It was a fiction that he needed, and it clicked into place with some essential romantic dichotomies.

Keats's attack, as we know, was largely inspired by the lectures of Hazlitt, who analyzed the phenomenon of ego-tistical sublimity with subtlety and cogency. Hazlitt's chief quarry was also Wordsworth, but some of his most suggestive evidence comes out of several passages in which he compares Wordsworth and Rousseau. In his essay "On the Character of Rousseau," published in *The Round Table,* Hazlitt argues that the dominating faculty of Rousseau's mind was "the most intense consciousness of his own existence," a conclusion that is perfectly consonant with our own current readings of Rousseau.[24] As a result of this consciousness, Rousseau could not look out at the world with empathy but, instead, "filled all objects with himself" (89). Hazlitt treats Wordsworth as Rousseau's exact counterpart, differing only because the latter wrote in prose. Still, that difference does lead to some curious discrepancies in their ways of approaching the minutiae of nature. Though both "wind their own being round whatever object occurs to them," Rousseau (as Hazlitt pictures him) comes to the things of nature in perfect frankness, with an open stress on the facets of his ego: he "interests you in certain objects by interesting you in himself" (92). Wordsworth, on the other hand, appears to be focusing on the object itself, the linnet's nest or the song of the cuckoo; but in fact "Mr. Wordsworth would persuade you that the most insignificant objects are interesting in themselves, because he is interested in them" (92). In this passage Hazlitt argues that the prose writer can express his feelings more directly than the poet, whose medium compels him to fill his poems with objects so that he can give his feelings symbolic embodiment. Rousseau is therefore the more candid and straightforward of the two, while Wordsworth's world, as Hazlitt reads it, is not as evenly divided between nature and the mind as he would appear to claim. Yet both, Hazlitt concludes, are among the greatest egotists that we know.

Hazlitt looked at Rousseau and Wordsworth from the other end of the spectrum, the one fascinated with the exploits of the empathetic consciousness. Here was the place for *Einfühlung,* what Novalis saw as an inborn capacity (*Naturorgan*) for the most intimate understanding of other creatures, and what Hazlitt and others saw as the outstanding characteristic of Shakespeare's imagination.[25] This too was a form of romantic engagement with the world, another mode of experimenting with the commensuration of mind and nature. The most familiar version to us now is Keats's "negative capability," the capacity for remaining in uncertainties and doubts rather than imposing fixities upon experience; in terms of the empathetic consciousness it meant the capacity for withholding one's own assertiveness so as to be filled with the essential content of another's being.[26] With Shakespeare, the great model for the romantics, it meant that (in Hazlitt's words) "he had only to think of anything in order to become that thing, with all the circumstances belonging to it."[27] Such empathy, according to many of its supporters, was the hallmark of genius, of the superior imagination. The energies of self were as active and intense for the empathetic consciousness as they were for the egotistical sublime, but the latter practiced the imposition of self on the world while empathy sought only for the submission of self. To put it differently, the proponents of empathy knew that when consciousness entered the recesses of another's being it was necessarily intrusive, impinging where only the inhabitant could properly belong. Yet this was an intrusion with no trace of arrogance or aggressiveness. The empathetic consciousness wanted nothing more than to assent to the validity of another being; it had no desire to assert the superiority of its own. The purpose of empathy was not dominance but knowledge—the kind of knowledge it was nearly impossible to achieve in Sterne's world. Most of all empathy wanted to know what it felt like to be a Desdemona or, in Keats's fine example, a sparrow pecking around in the gravel outside one's window. Rousseau, in Hazlitt's reading, could never achieve that kind of knowledge of others because he would rather explore with elaborate precision what it felt like to be looking at Desdemona or the sparrow, and how such looking entwined with and affirmed his private *sentiment de l'existence*. And that, for the proponents of empathy, was precisely the problem. Empathy sought out the intricacies of the object, not the subject; yet consciousness could know another being only to the degree that it ignored or played down the operations of its own perceiving mechanisms. It was very difficult, as Keats knew well, to resist the tug of one's private consciousness: he said in a letter to Benjamin Bailey, "I am not old enough or magnanimous enough to annihilate self."[28] Such extinction of the personality required a generosity of the spirit (empathy has to be seen as a gift of the self) that even the most willing could not come up with readily. It is, in effect, a renunciation of the autonomy of one's selfhood. And there were those who would always be ungenerous under any circumstances because the processes of consciousness could be a source of precious insight as well as considerable pleasure. The modern egotists— so argued their opponents—came to nature through the mediation of a self they found so fascinating that, in the end, they never got to nature at all. What should have been a conduit became, instead, a seductive detour. In an incisive passage from *Über naive und sentimentalische Dichtung* Schiller recalls his first acquaintance with Shakespeare, and how his initial readings of the dramatist had been wrongheaded in premise and approach:

> Durch die Bekanntschaft mit neuern Poeten verleitet, in dem Werke den Dichter zuerst aufzusuchen, s e i n e m Herzen zu begegnen, mit i h m gemeinschaftlich über seinen Gegenstand zu reflektiren; kurz, das Objekt in dem Subjekt anzuschauen, war es mir unerträglich, dass der Poet sich hier gar nirgends fassen liess und mir nirgends Rede stehen wollte.[f] [29]

Shakespeare was simply not that kind of poet but another, the kind who treats objects with dry truth and is wholly possessed by them. Schiller's typologies of the naive and sentimental, which derive in great part from such distinctions, are actually elaborate and somewhat fuzzy speculations on the commensuration of mind and nature in the modern world. His egotists are the sentimental poets, melancholy, uncomfortable, and self-obsessed; but they are quite unlike the Rousseau or Wordsworth portrayed by Hazlitt because the sentimental poets are too distanced from nature to be able to dominate or obliterate it through the energies of consciousness. They share all the pain and self-awareness of Hölderlin's Empedokles but without the philosopher-poet's compensating option of self-immolation to achieve the desired reunion. The sentimental poets provide the requisite counterweight to the Keatsian myth of a smug, self-satisfied egotistical sublimity: they want the intimate knowledge available only to the naive consciousness but they are prisoners, often unwitting, within the confines of their private selves.

Despite the confidence with which Keats and Hazlitt put forth their strictures, there are qualifications apparent even in their most forceful arguments. Hazlitt recognized all the feats of mind that emerged from Rousseau's interminable self-concern even as he deplored the mode of egotism that made those feats possible. And Hazlitt acknowledged several times that Wordsworth's limitations ("He can give only the fine tones of thought, drawn from his mind by accident or nature") led to poems as good as *Resolution and Independence*.[30] Keats stood in awe of Wordsworth though he knew how insufferably priggish Wordsworth could be. And Keats also admitted that the burden of other selves upon his own life could be discomforting, even overwhelming: "I wish I could say Tom was any better. His identity pressed upon me so all day that I am obliged to go out."[31] The contrary to the dissolution of his selfhood in that of the sparrow is the openness of his selfhood to penetration by others. In either case his autonomy gives way to the impetus of another's identity. He was not completely at ease with such vulnerability.

Much of this uncertainty crystallized when the proponents of empathy sought for a definition of poetic genius. It was a commonplace, in certain circles, to identify the most complete forms of genius with the capacity for empathic projection. The greatest poets, it was argued, know how to efface themselves so thoroughly that the perceiver disappears into the material he is shaping and the object shines forth as it is in itself, in all its own harmony and radiance. Coleridge (whose theories covered, at one time or another, nearly every variant in the relationship of consciousness and nature) had a precise understanding of the exploits the empathetic consciousness was capable of performing. Yet, though he esteemed its capacities, and even identified them with certain characteristics of poetic genius, Coleridge could still recognize what there was to be said in favor of the poet who was always conspicuously perceptible in his work. In a letter to William Sotheby of 13 July 1802 Coleridge acknowledges the extraordinary difficulty of achieving empathy:

> to send ourselves out of ourselves, to *think*
> ourselves in to the Thoughts and Feelings of
> Beings in circumstances wholly & strangely
> different from our own / hoc labor, hoc opus /
> and who has atchieved it? Perhaps only Shakespere.[32]

Later, in chapter fifteen of the *Biographia Literaria*, he lists among the qualities of Shakespeare's (i.e. poetic) genius "the utter *aloofness* of the poet's own feelings, from those of which he is at once the painter and the analyst."[33] But by the time of the late comments recorded in *Table Talk* Coleridge had learned to give the proper due not only to Shakespeare, who was never reflected in his work, but also to Milton who, as Coleridge asserts, is present "in every line of the Paradise Lost."[34] All of Milton's characters, Coleridge says later, are only extensions of himself, with nothing like independent life. Yet Coleridge does not consider this a drawback but simply the way Milton works, and that way, which looks forward to Emerson, has a remarkable value of its own: "it is a sense of this intense egotism that gives me the greatest pleasure in reading Milton's works. The egotism of such a man is a revelation of spirit."[35]

With Keats the acts of the empathetic imagination were too new and potent for him to have reached the seasoned judiciousness of Coleridge's late statements. He considered anything less than full self-effacement to be a lesser form of the imagination; and sometimes, it seemed, the lesser form was really no kind of imagination at all. In his letter that introduces the phrase "the wordsworthian or egotistical sublime" Keats specifically distinguishes such sublimity from "the poetical Character itself . . . that sort of which, if I am anything, I am a Member."[36] Keats's eagerness to clarify his admiration of Shakespeare as well as his own instincts for empathetic comprehension led him to toss any other kind of imaginative knowing into an abyss of self-admiration. Only empathy, it seems, is poetic. Of course Keats could not hold to this extravagance for more than one letter but his attitude does show how positions on the scale of commensuration can freeze into fixed typologies. In *Über naive und sentimentalische Dichtung* Schiller fell into a somewhat more subtle version of this dilemma in his attempts to clarify naiveté, the sentimental, and the qualities of poetic genius. Near the beginning of the essay he simply identifies the characteristics of the naive with the elements that make for genius: "Naiv muss jedes wahre Genie seyn, oder es ist keines. Seine Naivetät allein macht es zum Genie."[g] [37] So much, it would appear, for the sentimental poet's pretensions to talent, since in his deepest self he is radically different from the naive. As the essay moves on, however, Schiller finds more confidence in himself and more value in the sentimental mode, which he persistently identifies with the dominant contemporary personality. The naive is perfect in its way but that way is finite, bound within the things of this world. The naive poet can be absorbed by objects, but he has no awareness of the ideal which can be intuited, if not achieved, by his self-obsessed, sentimental counterpart. By the final section of the essay Schiller's early identification of the naive with genius has given way to an elaboration of the limits of the naive as well as its obvious value. Now he has come to see the problems in the naive's unreflectiveness, in its heavy dependence upon external experience, and in the necessary circumscription of its activities. And in a more confident gesture toward an equilibrium of the

imagination he begins to speak of the characteristics and difficulties of the sentimental genius, which by this point in the
essay appears not only to exist but to be of equal status with
the naive, though obviously different in kind. Because it rejects
limitations (which it has to do in order to break loose and
reach for the ideal), the sentimental genius encounters the
danger of going beyond the possibilities of idealized human
nature to an extreme of enthusiasm. Its problems are therefore
the counterimage of those faced by the naive.[38] Schiller's attempt at a final equilibrium is not quite as poised as the position Coleridge eventually reached because Schiller was
caught in a mixture of conflicting inclinations and could end
only in ambivalence. But the movement of his essay as a whole
is dialectical, perhaps deliberately so. That shows his treatise
to be as much an exercise in self-understanding as an exploration of the implications of poetic types.

It was obvious that the more sophisticated endeavors to
identify genius with the empathetic imagination could lead to
some intricate attempts at balance. In some cases they even
led to an understanding that the limitations and values at one
end of the spectrum were the mirror image of the limitations
and values at the other. Schiller came to see that if one end
of the spectrum faces all the well-defined hazards of modern
egotism, the other runs the serious risk of limiting itself too
exclusively to the world around it. Keats, who had rudimen-
tary glimpses of some of these problems, found the benefits
of the mode he practiced to be worth all the difficulties. But
the activities of the empathetic imagination were not for everyone, which meant, in effect, that its judgment about liabilities
was not always accepted. What was embarrassingly egotistical
for Keats was normal and correct for Emerson: the mode in
which the mind merges with nature in Emerson's essay is
frankly utilitarian, with nature there to serve the mind as
source material for man's study of his own destiny. Whereas
Keats had made his human consciousness submissive so as to
take part in the sparrow's existence, Emerson announced in
Nature that "the instincts of the ant are very unimportant

considered as the ant's; but the moment a ray of relation is seen to extend from it to man . . . then all its habits . . . become sublime."[39] Emerson was not interested in reducing the primacy of the self but in affirming it, and that affirmation included some of the bluntest statements available about the dominance of the mind over its materials. In *Nature* he puts the point unmistakably: "Shakespeare possesses the power of subordinating nature for the purposes of expression, beyond all poets."[40] In fact, it was the passivity inherent in every form of the submissive consciousness that made it suspect to those who took stock of other needs of the mind. The loss of identity a total absorption in nature or other selves entailed could be distinctly upsetting, as even Keats was led to admit. Despite the occasional identification of the highest genius with the empathetic imagination, it was as characteristic of romanticism to fear the dissolution of the self's autonomy through a thorough immersion in things as it was to praise the capacity for identifying with the strange self inside of another's being. To lose oneself, even temporarily, meant to let go of the ultimate point of stability in a churning world, the final asylum, which Wordsworth called "that last place of refuge—my own soul."[41] It was no petty egotism that caused a poet like the Lamartine of *Le Lac* to cherish the core of his perceiving consciousness. That core was the functional center of his own being, and its dissolution, however brief, was too high a price to offer for the privilege of knowing another's being.

Further, without a firm hold on that center of self the romantic poet would lose out on one of his most characteristic opportunities. It is surely part of the genius of the romantic lyric that it can meditate on the processes of consciousness in poems that are themselves examples of those processes at work. One need not turn to *Resolution and Independence* or *Le Lac* to see that happening. Keats himself was one of the most gifted interpreters of the efforts of the romantic mind to grasp and control experience. His *Ode to a Nightingale* offers a brilliant mimicry of the movements of consciousness, talking of and rendering those movements in an intricate pat-

terning that is a model of romantic self-awareness. There is
nothing in the poem about empathic projections but there is
a good deal about the struggles of the mind to reach accommodation with a nature that will not give easily of itself. What
seems to be a triumph of the mind, a penetration to the dark
center of the nightingale's grove, turns out to be no more than
a probable illusion. He does not have to fight off the impress
of other selves but to grope his way toward them, and few
romantic poems have been more effective in rendering this
intricate hunt and its sudden collapse. In a way Keats's ode
is a piece of self-rebuttal, what must have seemed a harsh but
necessary perspective to the excitement of his moments of
empathy. It can stand as the requisite balance to all the po-
lemics for the empathetic consciousness.

It was inevitable that between the two extremes of the spectrum there would be varying forms of arbitration, attempts
to make use of the benefits of each extreme while avoiding
their obvious difficulties. We have seen how Wordsworth ex-
tolled the marriage of mind and nature as the coalescence of
equals, while Novalis argued for an I-Thou relationship giving
due respect to both sides. For a theorist like Friedrich Schlegel
and a practitioner like Byron the alternative to the extremes
took the form of a special mode, the dialectical alternation
of chaos and order, breakup and renewal, which was romantic
irony.[42] As we have seen, one of the basic suppositions of the
romantic ironist is that there is a chaos at the center of things,
an anarchy that usually can be identified with the simmering
complexity and diversity of experience. Opposed to that
chaos, and poised to make use of it, is the mind of man, the
imagination imposing order upon lawlessness and discord.
Schlegel saw chaos as pure potential. He argues in one of his
fragments that "nur diejenige Verworrenheit ist ein Chaos,
aus der eine Welt entspringen kann."[h] [43] And he asserts in a
neighboring fragment that it is only the ironist who understands the whole meaning of that potential: "Ironie ist klares
Bewusstsein der ewigen Agilität, des unendlich vollen Chaos."[i] [44]

But of course he is conscious of more than chaos alone. The ironist has to be extraordinarily sensitive to the totality of experience, not simply to one force or element within it. As Schlegel says in another fragment: "zur Vielseitigkeit gehört nicht allein ein weitumfassendes System, sondern auch Sinn für das Chaos ausserhalb desselben, wie zur Menschheit der Sinn für ein Jenseits der Menschheit."ʲ ⁴⁵ Byron was much less comfortable with chaos than Schlegel was, though he too affirmed the dialectic of dissolution and regeneration, what Schlegel called the "steten Wechsel von Selbstschöpfung und Selbstvernichtung."ᵏ ⁴⁶ The long history of the Byronic hero shows that he sees men more often as victims of chaos than as creative manipulators of it, though his greatest poem reveals a successful way out of that dilemma. Byron's imagination of chaos was most fully realized in *Don Juan*. His poem continually posits an ordered world of social harmony and balanced stanzas, and continually breaks up that order through the disruptive passions of its protagonists and the wandering attention of the poem's narrator. Confusion succeeds to order and then order to confusion in an extraordinary dialectic that is one of the major triumphs of the romantic imagination. Schlegel, as we saw, admired Sterne's ability to create an image of chaos by seeming to give in to the overwhelming drive of the world's complexity and then reestablishing, for a while, the ordered movement of his mind and his book.⁴⁷ Byron does the same, assenting to the pressures of chaotic impulses and then triumphing over those pressures through the organizing skills of his imagination. But Byron's moments of triumph are themselves perpetually countered by an overwhelming sense that the world's chaos is catching up with him, that the order he has created will once again be subsumed within the flux of things. A romantic ironist such as Byron never denies chaos, nor does he claim that he can ever finally win out over it. He is always fully aware of his own insufficiencies. His job, as he knows, is to show both order and its opposite, consciousness and chaos, in action.

Yet romantic irony is more than a reproduction of the incessant swing from chaos to order and back again, which the ironist sees as the underlying pattern of cosmic activity. The very existence of the mode is also a subtle assertion of the capacities of the mind to impersonate the forces threatening its own order. In every case the romantic ironist reproduces the disorder of chaos in his work; but this is actually an artful semblance of disorder, a controlled mimicry of the anarchy that is always out there threatening to swallow up all the fixities of human experience. Because his mode is radically paradoxical, combining contraries in a counterfeit of confusion, the romantic ironist such as Byron or Tieck can have it all ways at once. He acknowledges that the swarming complexity of the world can absorb him and his order, unsettling him and compelling him to submit, calling his self-sufficiency into question; yet his acknowledgment appears within a comprehensive system of artifice—his novel or his poem—that he has himself created out of his own independent resources. Thus, he reproduces the disturbing alternation of breakup and renewal, disorder and order, within a structure shaped and dominated by his own mind. Of course all art is ultimately shaped by the mind; but in the case of romantic irony, it is peculiarly fitting and ironic—indeed an act of triumph—to assert the mind's control of the art work, because of the specific threats to its order and autonomy the ironist's mind sees. Eventually, there is not only a return to order within the work but (as in Tieck's *Gestiefelte Kater*) an ultimate, encompassing order which is the work itself. Romantic irony accedes to chaos, as it must; but even as it does so it affirms the genuine, if impermanent, sovereignty of consciousness. Schlegel liked to point out that the ironist transcends everything limited, even the shifting processes of experience in which he is compelled to take part. The romantic ironist accomplishes this transcendence through a complex and dazzling mode that is a masterpiece of inventive coalescence.

The structure of romantic irony is peculiarly fitted for such coalescence because it is dialectical, containing within itself some of the essential functions of both the dominating and submissive consciousness. In its occasional surrender to chaos (which is, in fact, an imitation of such a surrender) it is overwhelmed and absorbed by the restless density of the world, losing itself momentarily through total immersion. Irony is to that degree negatively capable. It remains open to complexity and uncertainty, and such openness, as Keats argued, is an essential characteristic of the receptive consciousness.[48] Further, it recognizes that the order of self we have created can be dissolved, for a while, in the teeming disorder of experience that seeks to swallow up all other identities in its own. But of course romantic irony is also sublime to the degree that it counters the thrusts of disorder with instances of the mind's ability to give shape to the scattered fragments of experience: as we saw in the last chapter, whenever the form of *Don Juan* crumbles into a comic mass of absurd digressions and startling rhymes, the narrator pulls together the pieces of his poem and asserts the control of consciousness once again. This capacity for self-recovery is one of the defining activities of romantic irony. With the distancing it obviously requires, the ironist's talent for the retrieval of self is one of the characteristics that distinguish him from the naive poet and the man of negative capability. Those others are thoroughly immersed in the nature they illuminate, allied with it if not fully identified with it. But for the ironist to complete his dialectic, he must exercise an element within himself that is necessarily and permanently estranged from experience. That element sees the world as forever unlike the mind, and it therefore compels the ironist to be separate and aloof from all things, insofar as he is able. Moreover, it is part of the ironist's business to do something with his alienation. The isolation of self that infuses Byron's poems from the earliest stages of his career is established in lesser work such as the Eastern Tales, and is given a fuller though still frustrating development in *Manfred* and *Cain*. In *Don Juan*, however, Byron learned how to put his isolation to extraordinary creative use: he transformed it into the requisite distancing of the ironic poet, the creator who must always keep alive within himself a stratum of personality that remains purely objective. With Byron as the model for this process, one can look back at Schiller's sentimental poet, who is compulsively and unwillingly estranged from experience, and see how the sentimental figure is the first step toward the triumph of alienation recorded in Byron's finest poem. But again one has to realize that the ironist's alienation, however necessary, is insufficient by itself: in order to be the complete imitator of experience as he reads it, he must practice humility (or a semblance of it) as well. The essentials of his mode require him to have an enormous appetite for variety. After all, his ironic work contains a number of dialectical patterns: not only does he mimic the movement from order to chaos but he also imitates the dialectic of the mind's relation to nature, the oscillation from dominance to submission. The ironist is therefore a consummate manager of antitheses. He is alternately detached and assimilated, aloof and involved, sublimely capable of manipulating the disruptive forces he can never fully conquer. If he sees human achievements as necessarily incomplete (the return of disorder shows how provisional those achievements are), he can at least offer an accomplished instance of their success as well as their incompleteness. *Don Juan* is one of those instances, a genuine triumph even though an ambiguous one.

Of course there are limitations within irony too. The ironist is probably not capable of empathy as long as he chooses to act as an ironist. When he assumes a submissive relation to experience, it is only because experience compels him to do so. He is not interested in exploring the selves of others but in supporting the ordering skills of his own self. Like all practitioners of the active consciousness, the ironist has to go without the rare and moving knowledge of what it feels like to have another kind of being. That is a considerable loss. But in compensation the romantic ironist has that unusual capacity for self-retrieval to which I have referred, the ability to pull himself out of the moments of chaos and back into a system of order. And if empathy is outside the range of his interests, he compensates for that loss with a detached and severely objective knowledge of what he is in himself. In fact, his talent for self-distancing carries him so far that he can mock his own pretensions to order and upset the very apple cart he has been carefully putting together. Schlegel sees this impulse toward self-parody as creative caprice, one of the wittiest and most effective tools of the romantic ironist. In one of his aphorisms he speaks of irony as being "die freieste aller Lizenzen, denn durch sie setzt man sich über sich selbst weg."[l 49] In another he points out the presence in certain poems of what he calls a transcendental buffoonery: "Im Innern, die Stimmung, welche alles übersieht, und sich über alles Bedingte unendlich erhebt, auch über eigne Kunst, Tugend, oder Genialität."[m 50] With this ability to undercut his own claims to an ultimate order the romantic ironist protects himself against overweening self-assurance. He knows that such pride of self is the trap that exposes the most extreme forms of the egotistical sublime. Byron at his self-mocking best is an antidote to Emerson at his most confident.

The enemies of romantic irony (particularly Hegel and Kierkegaard) argued that the ironist is excessively destructive, giving credence to nothing and questioning all assertions about order, even his own. This attack does have a certain accuracy: the romantic ironist agrees with the man of negative capability in preferring to remain in uncertainties and doubts. He distrusts all reverence of the absolute because fixities are necessarily suspect in a world where chaos is always ready to break out and usually does. The ironist is too aware of the uncertainties in things to trust fully what Keats called "consequitive reasoning."[51] Systematization, as Schlegel argued, must take its opposite into account or it can only falsify. Yet there is, finally, one value the ironist always respects, and that is the capacity of the mind to understand and reproduce the dialectic of self-creation and self-destruction, the alternation of order and chaos which informs the central patterns of experience. Though he emphasizes chance and the sporadic, wit and chaos, illusion and human insignificance, he ultimately affirms the magnificent capacity of mind to prevail, however tenuously, over that insignificance. Romantic irony, as we finally see, is self-consciousness aware of both the proximity of chaos and the strength of artifice. In its ability to weave contradictory tendencies of romantic consciousness into an inclusive dialectical whole this form of irony proves itself to be an unusually felicitous mode of association. In a curious way it seems to hold the whole spectrum of possibilities within itself. From our perspective, and for those reasons, romantic irony remains one of the most subtle and paradoxical experiments the romantics made in their probings of the commensuration of mind and nature.

ᏆᏫᎦ *FIVE* ᏫᎦᎦ

The Adequacy of the Imagination

The pressures for personal autonomy, for an order of consciousness that is both self-governing and self-sustaining, seemed to be compulsive for the romantics. That state was one of the conditions they could come to in that overall drive to internalize value which was among the defining processes of their period. To those who sought for it, an autonomous order of consciousness meant that the mind had created a system that could supply all of the major conditions it needed to satisfy itself, and that it could do so endlessly, with no help from outside. Consciousness could be as discontinuous with its surroundings as it felt necessary, and it could be so with perfect aplomb because of its remarkable ability to function satisfactorily according to its self-chosen schema. To describe the situation thus is, of course, to see its difficulties: so compact an order of being can be achieved only with considerable effort and luck, and perhaps can hardly be achieved at all. In fact, the evidence from Goethe or Byron or Stendhal indicates that moments of perfection were nearly always rare and fleeting, and usually had an ironic cloak cast deftly around them. Perfected autonomy would have to be a state of completely fulfilled desire, as it is in Schiller's naive poet. But the drive toward the internalization of value was invariably disturbed by a conflict of desire and capability as characteristic of romantic experience as the drive itself. That conflict, in its turn, touched the romantics at nearly every point where their skills as romantic personalities were involved.

Such autonomy does not come naturally but must be fought for, made by and for oneself in opposition to the pressures for subservience coming from outside. Figures like Vigny's Chatterton and Byron's Manfred faced forces that differed in their location on the chain of being but were alike in demanding subordination; and both the artist and the magician responded with an attempt at soul making that was, essentially, a grand creative gesture. Each had to devise a private order of being and to do so consciously, in full awareness of all that was being asked of his shaping spirit. It is clear, then, that the making of a self-subsistent consciousness is as much the business of the mind's inventive powers as is the making of art. Indeed, we know that in romanticism those two modes of organic shaping are very closely linked, as they had been for Sterne. Coleridge's *Dejection* is only one of the more cogent instances of concern over their association; Goethe's *Werther* is another. But these examples, with their records of ambiguous failure, ought to be cautionary as well as illustrative. As it turns out, all the assertions about the value of the autonomous inner life rely on an implied assumption that the imagination is adequate to create forms for the self-sufficient consciousness. Obviously much is at stake here. If, under the pressures for subservience, the imagination could make an authentically independent order of being, then it would have demonstrated not only that the mind can be self-subsistent but that what Hazlitt calls the "power of thought" is capable of handling the most difficult jobs.[1] The act would have shown, at once, both the autonomy of consciousness and the adequacy of the imagination. Simultaneous success in such critical areas is no trivial affair.

One way to begin with these dilemmas was to ponder images of adequacy in others. For those who did not have it that was a useful stopgap while they wondered whether autonomy was possible within themselves, or whether they wanted it at all. For those who did, it was the best way of testing their own success, examining how far it fell short of perfection. In any case that projection outward made the admirer of self-subsistence into a spectator, obsessed with disparity and distance. He could objectify his obsession in the imagery of absent

divinities, self-contained and aloof in a distant world of light,
as Hölderlin did in "Hyperions Schiksaalslied":

> Schiksaallos, wie der schlafende
> Säugling, athmen die Himmlischen;
> Keusch bewahrt
> In bescheidener Knospe,
> Blühet ewig
> Ihnen der Geist,
> Und die seeligen Augen
> Bliken in stiller
> Ewiger Klarheit.[a][2]

Alternatively, the artist could work his awareness of remote
perfection into a stereoscopic vision of his past and present
selves. Wordsworth did that in the *Immortality* ode with his
image of the observer, standing inland, watching "the Children sport upon the shore." In a moving variation of this
mode of perception he speaks, in *The Prelude*, of the remembered past as having a "self-presence" in his mind; that is, an
autonomous subsistence of its own. Though he is one of the
more skillful successors of Rousseau, what Wordsworth sees
of his old self is so integral and independent that, in musing
on it, he seems "two consciousnesses, conscious of myself /
And of some other Being."[3] It was possible, of course, to see
absolute self-subsistence not just in gods or children but in the
system of organic nature, the radical prototype for an autonomous order, which found all that it required within its own
confines. The fortunate possessors of autonomy were thus
seen as more natural than those who did not have it. The
latter looked on at those who did with baffled aspiration.
Schiller makes these points explicitly in *Über naive und sentimentalische Dichtung,* and he does so through the same
image of the abstracted observer, which was to be used later
by Hölderlin and Wordsworth:

> Besonders stark und am allgemeinsten äussert sich diese
> Empfindsamkeit für Natur auf Veranlassung solcher Ge-

genstände, welche in einer engern Verbindung mit uns ste-
hen, und uns den Rückblick auf uns selbst und die
U n n a t u r in uns näher legen, wie z. B. bei Kindern und
kindlichen Völkern.[b] [4]

Such objects compel us to think of ourselves as we once were,
and the comparison with our present state of imperfect
achievement is humiliating. Furthermore, they remind us of
nature because they exemplify the coherent order and radical
innocence of the physical world, as well as its unlimited potential. We, the observers, have none of those qualities. We
are unnatural because we have become limited and fragmented, while the child, on the other hand, is all harmony,
strength, and integrity, as nature is. And he is integral precisely
because he is complete and has within himself all that he
needs.

Schiller had begun his essay by extolling nature's "Daseyn
nach eignen Gesetzen, die innere Nothwendigkeit, die ewige
Einheit mit sich selbst,"[c] and he finds this autonomous completeness in birds and flowers as well as in children.[5] But such
self-subsistence is more than the property of these unconscious
beings alone, for when Schiller says later that man can be as
pure as nature, he is not only speaking of children but of the
naive poet, who is unified, autonomous, and creative, with a
perfect configuration of consciousness, which puts him absolutely, and with no effort of will, in harmony with nature.
This personage is not subservient to his world but a partner
to it, and he is its equal in self-subsistence. Unlike Rousseau
the naive poet rejects nothing, but, instead, makes full and
adequate use of all the richness that experience affords. As a
poet he can do whatever he wishes. He is naive because his
skill and self-sufficiency are innate and prelapsarian, not
earned. On the other hand, if his subjective wholeness is as
instinctive as that of Rousseau's equally prelapsarian primitive, the naive poet has what the savage could never conceive
of, the perfected consciousness of the artist. We envy him
because of his achievements as well as his coherence. Only the

naive can combine spontaneity and freedom with the accomplished forms of intuitive genius. Still, there are aspects even of his own situation to which the naive poet cannot respond simply because his wholeness came to him naturally and without effort. Unaware of disparity, he is also unaware of the full meaning of self-containment because he cannot know all the threats to consciousness.

His sentimental counterpart, on the other hand, is unnatural; that is, if instinctive harmony is the hallmark of the natural. In harmony with nothing, he cannot share the Rousseauistic mode of self-containment because the sentimental poet longs for an unachievable shape of consciousness which will bring him into tune with the ideal. Irrevocably postlapsarian, he has all the awareness that the naive lacks but he has it only because he has reached the most abrasive stage of self-consciousness. Still, it is because of such self-consciousness that he finds ways to objectify, if not to solve, his problems. The sentimental poet lives in a state of separateness and betweenness, attached neither to nature nor the ideal. The odd and tense combination of the willed and the enforced, which seems to be endemic to post-Cervantean separateness (the Don was definitive there too), has a special meaning for the sentimental poet. Though he is Quixotean in his awareness of an ideal that is not in harmony with the present state of things, he is in other ways like the characters in Sterne, compelled into separateness by the conditions of experience. In his own case, though, he shares the world with a model of self-sufficiency who is in perfect control of the possibilities of experience available to him; and though those possibilities may not be all that the sentimental poet wants for himself, they are more than he has right now. Schiller's typologies reverse the relations of autonomy and discontinuity that had been adumbrated in Milton and polished in Rousseau. The self-sufficiency Satan said he had and Rousseau actually achieved stresses their moral separateness from all those around them. They wanted autonomy for a number of reasons, not least for the most basic reason of all, that the standards of others could not apply to them. In Schiller, however, the successfully autonomous figure is the one that is most in harmony with his surroundings, while the discontinuity suffered by the sentimental poet makes it impossible for him to be at one with himself, not to speak of his environment. It is not, however, as though he could have chosen otherwise. The essay focuses on him not simply because it was written by a sentimental poet outlining his malady but because his is peculiarly the condition of the modern poet. He is as much the prisoner of history as he is the victim of his own unrelenting self-awareness. Indeed, he is the latter because of the former. The naive poet is the anachronistic figure, a throwback to an earlier state of culture. What this means—to pile on another paradox—is that the figure in harmony with his environment is out of place in his age. The sentimental poet is the one who is ironically congruent with all that history has brought upon us.

His state, characterized by a persistent awareness of loss and disconnection, is also imbued with the pain of personal inadequacy: he knows that he is almost certainly incapable of reaching what he wants. Still, it is because of such self-consciousness that he finds ways to objectify, if not to solve, his problems. In order to turn his insufficiency into art, to make the qualities of his condition into forms of imaginative discourse, the sentimental poet finds new ways of using old genres of poetry, the satire, the elegy, and the idyll.[6] Through each of the genres he will render, with full perspective, all the imperfections of his present state. Lukács has argued that Schiller subjectifies the issues of the naive and sentimental, turning the genres from literary categories into modes of feeling: "Er subjektiviert ununterbrochen seine Darlegungen und macht demgemäss aus objektiven Tatbeständen stets subjektive Empfindungs- und Denkweisen."[d][7] In fact, that is exactly what Schiller had said he was doing: "ich sehe bloss auf die in diesen Dichtungsarten herrschende E m p f i n d u n g s w e i s e."[e][8] The feelings Schiller speaks of are inherent in the genres, and the skilled sentimentalist can turn them to the benefit of the distraught modern imagination, refurbishing the feelings so that they tell of the new alienation. The paradox is neat, ironic, and fruitful: he shapes traditional attitudes into forms that are imaginatively adequate to express his own personal insufficiency. In a strange and subtle way the sentimental poet, like Rousseau on his island, wins by losing.

Schiller's essay is an unsteady but effective combination of cultural history, aesthetics, and the psychology of creativity. His formulations point to what would be the specific problems of the romantic artist, who has to make a place in his art for all the promptings of the romantic consciousness. The artist shares the same urge toward the internalization of value Satan prefigured and Rousseau exemplified, but he has his own version of the need to find external correlatives for the conditions and values within. For Schiller the process came easily, at least within the theoretical framework of his essay, and there was no questioning the competence of the literary forms. If the sentimental poet could not himself be as self-subsistent as the naive, he could admire the naive's private coherence and look forward, through the genres, to his own. Further, the myth of the naive and sentimental is in itself an extraordinary imaginative construct, sufficient to place the sentimental poet within the context of past and current history, even to help define his personality in terms of his placement in time. The myth owes much to Schiller's instinct for dramatization through foils (e.g. with the brothers in *Die Räuber*), and the potential for a narrative framework is clearly implicit in the ordering of the personal modes sketched out in the essay. If he cannot now possess the ideal, the sentimental poet can at least possess his own situation through his organized description of it. However tentative the configuration of types he draws up, it succeeds in giving him a sense of his own and the world's order, showing him how he clicks into place within the modern system. And if that was all he could do for now, it did surprisingly well. His job at the moment (a moment that continued at least through Wallace Stevens) was to find what would suffice. He discovered that the act of finding, most of all the embodiment of that act in the myth of the naive and sentimental, could get him through. His myth had about it a temporary but effective completeness and satisfaction.

The conflict of desire and capability was never more intense than at this point, where the sentimental poet had to find his sense of vocation. His mind was attentive to itself, to the process of its searching; but it also listened for echoes and evidence of that which it did not have. Every pastoral from the time of the Renaissance performed the second of these activities; but it was only from the mid-eighteenth century, when the awareness of the mind's processes began to weave itself into imaginative structures, that the first activity came in with full force. From this came Schiller's emphasis on the genres and the more subtle instance of the myth itself, all of those instruments through which his imagination could find both ease and self-understanding. The actions of the sentimental poet's mind are twofold, and his attention must therefore be multiple. First, the mind has to focus on its own presence and the conditions in which it is working; second, the mind must also dwell on an absence, on the painful unavailability of that which it seems to need most of all. The task of the imagination, then, is to find a mode of speech, as Schiller did, through which it can combine both duty and nostalgia. It needs to render in objective form what it can do, here and now, to make use of what it has. Alternatively it must learn to honor that which has gone by and is irretrievably lost. The givens of Schiller's sketch are written large in the extraordinary reach of Hölderlin's informing myths.

The poet in Hölderlin's hymns senses that what he values most is not here but elsewhere, at some other point in time or else in Greece, where one can at least walk through the places of absent glory. Like Schiller's sentimental poet he is the man between, obsessed by remembrance and prevision, thinking only of the self-subsistent gods who have been among men and will come again. It is his business, as the poet in a dark time, to keep those old values present and alive within himself, through memory or anticipation. He is a living repository, and a most anxious one. As artist, then, he has to create forms that speak eloquently of absent good and, at the same time, render the way he feels about its absence. The world shaped by his imagination will have to focus on himself as center, partly because he sees himself as a representative contemporary, and partly because he is most concerned with his own duty and his longing. Out of that subjective center his imagination will project a myth that objectifies all his loss and desire, a myth that sees the present as a dark night for his own soul and for all others as well. The myth will place brightness and the presence of autonomous divinity both before and behind him. His task is to make clear that the gods have departed primarily because our current state of being is hopelessly incapable of bearing their dazzling presence. The night we are in is therefore an image of our present inadequacy. We are in this interim darkness because of the absence of the gods; and we are in it for yet another reason, because (the gods show their mercy here) it is all that we can now tolerate. We cannot bear light and we do not yet deserve it. Everything that the poet-prophet feels within himself is put out there in the shape of his poetic world. There has to be an exact congruence between the order of self and the order of his myth, with the myth an objectification of his representative inner state.

More skillfully than any of his contemporaries, Hölderlin managed the shaping of a myth reconciling prophecy with privacy, the seer's need to speak out with the requisite subjectivity of the romantic who was repelled by contemporary social value. His control is extraordinary: the syncretic myth he builds out of classical, Christian, and Germanic worlds dissolves the distinctions among his sources, making Christ and Dionysus part of a coherent package along with Teutonic deities and a series of demigods, human and natural. This syncretic fusing of the disparate transforms the past into an eternal present, absorbing time into form and plot into ritual.

In *Brot und Wein* the wine of Dionysus emerges again in the Eucharist, whose bread is a product of the earth's ancient hierogamy with the sun; and in *Der Einzige* Christ is the brother of Herakles, as strong as any of his siblings and, for this poet, most beloved of all. Blake, Hölderlin's cockney counterpart as a maker of myth, called the result of such temporal maneuvers "a vision of the eternal Now," and he was able to place within the same imaginative structure figures and locations out of the Bible, the modern world and his own devising.[9] London and Jerusalem work as comfortably together in his myth as do Adam and Milton. Clearly, what Blake and Hölderlin did through their syncretic modes is an exact correlative to what Rousseau did in the enclosed privacy of his deepest consciousness. In each case the boundaries of time and place collapse, and the categories become mere tools, subject to the needs of the mind that controls time and place in perfect mastery. This is a version of the Satanic desire to dissolve all such categories into modes of the autonomous mind, but this version has an undevilish purpose: the poet must teach men to resist the urge to chaos, what Hölderlin calls in *Mnemosyne* the longing for the boundless. Of course there is nothing in Rousseau comparable to the enormous mythic structures in Blake and Hölderlin. The urge to think in terms of figures and narratives is one that Rousseau gave in to very frequently, but only in *La Nouvelle Héloïse*, and to a lesser extent in *Emile,* does it find extended external form.[10] Ordinarily it released itself in reveries. In Blake and Hölderlin, however, the impulse to create through persons and stories is dominant, compelled perhaps by the need to work in a larger cultural framework than that Rousseau employed in his fictions (that is, if we do not consider the *Discourses* as fictions). But even with these distinctions the same factors are at work in all three: the control of the commanding consciousness over time and place, its reshaping of their categories for its own needs, ultimately the obligation to assert the value of mind against all the antagonistic forces outside. The identity of these actions in such disparate creators shows that, whatever their differences of mode and temperament, the mythographer and the compulsive recluse must be responding to the same demands of the romantic imagination. None of the romantics could do more with those demands than Rousseau or Hölderlin did, and the most ambitious among them attempted no less, whether their field was the recesses of the mind or the widest reaches of the cultural imagination. Finally, though, we need to return to a point already indicated, the fact that Hölderlin actually worked in both fields at once (Blake did too, but in a different modality). Hölderlin's myth puts into objective form all the contours and needs of the poet's forlorn soul: cultural loss is private loss written large, and as representative man he suffers for everyone.

Hölderlin differs most sharply from Rousseau and Blake in two crucial areas, his attitude toward the present disjunction and his feelings about the autonomy of consciousness. Blake posited a division that began with the Fall, that is, with the triumph of Urizen and the consequent creation of the physical world; but he argued that restoration will occur once the world achieves that wholeness of consciousness and the awareness of the proper business of man that now characterize Blake's poet-prophet. With the restoration the world will become, totally, imagination. Indeed, the poetic consciousness will contain what was once the world. Rousseau noticed division and a Fall everywhere, particularly in his own life where a number of versions had occurred; but his experiences during revery, above all at the Lac de Bienne, are concise instances of restoration, renovations of the old wholeness through a union with the world's most important elements, nature and the radical structures of his own self. In those moments, as we have seen, he needed nothing more than the most essential aspects of himself. Hölderlin's victories of the imagination, surpassed by no one else in his time and few thereafter, are the work of a poet whose anguish and art are built on his sense of separation. He is the master syncretist, but he is still, in part, a sentimental poet, with the dominant mood in his work an awareness of spiritual deprivation. Further, though the forms of his imagination have an admirably self-sufficient structure, there is no room in Hölderlin's myth for an autonomous poetic consciousness. In fact, the situation is quite the opposite. Passages such as the fragmentary ending of "Wie wenn am Feiertage" point to the immediate dangers faced, in the modern world, by the prophetic consciousness, and all through the major poems there are pained revelations of the difficulties of his job: somehow he has to establish a balanced relationship between the gods, whom he serves, and men, to whom he speaks. To do that properly he has to remain pure, which for Hölderlin means being humble. And humility, in Hölderlin's world, could never be compatible with an assertion of absolute autonomy. The myth he built through his poems is as coherent and independent as it is complex and inclusive but he cannot, himself, be more than a servant. Autonomy is the property of the gods and demigods and heroes, not men such as he is, even though he has been chosen by the gods for prophecy. For Hölderlin this means that he will discover autonomy in his creations but not in himself. Were he to insist otherwise, he would court the hybris that threatened Empedokles in Hölderlin's play about the philosopher, and run the further risk of turning the separation from the gods he now feels into an even more desperate agony. It is fitting that Empedokles' penalty should take the form of a separation since his fault had been an insistence on his mind's independent powers. This homology of sin and punishment is one of Hölderlin's aptest ironies, a sardonic, Dantean view of the relation of transgression and retribution.

But these threats do not exhaust the difficulties. Successful autonomy is so awesomely difficult to comprehend that, when the poet does encounter it in action, he may well question whether his art is adequate to contain all that he sees. Hölderlin's lyric on Buonaparte presents a test case:

> Heilige Gefässe sind die Dichter,
> Worinn des Lebens Wein, der Geist

Der Helden sich aufbewahrt,

Aber der Geist dieses Jünglings
Der schnelle, müsst' er es nicht zersprengen
Wo es ihn fassen wollte, das Gefäss?

Der Dichter lass ihn unberührt wie den Geist der Natur,
An solchem Stoffe wird zum Knaben der Meister.

Er kann im Gedichte nicht leben und bleiben,
Er lebt und bleibt in der Welt.[f][11]

The heroes in Hölderlin's poems have all the resonance of self
one associates with demigods. They represent the perfect realization of the most intense forms of being, a fulfillment more
complete than any ordinary man could expect to achieve. The
Jüngling of this poem is a hero who can be found in the
company of men, that is, he is a proximate figure, but his
extraordinary self-containment and intensity separate him
from other men even while he is among them. He is both near
and distant, as palpable as the spirit of nature but equally
aloof and impossible to grasp. Hölderlin, with no naive poet
to use as a model of harmonious autonomy, looks on at present autonomy in the person of Buonaparte.

Though Hölderlin is as obsessed by the self-sufficient consciousness as anyone in his time, his reading of the contemporary world, as well as the conditions he established in his
myth, forced him to put autonomy outside of himself, in the
divine and divinely touched persons who populate the myth.
Thus, he filled his poems with exemplars of self-sufficiency,
most of them drawn from ancient myth and modern history
rather than the literary imagination; yet they were in no sense
models that the poet-prophet could, or should, follow. He
was held back by that which differentiated him from the heroes: all the difficulties and inadequacies of ordinary mortality. Hölderlin's lyric on Empedokles, a companion-piece to
"Buonaparte," places the poet precisely in relation to the hero:

Das Leben suchst du, suchst, und es quillt and glänzt

Ein göttlich Feuer tief aus der Erde dir,
Und du in schauderndem Verlangen
    Wirfst dich hinab, in des Aetna Flammen.

So schmelzt' im Weine Perlen der Übermuth
Der Königin; und mochte sie doch! hättst du
    Nur deinen Reichtum nicht, o Dichter
        Hin in den gährenden Kelch geopfert!

Doch heilig bist du mir, wie der Erde Macht,
Die dich hinwegnahm, kühner Getödteter!
    Und folgen möcht' ich in die Tiefe,
        Hielte die Liebe mich nicht, dem Helden.[g][12]

This hero is dying into life, not quite giving up his life in order
to save it, but melting into the divine, much as Cleopatra
allowed her pearls to dissolve in wine. His action has nothing
to do with escape but, rather, with passionate devotion: his
Reichtum has been *geopfert*, all that wealth of the spirit of-
ferred to the earth's holy might. The image of inner riches,
that part of him he can spare less than Cleopatra can spare
her baubles, is left indefinite. *Reichtum* is a large enough word
to contain all the intricacies of an awesome personality as well
as the poet's astonishment at the nature of a hero. If the word
does not melt the distance between poet and hero (nothing
can), it at least brings them together in a context of impression
and reaction. It is as much a word about the poet as about
the object of his awe, its tone defining their relationship with
complex precision. And it simultaneously defines the difference between the hero's and the queen's actions, his wealth
and hers. Her wanton arrogance (*Übermuth*) is as aggressive
as his exuberance; but the difference of expenditure serves
only to degrade her, just as the ironic likening of the wine
glass to the seething chalice of the volcano serves to mock her
petty actions. Cleopatra, no demigod, is closer to our own
kind: hers is the self-sufficiency of regal insolence; his is that
of an aloof personality that answers only to the divine. All
that he is and has is contained within that relationship. He

needs nothing more than to be himself in the presence of the divine in order to achieve complete independence from the exigencies of experience—all those demands coming out of the world from which the awed poet watches his hero. Yet it is an independence concomitant with the most complete giving. Empedokles' self is so thoroughly possessed by the fiery One that it wants to confirm the possession in full literalness. Cleopatra's self is possessed only by its arrogance, so much so that she is subservient to her own willfulness: it is *der Übermuth der Königin* and not the queen herself that melts the pearls in wine.

Empedokles' passion is consuming but not simple. He stands there in shuddering desire (*schauderndem Verlangen*), his ecstasy mirroring the seething and flashing within the volcano. His leap into the divine fire is therefore a plunge toward passionate union, different in object from any union that Cleopatra could know but drawing ironically on images that are also appropriate to her own sort of passion. The immolation of Empedokles' treasure is a sacrifice following upon a gesture of intense desire. Only the most thorough oneness can appease that desire; palpable treasure will not do. Nor, for that matter, can other kinds of love be sufficient substitutes for such a union. The poet, envisioning the hero up on Aetna, acknowledges his inadequacy, his inability to reach the degree of renunciation achieved by the hero. Passion directed to his own kind rather than to the gods is the hindrance to his attempts at high spirituality. He is held back by his humanizing love (compare "Menons Klagen um Diotima"). Thus, the poet's submission to his humanity separates him from his hero, while the latter's absorption in the divine, that love which undoes his humanity, separates him from all other men. This is, in effect, another version of that distance from mere humanity embodied in a different dimension in "Hyperions Schiksaalslied." The Empedokles of Hölderlin's play deluded himself into thinking that he was self-sufficient in relation to nature and the gods, and that he was therefore independent of them. The Empedokles of the poem, all arrogance gone, is independent only from men. As Empedokles stands at the edge of the volcano he partakes of the spiritual remoteness and self-containment that for Hölderlin were necessary attributes of divine and quasi-divine beings. Empedokles is *heilig* because, though no god, he shares those attributes. He is as holy as a man can be and still be a man. His complete holiness will come only when he vanishes in the fire. Then he will no longer be the mortal, self-contained Empedokles; he will be absorbed within the divine self-containment.

In "Buonaparte" and "Empedokles," lyrics of his early maturity, Hölderlin sets forth one of his major preoccupations, that startling combination of proximity and remoteness that made the poet's contact with superior beings so difficult and unsettling. *Patmos* puts it precisely: "Nah ist / Und schwer zu fassen der Gott"; the God is near and difficult to grasp. The poet-prophet's present job is to stand between men and this autonomy to which we do not, for now, have access. He must show that our own separateness is not that of aloof beings but hungering ones, that our distances are enforced, not desired:

> Drum, da gehäuft sind rings
> Die Gipfel der Zeit, und die Liebsten
> Nah wohnen, ermattend auf
> Getrenntesten Bergen,
> So gieb unschuldig Wasser,
> O Fittige gieb uns, treuesten Sinns
> Hinüberzugehen und wiederzukehren.[h] [13]

As sentimental poet he stands between eras of harmony and reconciliation, the feasts that have been and those (sketched out in *Friedensfeier*) that are to come. Hölderlin's success in coordinating these difficult postures had been prefigured, to a degree, in the hypothetical success postulated in Schiller's essay, but his remarkable achievement far exceeds the revitalization of genre Schiller saw as the best prognosis for the art of his time.

Hölderlin overcame the difficulties of contemporary soul

making by building a place for the anguished poet into the order of his imaginative world. The difficulties were prevalent at the time: if the poet needed to make a viable work as well as a self, all the logic of the creative process would seem to dictate that he should finish the self before or within the work—even if the work turned out to be no more than a rendering of the imperfections of the self. Though that logic was not always honored, its implications could never be ignored. Goethe, profoundly aware of these problems, had found an exemplary instance in Werther, who tried to ignore the logic and died for it. In an unusual moment of self-awareness, however, Werther faced up to the cost and inadequacies of his cherished autonomy. During the entry of 9 May in Book Two he complains that a prince with whom he has been visiting is a pleasant but somewhat narrow dilettante who pays more attention to the intellect and abilities of his guests than to their hearts; but Werther says that, unlike the prince, he is proud only of his heart because the heart "ganz allein die Quelle von allem ist, aller Kraft, aller Seligkeit und alles Elendes."[i] [14] These are, of course, the same terms of autonomy that Satan had made definitive. As Werther presents them they contain all possible attitudes, just as Satan's comments had done in the passage arguing that the mind is its own place. The heart holds all potential within itself, and has the strength to realize that potential. Two letters afterward, writing once more about his visit to the prince, Werther indicates that he is still able to sketch, though apparently not much, and he says that the best product of his visit is his drawing. Of course this confidence cannot last, and by 3 November Werther has gone the same route as Satan, from an assertion that all possibilities are open to an admission that there is now actually only one. After some harsh words about the unendurable burden of his resentment, Werther acknowledges that he is indeed still autonomous but that he can now create only unhappiness for himself. The language of his acknowledgment of insufficiency echoes the terms of his previous claim for complete independence: "in mir die Quelle alles Elendes verborgen ist, wie ehemals die Quelle aller Seligkeiten."[j] [15] Once there had been a Paradise within him but now there is not so much a Hell as a desert, a wasteland in a landscape that used to be lush and creative. In terms that prefigure Coleridge's similar laments he bewails the loss of "die heilige, belebende, Kraft, mit der ich Welten um mich schuf."[k] [16] His dessicated soul is an exhausted fountainhead, a leaky pail, parched earth—for once, his images are accurate. In fact, the whole passage is a model of incisive self-awareness, and perhaps for that reason it is also one of the most pristine examples available of the relation of autonomy to various capacities of the romantic consciousness. In this entry Goethe brings in the Satanic insistence that we alone create the tone of our world, and he combines it with the man of feeling's demand for the fullest pitch of emotional experience. Goethe conflates the two modes simply by changing the source of autonomy from the mind to the heart, from the *Verstand* ("understanding"), which the prince—and Satan—had found valuable, to the *Herz* ("heart"), which Werther esteems above everything. And with this change as a basis Werther can expostulate on the conditions of romantic creativity, making clear that his inability to enliven his world is ironically related to his cherished autonomy: when he admits that he can blame no one else for his resentment, since the source of all his misery is within himself, he is forced to acknowledge that his spiritual aridity is also the offspring of his inadequate soul, and that he owes his barrenness too only to himself.

This bitter confirmation of Werther's autonomy helps us to understand the conditions of a mode of self whose ironies pervaded romanticism. By the last pages of the book, when he had closed his Homer and opened his Ossian, Werther had brought to fruition an order of self that was as successful in defining a kind of experience as it was, for him, self-destructive. Here the book was most influential, setting up a framework for confronting unlikeness that made crushing failure almost a precondition for a kind of subjective order. In moments of relative stability preromantic heroes had organized their sense of society's insufficiency into a tenuous dialectical interplay, one in which that sense faced an equal and opposite awareness that there were pressures within the self that mocked all attempts to contain them. The pervasive impression of explosiveness in the literature of the *Sturm und Drang* is only one more version of a recognition that the public container and the private contained were radically disproportionate. All compromises were founded on a gamble that one would not blow up. The pistol shot that ended Werther's pain and ricocheted through his imitators is therefore wonderfully apt. But the order of self that Werther achieved before his suicide became for others enough to postpone self-destruction if they were able to realize that in the act of suffering they could make use of those same personal characteristics whose frustration had led to the suffering.

Werther himself seems to have seen the point. At the beginning of the novel his creativity can no longer objectify itself fully; he is unable to put all that he feels into the independent existence of an art object. Werther looks for forms to bolster his sagging work as an artist but he comes up only with some silhouettes and incomplete sketches, nothing fully formed, rounded, or molded. He can only talk about art, not produce it. And when he talks about the rules of art, the best image he can come up with is one that likens exuberant poetic genius to a stream bursting its banks; that is, to an image of the collapse of order. Yet there are times, especially at the beginning, when Werther seems quite comfortable with his inability. In the second letter of the book he reports how he is utterly absorbed in the sensations of the present moment, alone and glad to be alive in such wonderful surroundings; yet there is nothing that he, as an artist, can make out of that moment: "ich könnte jetzt nicht zeichnen, nicht einen Strich, und bin nie ein grösserer Maler gewesen als in diesen Augenblicken."[1][17] Werther, it is clear, does not see any contradiction between his qualities as an artist and his inability to put his feelings into the shape of an art object. He can satisfy the impulse of his talent merely by evincing the feelings the talent would be used to express. Thus, he can function comfortably, with no need of externalization, by drawing on the energies of his inner life. He needs nothing more than what he can generate within himself. Two letters after this Werther goes even further, spurning all outside influences, finding more than enough impetus coming from within himself. Declining an offer of some books, he argues for his inner self-sufficiency: "ich will nicht mehr geleitet, ermuntert, angefeuert sein, braust dieses Herz doch genug aus sich selbst."[m 18] The contradictions, if they are such, begin to work themselves out as Werther finds himself more and more frustrated about his failures at love and art, and, with that, more and more passionately disturbed about his frustration. In fact, the working out is done through the shape of a deadly, but temporarily efficient, subjective order.

What Werther did was to create a self-perpetuating process of self-consumption. All the pain that came out of baffled love or the choked up channels of creation was put to use by the self, which was seeking a way of sustaining itself. First, there has to be a distancing of the self from its content, a full self-consciousness, however implicit or subliminal its workings. The initial result of that awareness is a thorough recognition of the pain one is going through, the suffering one is compelled to have by the exigencies of bourgeois life. Then, after the recognition of pain comes a bitterness over the fact that one has to have that pain, that one is forced to suffer under the pressure of alien systems of value. In a sense, of course, this is part of the cost of self-consciousness: to reverse Emerson, better the mindlessness of the ant than the mindfulness of the self-aware human. But even that cost has its use. The bitterness that comes from the recognition of enforced suffering is added to the sum of one's suffering, making one even more miserable and giving one even more reason to feel bitter. The hero feeds on his own substance and that feeding makes him grow; and the more he grows the more substance he has to feed on. The entire process, based on the perpetual replenishment of unhappiness, is circular and self-sustaining. As a result it estab-

lishes an independent mode of the self which needs little from
outside except a cause for frustration. The failed artist can
create a special order of personality whose continuity is based
on the activity of self-consumption. As the hero, slipping into
the melancholy of the *mal du siècle*, fights and loses, he can
also learn to win, at least for a while.

Here too Rousseau was a model, teaching others how to
bring it off without destroying themselves. In the *Deuxième
Promenade* he speaks of his imagination's current state of
decline and of his need to think back to earlier times in order
to show what he had been. Specifically he wants to go back
"au tems où perdant tout espoir ici bas et ne trouvant plus
d'aliment pour mon coeur sur la terre, je m'accoutumois peu
à peu à le nourrir de sa propre substance et à chercher toute
sa pâture au dedans de moi."[n][19] He makes the same point in
the *Huitième Promenade,* though there he complains that his
exhausted imagination now has little left with which to feed
his heart.[20] Rousseau learned to draw on his own substance
as a defense against the world's infidelity. It was a way of
giving himself what the world would no longer give him; that
is, if it had ever been able to give him anything at all. Any
weakening of the process would come not from a paucity of
resources but from the dessication of those sources within
himself that served to feed him. Yet the sense of decay hinted
at in the *Huitième Promenade,* the feeling that his imagination
was winding down, is clearly not supported by the other
walks, especially the *Cinquième.* What he could do does not
show a dessication but a purification, the last practices of a
master of subjectivity. In any case, Rousseau's self-feeding
(including the pleasure it gave him as well as the pleasure he
had over that pleasure) is very different from the self-feeding
of Werther, who offered himself only the nourishment of pain.
Eventually Werther's self-perpetuating self-consumption had
to create a kind of claustrophobia, a sense of being bottled
up within. Goethe is especially sardonic here, making the
mode of Werther's suicide seem apt and inevitable: he has to
blow a hole in himself in order to get out. Through that self-

entrapment Goethe demonstrates once and for all that autonomy alone is not enough for the artist, because the self can
be crippled as well as independent. He also shows that the
attainment of an ironic form of subjective self-subsistence may
be all the creativity that some fragmented souls can muster.

It is clear from the example of Werther, and from analogues
made by authors such as Sénancour and Coleridge, that the
inability of the romantic consciousness to internalize the warm
life of nature is a symptom of radical disorder. Werther objectifies his own inadequacy in the imagery of water and blood.
He stands before nature and laments that what he sees cannot
pump a drop of bliss from his heart to his brain.[21] Of course
this is the classic trope of the wasteland, but it also parallels
Werther's likening of untamed genius to a raging river. Coleridge puts the same problem in terms of dullness rather than
dryness. In his ode on *Dejection* he complains that even his
pain is indolent and cannot rise to a pitch where he could
mourn his loss with the proper intensity. And that dreariness
within is matched, as it has to be in romanticism, by a failure
of his imagination to perceive with its fullest capacity. He
looks out at the landscape with a blank eye, and though he
sees the things of this world well enough, he cannot bring
them to life within himself: "I see them all so excellently fair,
/ I see, not feel, how beautiful they are!" The problem could
not be put more precisely, and Coleridge goes on, with equal
precision, to attribute the inadequacy of his imagination to
a failure of the powers that only an autonomous consciousness
can have. He cannot feel the life in nature because he has been
unable to put any life out there; and there is life in nature only
when the soul, exercising its beauty-making power, enlivens
what is otherwise an "inanimate cold world": "O Lady! we
receive but what we give, / And in our life alone does Nature
live." To enliven nature we require only a lively consciousness.
The mind is its own source of invigorating power; nothing
else can do the job. Thus, when the omnipotent consciousness
is reduced to a state of dullness or dryness there is nowhere

outside itself where it can go for refreshment or renewal. Coleridge is left alone in his dreary desert. And since the responsibility for such defeat is entirely his own, he cannot share the guilt—drowsy though it may be—with anyone else. Like Werther he can condemn only himself.

Still, Coleridge can do several things that Werther cannot. At the end of the poem, when he discovers that the high winds he hoped for had actually been howling out there for some time, the poet finds that he is able to read into the wild sounds of the wind all manner of moans and cries of pain; and though these are no more than projections of his own private condition, they are projections all the same. As it turns out he can put life out there once again, even though that life is limited to expressing itself in sounds as unhappy as his own. Coleridge's enlivening of the wind shows that his unaided consciousness can still invigorate the things of this world. Further, as if to give a broader context to these actions, he turns here to old forms of artifice, drawing on ancient modes for the shaping of his private lament. The poem is an ode, of course, but it is also an elegy for Coleridge's departed powers. Elements of that mode emerge at the end when he reads images of affliction into the storm: there he works in true elegiac fashion, making all nature mourn along with him for the loss they have suffered. At that point *Dejection* accomplishes the renewal of ancient modes, which Schiller called for in his essay on the naive and sentimental poets. But there is more to be observed here than some sad facts about Coleridge or some partial renovations of literary history. All these subtleties of maneuver and tone make clear that the poem rests on an intense paradox, and in many ways we have to be grateful for this happily mistaken instance of self-analysis. Coleridge's claim that he has lost his shaping spirit of imagination is belied by the very form the claim takes, the ode on *Dejection*. The poem is infused with confessions of ineptitude but in fact Coleridge has learned, for at least one more time, to turn ineptitude into magnificent art. In the poem he acts out the bipartite duties of the sentimental poet: he goes over the current conditions of his consciousness, analyzing their relation to what nature has to offer; he laments the loss of that which he needs most of all. At the end he reveals that his enforced discontinuity can be overcome for a while, and that a perfectly articulated self might not, after all, be necessary for an articulate imagination.

The example of Coleridge shows how it is possible to deceive oneself about adequacy, discovering it there where all good guesses would have assumed it to be lost. Obviously the reverse can also be true. As we have seen in Satan and could notice in any number of romantic figures, one can convince oneself that all the capacities are there when the briefest experience would prove, very quickly, that they are not. In either case the creation of a character who builds his life on the autonomy of his consciousness is clearly a difficult and complex business, and for that reason a mere image of attainment may suffice. If there is no authentic autonomy in the characters the poet creates, there is certainly a recognition on his part that autonomy is the requisite step prior to all other kinds of achievement; and if one is in a hurry for achievement, a character with a semblance of autonomy will do. Werther's was genuine, though limited and exhausting. In some of Goethe's successors, in Chateaubriand to a degree and most clearly in the early Byron, a satisfaction with façade replaced the sense of hard-won independence that emerges from Rousseau's revelations of self in the *Rêveries* and from Goethe's depiction of Werther's real sorrows. *Childe Harold's Pilgrimage* begins with a sketch of a personality, thrown together in ten stanzas so that the Childe could get on with his business as a melancholy traveler. His motivation is actually a package of commonplace emotions and observations brought in to give quick content to an attitude. The Childe himself is no more than a point of view with a built-in evaluative framework, ensuring that certain things will be sought out and commented on in a certain way. His autonomy is like that of Satan, only asserted, never shown at work. Put another way, *Childe Harold's Pilgrimage*, like Schiller's essay and Coleridge's *Dejec-*

tion, is a gesture of the mind "in the act of finding / What will suffice." One could argue further that Byron's whole career is a quest for sufficient imaginative forms, and that he finds these only in *Don Juan*, where the genuinely autonomous self of the narrator speaks through an imaginative mode that is perfectly adequate for every experience. The self-subsistence of the narrator in *Don Juan* supplants the problematic independence that was the best Byron could achieve in his earlier characters.

To reach that point of success, however, he had to work through an uneven series of poems, which show him thickening and adding content to the skimpy selves of his earliest figures. The process culminated in the poem about Manfred, whose hero was more coherent than any before him and most aware of what he needed to do. Manfred was more carefully put together than any of his Byronic predecessors, with the elements of the independent consciousness more precisely spelled out and tested in specific actions. Byron, like Goethe, was a connoisseur of attitudes, a collector of defiant relationships to experience. By the time he reached Manfred he had run through the spectrum of autonomy from Rousseauistic sensibility and withdrawal, as in *Childe Harold*, to Satanic involvement and aggression. In the process he piled more and more attributes onto his heroes. With Manfred, however, most of the other qualities had been burned away, and at the end of the poem there was left only the most essential Satanic assertion, the argument that the mind alone has the right and capacity to evaluate its own situation. But he arrived at that stage of the purest self-subsistence only after coming to see that he was insufficient in spiritual power, that is, the power literally to control spirits. Of course he does raise seven of them at the beginning of the poem, but the seventh, the spirit of the heavens, discloses that the power Manfred is using is not his own but borrowed from some unspecified source. If the spirit's sardonic claim of hegemony—that is, his assertion that Manfred's skills are "lent thee but to make thee mine"— turns out to be true, then Manfred's imperious gestures can lead only to his own self-destruction.[22] Every manifestation of those powers will draw him further into a trap of his own devising. But Manfred, ignoring the import of the spirit's contention, argues instead that the power he owns has made all the spirits his subjects, and that the mind controlling them "is as bright, / Pervading, and far darting as your own" (I, i, 155-56). In this war of words and forces both Manfred and the seventh spirit prove to be partly correct, which complicates the results considerably. When he intrudes into the hellish court of Arimanes, the regal hall where contact can be made with the dead, Manfred asks for, and is granted, an encounter with the specter of Astarte. Though his trespass forces an admiring discussion of the relative strength of his and the spirits' powers, Manfred clearly has no sway over Astarte's appearance, since he can neither bring her up on his own nor keep her here once she has arrived. Yet if there are severe limitations on what he can do, Astarte's departure obliges the spirits to recognize that the powers Manfred does have, though limited, are more than sufficient when they are self-directed: if his abilities are inadequate and possibly illusory when applied to outside forces, they are genuine and irresistible when he turns them upon himself—as he does when the figure of Astarte disappears despite all his pleas: "Yet, see, he mastereth himself, and makes / His torture tributary to his will" (II, iv, 528-30). Manfred has learned that if his mind cannot give him the spiritual strength of an immortal, he can at least do what a mortal does best, show the moral force of the autonomous will.

The result is a continuation of the same kind of fractional success that had turned up in Milton, Goethe, and Coleridge. Autonomy is acknowledged, indeed demonstrated, but with qualifications revealing that its possessor finds his strength only in failure and only as he turns that strength upon himself. Manfred's confrontation with the Abbot at the end of the play pits a communal system, which offers institutional ethics and promises of salvation, against a private order, which can offer only personal laws and self-induced suffering. His answer takes the issue to a pitch of self-awareness that it never had before. He speaks not merely for the Byronic hero but for that line of autonomy that struggles for its own in Heaven or society and finds in the end that Paradise has never been a genuine possibility. Manfred's words, with their echoes of *Paradise Lost,* are the *locus classicus* because they offer a lucid distillation of the whole history of half-successful autonomy between Milton and Byron:

> Old man! there is no power in holy men,
> Nor charm in prayer, nor purifying form
> Of penitence, nor outward look, nor fast,
> Nor agony, nor, greater than all these,
> The innate tortures of that deep despair,
> Which is remorse without the fear of hell
> But all in all sufficient to itself
> Would make a hell of heaven,—can exercise
> From out the unbounded spirit the quick sense
> Of its own sins, wrongs, sufferance, and revenge
> Upon itself; there is no future pang
> Can deal that justice on the self-condemn'd
> He deals on his own soul.
>
> (III, i, 66-78)

The mind is both efficacious and futile, its strengths undoubted but only as they relate to its capacities for self-punishment and a kind of elegant decline. Yet there is no easy acquiescence on Manfred's part, even though there are elements in it of the success-in-failure we have seen in Werther. Byron's garish drama is tentative and exploratory, not the end of a tradition but the turning of one. Rather than accepting the history of Satan as an apt image of the fate of the unregenerate mind (the temptations of his old Calvinism could easily have stopped him there), Byron turns that history into an instance of what can be tried—though it is all that can be tried—by the mind that can accept no other premises than its own. Limitations and opportunities are equally visible here, the former granted since Satan, the latter effective since the mind had become, for many, not only its own place but the only place. It was not just the Abbot's system that was insufficient but all others as well. Manfred drew all value into what Wordsworth, in a similar gesture, had called "that last place of refuge, my own Soul." No other locale of value seemed to be available in the immediate world. Wordsworth, after his own retreat into the self, found a new locale in a paradisal valley, and later in accepted institutions. Blake, with the same desire, knew only that the system had to come out of himself. Byron saw that the order of the insular self would have to suffice, and that if Manfred was not a final answer, it was a way to clarify the possibilities. Manfred's melodramatic aggression is designed less to update Satanic defiance than to define the limits of human opportunities. If he cannot negate death, he can at least have a say about the mode of his own dying. But then after all he does die, inevitably and almost willingly, burned out by his own dry heat. Even Manfred turned out to be a dead end, the last Byronic instance of self-sufficiency collapsing into self-consumption. *Don Juan* was the necessary next step.

SIX

Self, Society, Value

The ending of *Manfred* seems ambiguous because the conditions of conflict are never overtly defined. Who, after all,
is Manfred struggling with in the various encounters at the
end of the play? He rejects the institutionalism the old priest
represents, not only because no one else can tell him what to
do but also, he says, because no one else can punish him as
much as he can punish himself. In the final scene, with a
deftness of touch that blends irony with melodrama, Byron
has Manfred spurn the devils in a blatant echo of Satan's own
words. He even includes a reminiscence of Satan's remark
about the indestructibility of spiritual essence:

> The mind which is immortal makes itself
> Requital for its good or evil thoughts,—
> Is its own origin of ill and end—
> And its own place and time: its innate sense,
> When stripp'd of this mortality, derives
> No colour from the fleeting things without,
> But is absorb'd in sufferance or in joy,
> Born from the knowledge of its own desert.
>
> (III, iv, 129-36)

Yet if the mind is that strong, why does it choose to punish
itself? Obviously because Manfred does not share Satan's
morality but only his insistence on the strength of consciousness. Indeed, it is clear that Manfred, the Abbot, and the devils
all agree that he is a flagrant sinner, and they disagree only
on who is to punish him for it and whether he can be saved.
Further, the Abbot and the devils are equally institutional,
though on opposite sides of every imaginable fence. On in-

spection it turns out that they are part of the same institution, the vast edifice embodying Judaeo-Christian ideas of good and evil in a value system where abbots and devils have precisely assigned places. It is odd to find a hero who spouts Satanic assertions and yet agrees with his institutional opponents that he is, after all, a sinner. That may be part of the reason why Manfred was not a useful way out for the problems that Byron saw. In any case, the relation of Manfred's autonomy to the value system represented by his opponents is far less clear than he claims. There is, it appears, an uncertainty in Manfred of which he is not overtly aware. That same uncertainty, as it turns out, is endemic, not only among Byron's pre-*Don Juan* figures but among romantic heroes as a group. It is, indeed, one of the essential conditions in which the romantic hero has to function, however much he feels that he is fully aware of himself.

Self-awareness, a recognition of the demands and complexities of his private being, is basic to the position of the romantic hero.[1] From the earliest exemplars, like Saint-Preux and Werther, to the late instances in the heroes of Stendhal, these figures take for granted the centrality of the suffering and active ego. Concomitantly, they like to think of the world outside the self as a corporate entity that cannot penetrate to those recesses of being from which all awareness starts. One of the characteristic tropes related to this field of conceptions occurs frequently in *The Prelude*, where among the glories of the self is the ability of its faculties to expand outward in all directions ("Thus daily were my sympathies enlarged"), absorbing and thereby affecting more and more of what is outside of itself.[2] Wordsworth had a greedy self that could nearly always enrich itself from whatever material was at hand. That, for some, was a kind of health, though perhaps it was no more than luck, the fortunate combination of a particular self and a special set of circumstances. In any case, the sickness unto death for the romantics comes when the direction of energy reverses and the world impinges upon the self. The self is then proven to be by no means beyond the reach of hostility, since it can disintegrate under pressure into a madness like Hölderlin's. But those situations are comparatively rare, and when no recovery is possible, or the impingement becomes intolerable, one can usually choose retirement or annihilation. Suicide, for the romantics, was never without a sense of victory.

Accompanying this self-awareness and in part determining its degree is a sensitivity to the boundaries of self and nonself, boundaries to the distinction of which the hero devotes a great deal of energy, care, and alertness. Rilke's Malte Laurids Brigge (who descends from the romantic hero through Baudelaire, Dostoyevsky, and Jens Peter Jacobsen) has become so palpably aware of the boundaries of self and nonself that he can feel his being ending at his fingertips.[3] Outside of the self is the other, which for the romantic hero means society and social values as well as nature and other selves, all that Emerson included in the NOT-ME. For the hero the question seems to work out to the choice of limiting his boundaries or expanding them to include the values of the other, thus drawing those values in to the components of his private being. To a few, like Wordsworth, expansion seems possible without any real loss of integrity, since many of the values are in no ultimate sense hostile but quite in harmony with the self's own demands. Wordsworth was able to test inharmonious values and then reject them after a struggle, much as the body rejects an alien element; his bout with Godwin was not only metaphorically a sickness. Still, for all romantic heroes the choice of inclusion can never be without pain or ambivalence, nor is the result, for most of them, ever really a peaceful one.

The difficulty comes about because in the other are included all sorts of affirmations, from religion to politics to the place of the individual in a moral universe that society considers explicable. His uneasiness over how to take these affirmations makes it inevitable for the hero to become suspicious of an authority that, in an exposed position of its own, has to expound and defend the values it signifies. The hero knows, or learns, that a rejection of what society offers him means a drawing in of boundaries and thus a frustration of the expansiveness that comes naturally at an early stage in his career. This is what occurs in the confrontation, in Vigny's *Chatterton*, between the poet and the mayor of London, where the conditions of the exchange between the poet and bourgeois society are made explicit. Chatterton could then no longer deny the incompatibility of values so different that not even a truce (let alone a harmonious unification) was possible for them. Childe Harold found more tolerable than did Chatterton the purer distillation of self that comes about when the values of the other are rejected, though even he, from his withdrawn position, felt it necessary to condemn the insane brutalities of war. Hölderlin's Hyperion, on the other hand, accepted war gratefully as a means of realizing what appeared to be the joyous compatibility of his own values with those he was certain were around him. And for the heroes who chose either retirement or deliberately antisocial acts (René or Karl Moor), the boundaries were never quite immune from attack by the vestigial remnants of some set of values that the hero thought he had left behind.

Clearly, then, there is a variety of potential relationships between the romantic hero and the normative values of his society, ranging in a spectrum from imperfect assimilation to an apparently thorough rejection. But whatever his situation, a rhythm of attraction and repulsion creates an ambivalence in his relation to the outside world that seems basic to the hero's position. In fact, in this tug of impulses lies much of the romantic agony. Yet conventional opinion about the hero and his role vis à vis society assumes the absolute moral isolation of the romantic hero, probably because the heroes themselves so often insist upon their independence from external frames of reference. Analogies that cannot survive close examination are used to support this opinion. A representative sample appears in Clara F. McIntyre's "The Later Career of the Elizabethan Villain-Hero," where we find the assertion that Mrs. Radcliffe's hero Schedoni, perhaps the most significant Gothic villain, is a modern counterpart of the Elizabe-

than villain with his ambition, selfishness, great intellectual
power, and deliberate violation of the accepted values of society.[4] And since Schedoni directly influenced Byron and the
later romantics, Miss McIntyre argues that the full-blown romantic hero is little more than a continuation, with some
effects drawn from Schiller, of the Elizabethan villain-hero.
But her argument shows no awareness of the complicated
genealogy of the romantic hero (where, for example, does the
man of sensibility fit in?), and it rests on a shallow reading
of the texts in question.[5] Miss McIntyre dismisses too easily
Schedoni's remorse over the near-murder of Ellena, and mentions only those aspects of Schedoni's personality that fit in
with her definition (actually Clarence Boyer's definition) of
the Elizabethan villain, ignoring Schedoni's bleak, brooding
melancholy, the touchiness of his pride, and particularly the
repressed remorse and guilt over the murder of his brother.
Schedoni could never silence the traces of moral recrimination
from the past or allow himself to sacrifice his daughter to
further his own affairs. Without an understanding of the Satanic elements involved here—the cold ambition mixed with
agonies over the past—neither the complication nor the unity
of Schedoni's character comes clear, and the remorse over
Ellena is not seen for what it really is, the horror at the near-
murder of yet another close relative.[6] The complexities and
ambivalence in Schedoni, coupled with his unshakeable grandeur, fascinated the romantics, and these were the characteristics they built upon for their later heroes. The Elizabethan
villain was only one of the many influences converging to
form the romantic hero.[7]

In fact, the attitude of the hero toward society tends to be
paradoxical and ambivalent, rarely if ever as pure and unequivocal as it is usually said to be, or as he says it is. This can
be shown with a variety of figures extending in time and type
from the outlaws of Goethe and Schiller to Julien Sorel, the
roots of the ambivalence going far back into the history of
the romantic hero. It is true that the figure of the hero takes
on a number of forms, and that even Byron, who absorbed

so much of the tradition and who for many is synonymous with the romantic hero, cannot exhaust all the varieties of the type. But if we can speak of such a being as the romantic hero, and do not want to pluralize hero as Lovejoy pluralized romanticism, then we should be able to show certain radical agreements in attitude among most of these figures. One such agreement, which is probably central to their whole mode of action, is their unresolved ambivalence toward those values of society that seem continually to press against the boundaries of the self and demand recognition.

Taken as a group, the heroes differ in the degrees of their social awareness (though none is ever without it) and of their active commitment to a meaningful confrontation with society. Obviously, creative engagement need not imply any positive support of current values; indeed, the situation nearly always indicates the opposite, and even when the hero has, like Götz von Berlichingen, a definite set of values in mind, it usually differs from the set at hand and he is therefore considered a public rebel. Society, for such figures, is not something to be scorned from a citadel of the self. Its impingement upon the self is too drastic and insistent. Engagement is the only feasible mode of release for such pressures. The political rebel—Hölderlin's Hyperion, for example—will try to reorganize society along more tolerable lines. Others, the noble outlaws in particular, will flout it for profit or for spite. In any case, the position the hero takes is rarely a stable one, since he is a composite of too many factors continually at war with one another. He cannot play a consistent role because of his shifting feelings toward the role that he chooses to play.

Such dilemmas rest on romantic paradoxes of the sort that trapped Hyperion. In an era when revolutionaries struggled for changes in the structure of society as well as in the relations of master and slave, conscience demanded engagement from those to whom life meant more than sluggish acquiescence. On the other hand, both the age and part of the tradition of the romantic hero insisted upon the privacy of the individual self, its uniqueness and apartness.[8] An earlier version of a similar concatenation of qualities appears in the man of sensibility, who prides himself on his ability to feel profoundly and also demonstrates whenever possible his awareness of the sufferings of others, their ills and misfortunes. But the difference between, say, Mackenzie's *Man of Feeling* on the one hand and Hölderlin's *Hyperion* on the other rests in a peculiar balance of the qualities and a special relationship to sympathetic experience. For the man of sensibility, whenever he demonstrates social awareness, reveals also that he can feel deeply. He is therefore a good man, capable of exquisite sensations that by their very existence reveal a noble and generous heart. It is enough for him merely to feel deeply and to make token gestures that offer little more than peripheral contact with other classes, gestures that always indicate an awareness of his own distinctiveness. For him, therefore, there should be no real ambivalence, no agonizing over contradictory impulses. He should be able, successfully and without conflict, to remain apart at the same time as he establishes a satisfactory (because essentially undemanding) relationship to the objects of his compassion.

But so fine a balance rarely seems to happen that easily. In his letter of 15 May Werther combines his desire to be beneficent toward "die geringen Leute" with a deep awareness that "wir nicht gleich sind, noch sein können."[a] [9] He feels it wrong that "Leute von einigem Stande werden sich immer in kalter Entfernung vom gemeinen Volke halten, als glaubten sie durch Annäherung zu verlieren";[b] [10] and of course he wants to do otherwise, keeping his rank in mind but spreading his beneficence among the inferior classes. Sensibility and separateness are neatly, if condescendingly, wedded in this passage. But later—using a unifying device that he employs frequently to give both structure and irony to his novel—Goethe has Werther repeat the remarks about rank but in a very different context. As usual with such echoes the words take on an ominous tone in the new situation. In the letter of 24 December in Book Two, written after he has left Lotte and entered the service of the ambassador, Werther again admits the necessity of an "unterschied der Stände," a distinction among social ranks; but this time he is the target of condescension, too high in the social order to be the object of charity but not high enough to be the equal of those with a long lineage. He wants to be left to follow his own ways: "ach ich lasse gern die andern ihres Pfades gehen, wenn sie mich auch nur könnten gehen lassen."ᶜ ¹¹ He wants modes of relationship in which aloofness and association are equally possible. Werther's exercises in beneficence are an attempt at such modes, and he succeeds in them because he can begin and end the exercise as he wills. But his uneasiness with the ironic reversal of positions noted in the December letter (of course he is totally unaware of the irony) signals his inability to control the difficult balance when he does not call all the signals. The ironies compound because there is, as it turns out, a link with society at issue here, and its presence calls into question all his assertions of independence. The snobbery he practices as a man of feeling is a precise mirroring of the snobbery he finds repellent in other classes. Werther is closer to what he disowns than he realizes, and that ambivalence, as the results show, is an exceedingly unstable mixture.

In Mackenzie's *Man of Feeling* the ambivalence takes a different turn. There, the effectuality of the hero of sensibility is always in question, and that issue is further complicated by Mackenzie's clumsiness in controlling the fine line between innocence and obtuseness. His point is to reveal the radical corruption of society's values in the face of Harley's radical innocence. Mackenzie does that quickly and with little effort. *The Man of Feeling* bears close relations to the pastoral vision, particularly as Empson has extended it: Harley is not simply a bumpkin confronting the world but a representative of a very different way of looking at things, based on a different organization of values. Indeed his ways of seeing, "like the mirrors of the ladies, have a wonderful effect in bettering their complexions."¹² But of course Harley does not know that, at least in the early pages of the novel. The man of feeling is fully aware of his sensibility, but he has no idea of his insensitivity to the actualities of things. His situation is in some ways the precise opposite of Werther's: Harley thinks his values are congenial with general experience when in fact they are essentially discontinuous with those by which the world, in its prudence, actually lives. He is a gull not simply because he is fooled by tricksters and thieves (many others are so fooled in the novel), but because for a long time he assumes that, however intense his sensibility, there is a continuity between what he is and what society requires of its survivors. Even late in the novel he is described as "sensible to judge, but still more warm to feel," a division of emphasis that, in the line leading to the romantic heroes, is usually fatal.[13] Harley does awaken gradually to a limited awareness of his moral isolation, much as Werther and Hyperion were to do; but he has nothing of the full recognition of incompatibility owned by Saint-Preux, or, later, by Julien Sorel. Like the sentimental poet, he is unwillingly discontinuous, but unlike that figure he is, for most of the book, unwittingly so as well. Though he never lays claim to autonomy, he is far more independent of social value than he knows or wants to be. Harley is able to enact his values only at home, in a limited world where he has some effectiveness in picking up the pieces of broken lives. But he does far less well with his own. Even at home his self is so distinctive that it can prove the extent of its separateness only through the ultimate act of separation. Harley slips out of life in a state of confusion and embarrassment. Then, finally, he is at ease, separated from the sensibility that had made him alien. As the narrator puts it: "I saw that form, which, but a little before, was animated with a soul which did honour to humanity, stretched without sense or feeling before me."[14] At the end he is as cold and unfeeling as the society that had gulled him. Like Clarissa and Chatterton, he is at one with the social order only when dead.

Obviously the romantic hero has behind him a complex and sometimes contradictory genealogy, including a series of self-sufficient villains as well as heroes of self-serving com-

passion. Both villain and hero share an impulse toward apartness as well as an awareness (conscious in the one, subliminal
in the other) that society can be used for the gratification of
self. Still we should never minimize the differences between
the gross egotism of a Montoni and the genuine compassion,
however dubious some of its impulses, of a Harley. It is only
for the latter and his sort that ambivalence is possible. The
kind of active commitment to which figures like Chatterton
felt driven required an involvement that clashed gravely and
painfully with that desire for self-sustaining subjectivity that
had been active at least since Richardson, not to speak of the
line of Satan. Reconciliation of these dilemmas seemed beyond
the reach of all but the most extraordinary. Shelley resolved
them, as we shall see, in some of his poems. But the Hyperion
of Hölderlin's novel, forced into a dilemma beyond resolution,
could only suffer and retreat into bitterness and remorse.

Hyperion wanted to revivify, in and for the present, the
values of the past. This meant, more than anything else, a
completion of the possibilities of self, the absorbing into his
own being of qualities he felt to be painfully lacking in himself.
To do this he had to engage in a society, the customs and
habits of which, he says quite explicitly, are not his own.[15]
The warning implications of his metaphors of play were lost
on him. A naive arrogance lies behind his feeling that he can
partake of society or not, as he pleases, and that he can achieve
heroism without a thorough involvement of self. To place
oneself in a situation of danger, as he did, is simply not enough
to forestall the difficulties he gets into. Like many another
romantic hero committed to a scheme of public action, Hyperion becomes alienated because he is different from the
vulgar crowd he leads and tries to help, and it takes him some
time to realize the import of that difference. In the name of
furthering freedom he is ironically associated with wanton
acts of pillage that flout the very values he has been trying to
impose. The novel charts his growing, painful awareness of
the hard realities of politics and of his own ambiguous situation as a redemptive figure. At the end he turns out much

like a conventional Byronic hero, isolated, with shattered values, and haunted by feelings of guilt over Diotima's death. Life has gone by for him, nothing is left, and he cannot cry. The revulsion and violence evident in the famous attack on the values of German society come less out of the bitterness of crushed hopes than from the sour taste of radical incompatibility.

Similar motifs had already emerged, though without the influence of the tradition of sensibility, in the earlier *Sturm und Drang* figures of Götz von Berlichingen and Karl Moor. Götz, part political rebel like Hyperion but also an outlaw like Moor, breaks his word as a knight for the good reason of taking control of a peasant rebellion in order to curb its destructiveness. Thoroughly pragmatic in his inclinations and actions, concerned primarily with a well-defined but impossible return to a vanished status quo, Götz is less a Prometheus than an unhappy anachronism well aware of what he is about. His attempt to lead the peasants is a grand moral gesture, forcing him into the painful choice of flouting one set of values in which he believes—the importance of a knight's word—in order to avert an irresponsible blood bath. Like Hyperion and Karl Moor, Götz is morally superior to those he tries to control, but he falls into a moral and personal disaster when his attempts fail.

Moor, on the other hand, has little of the political rebel about him, but he too registers the ambivalence even as he bewails his moral isolation. His motives (though even more personal than those of Götz, who at least wanted to salvage a way of life) are mixed enough for him to play the part of Robin Hood, at the same time as a massive pride leads him to set himself up as a judge when no other satisfactory one can be found. God no longer avenges human wrongs, therefore Karl Moor has to do so. But in his introduction to the play Schiller warned clearly, though with obvious futility, that Moor could not be reduced to one or another simple trait. Schiller calls Moor a peculiar Don Quixote and also likens him to Satan—that strange and reverberative combination, by

now thoroughly familiar, which Schiller brings together because they each stand for values that cannot square with the
values of the social order.[16] Himself the victim of evil, the
robber longs for a perfection clearly beyond attainment in the
ambiguous world Schiller drew up for him. Moor has "eine
Bitterkeit gegen die unidealische Welt."[d] [17] He attempts to
steer his way through so complicated a set of patterns of
morality—loyalty to the poor, to his gang of cutthroats and
to his own fear of harming the innocent—that he can resolve
the insufferable dilemma only by offering himself as a sacri-
ficial victim, for order has to be restored and vengeance belongs only to God.[18]

The examples of Hyperion and Götz (and to a certain extent
Karl Moor) point out the difficulties inherent in the very nature of romantic liberalism or, for our purposes, in the problems the romantic hero as political rebel faced in his role as
redemptive figure. Spiritual aristocracy forms the keystone
holding in shape the whole image of the hero, whether he had
committed himself to an active role in society or opted out
of it. None of these figures was without some sense of this
distinction, which they saw as the essential condition of their
status, the primary determinant of their whole mode of being.
Going along with that aristocracy, in fact taking an inevitable
part in it, was a sense of the self-sufficiency of one's private
values. Artistocracy of whatever sort, social or spiritual, implied not only distance and separateness but some form of
subjective independence, as it did with figures as different as
Werther, Manfred, and Ahab. Indeed, self-government in the
realm of value was seen as so essential to the elite status of
the self that it could be treated as a symbol, the defining
condition, of that status. The presence of an independent
framework of judgment (or even an assertion of such a framework) was meant to be taken as a sign of that distinction and
distinctiveness of self the hero had to have in order to be fully
himself—or at least himself as he envisioned himself. All of
this put the one who chose active engagement into a special
set of difficulties. His sensitivity and capacity for insight had

shown him what needed to be done in the social order, for others as well as for himself. He had to learn to take part in the world at the same time as he practiced and protected that autonomy of self and value essential to his most profound understanding of himself. Yet it was that same understanding that created and perpetuated the ambiguities and ambivalence. The hero's recognition of his private distinctiveness established any tendencies he may have felt toward separateness, and he could not help but feel tendencies of that sort. The self-awareness, which only he and his peers could possess, made clear to him how different he was from those with whom he had to deal. The urge toward a more encompassing relationship with what was (or with those who were) outside of the world of the self ran into the counterimpulse to explore the rich possibilities and rewards of spiritual aristocracy.

Shelley managed to obviate such difficulties with his politically involved heroes by treating the masses as if they were all, themselves, of an imposing spirituality; or, what amounts to the same thing, by mythologizing the whole affair, as in *Prometheus Unbound*, and thereby putting the action on a plane where he could conveniently ignore those who were to be led to Utopia. In *The Revolt of Islam*, for example, the plane on which the real action occurs becomes obvious, at the very beginning of the poem, in the allegorical battle between the eagle and the serpent. The key to Shelley's approach lies in the feeling of an immediately present or imminent apocalypse (note, e.g., the curious mixture of tenses in the song "The world's great age begins anew" at the end of *Hellas*). He focuses, therefore, on the extreme tensions involved in bringing to birth the moment of glory, and has no room or cause to deal with difficulties of the sort Schiller, Goethe, Hölderlin (in *Hyperion*), Vigny, and others found especially problematical. This is by no means to say that Shelley sentimentalizes. Rather, he works in a different mode, which demands other and less ambiguous approaches to the painful world of romantic politics.[19]

Still, solutions valid for Shelley could hardly be so for others who had a different orientation and could not harmonize their spiritual superiority with the selfishness and insensitivity of those they had to lead. For figures like Hyperion, rebellion, self-respect, and morality make an unstable mixture at best, and each of these heroes shipwrecks upon the realization that personal and public interests are separate and cannot jibe. The hero is usually the only one who breaks under this ambivalence beyond reconciliation, and his last positive act tends to be one that draws him away from immediate involvement, or an attempt at it, and toward some version of a sacrifice of self.

The later romantics set up a pantheon of heroes who were never quite happy in or out of society, whether plundering it or redeeming it. Most were like Byron's Corsair, the pirate captured because he sidetracked a battle in order to save innocent women, and then sickened at the murder committed by the woman who wanted to save him. None of these figures seems to have been able to make a full break of the sort Rimbaud achieved. In that inadequacy as in others they had a familiar predecessor: the Satan of *Paradise Lost* has moments of remorse and self-condemnation, and he condemns himself (however briefly) in terms of values such as respect for God and compassion for the innocent pair—values that come right out of the system he is supposed to have rejected. The psychological makeup of the complete villain has in it a necessary divorce from outside value, which is impossible to find in any of the heroes we call romantic. Awareness of this difference prompted Schiller to set up a true villain, Franz Moor, as foil to his brother Karl. Franz is closer to the conventional Renaissance villain, Iago or Richard the Third, than to his brother or any of Karl's counterparts in the literature of the time.

In the difference between these two brothers rests a distinction crucial to the understanding of the romantic hero as rebel, a distinction clarifying not only his essentially un-Machiavellian personality but the tenor of his modes of feeling as well. Franz—or Iago, or any of the pure, Italianate Renais-

sance villains—feels no compunction about lawlessness since
his own desires and their fulfillment are the only demands he
will acknowledge, the only sources or standards of value that
he will follow. Most villains of this sort show little awareness
of the society beyond the confines of the self. Social values
have meaning for them only insofar as those values can be
used or manipulated. Otherwise these figures function only
through their private self-chosen schema. In Ann Radcliffe's
The Mysteries of Udolpho Emily is, in effect, held prisoner
by Montoni, the new husband of her aunt. When she asks
"by what right he exerted this unlimited authority over her,"
he answers sardonically "by the right of my will; if you can
elude that, I will not enquire by what right you do so."[20]
Montoni is asserting the absolute discontinuity between the
values by which he functions and any values society may hold.
Emily's question assumes that there is a connection between
society and their situation; Montoni rejects that assumption.
His right, he says, is unlimited; the severance is complete. It
is that sort of total repudiation, a discontinuity not only asserted but held to and acted upon, which characterizes the
unmitigated villain. Schedoni, the quasi-villain from *The Italian*, attempts to act upon such a discontinuity but he is, as we
have seen, beset by an ambivalence caused by the unsuspected
presence within himself of values he was certain he had left
behind. For figures like Franz Moor and Montoni there can
only be a juxtaposition of incompatible value systems; there
can never be a penetration of one by the other. But it is the
latter from which the romantic rebel tends to suffer. The pressure of his discontent prompts him to set himself up as an
antagonist, an antisocial personality who works under a compulsion, never quite secure, to affirm the independence and
validity of his own values. The true villain feels no such compulsion because he is already so secure in his standards that
ambiguities and ambivalence cannot bother him. For the hero,
but never for the villain, one or another form of love—sex,
friendship, or general human compassion—seemed always to
get in the way, to reveal itself as still present in the selves of

those for whom antisocial acts become a mode for the completion of self. Love as the great romantic theme was not confined to the situations of a Werther or an Adolphe. It appears, in another form, in the compassionate remorse for those one has killed, however justifiably. Even Byron's Giaour, who swears that he mourns only for the woman he avenged, calls himself a Cain, whose crime he repeated and whose curse he bears.

The redeemers of society suffered no less than the criminals from ambivalence, though not in quite the same way or for the same reasons. Vigny worried more than most about the moral ambiguities involved when personal and public freedom clashed over active social involvement. Visions of victory could be offered in mythological or apocalyptic terms, as in *Prometheus Unbound* or at the end of *Faust*, but Vigny was more disturbed about present actualities and their cost to the poet. His whole work argues the necessity of the poet's status as pariah, he and society being what they are. But one has to note that the desire to serve is always there, and that Vigny's most compelling analogy to the figure of Chatterton (in both *Stello* and the play) is the military man of *Servitude et grandeur militaire*, that other pariah caught in the conflict of duty with a social position that is usually abnormal and absurd. If Docteur Noir warns Stello to stay out of the inevitably corrupting world of politics, the examples he offers of Gilbert and Chénier show poets who did insist upon engagement, although they suffered mortally from it. And Chatterton, Vigny's great image of the poet in conflict with bourgeois value (Gilbert struggled with royalty, Chénier with an uncontrollable revolution), has a grand vision of the ship of state with the poet as pilot. He gives up his urge toward commitment only after society's judgment on his nonproductivity has been borne in upon him, though he does have the last, beautifully ironic gesture of selling his body, useful only after death, to a medical school.[21]

This whole set of problems takes on other forms with that extensive group of heroes for whom an active relationship to society seemed not only undesirable but psychologically impossible. Here, with the familiar, uncommitted, isolated figures like René and Manfred, and with the equally familiar image of the agonizing secret sin, the insistence upon moral solipsism appears as part of the expected paraphernalia of the hero's character. Value, they insisted, is personal, individual, and self-created, a product of those private needs of the self that seem never to coalesce with the requirements of the social order. The mind, then, would become its own source for standards of reward and punishment, and thus one would feel the guilt of the secret sin according to the scheme of values one's own mind had established. This, at least, is what the heroes say, over and over again. But we ought to be skeptical about this peculiar masochism, especially when it comes to the source of the standards by which one punishes oneself. The hero is free, presumably, to choose the values he sees fit for the role he has assumed, since his thorough rejection of the social order creates a new relationship of self and outer world, new boundaries, and therefore new standards of value. A delightful irresponsibility seems on the verge of being accepted, an absolute liberty such as Gide offered in Lafcadio. But somehow it never appears to happen, and in one way or another the unsociable hero broods, agonizes, and suffers remorse, never adopting the complete freedom available to him. We return to the question with which the chapter began: why should someone feel sinful if he can, as it seems, choose to feel otherwise? Obviously, responsibility has not been waived at all; it has become guilt.

In Werther, who is a figure early enough so that we can see the process of isolation taking place (it is equally visible in Hyperion), much is still clear that later appears only implicitly. For Werther evinces throughout much of the novel a radiant urge toward happiness that depends in part (and dangerously) upon a compulsive insistence on personal freedom, an expansiveness of self so total as to be almost without bounds. He is, at the beginning, quite sociable, indeed an affable personality. But he analogizes, ominously, the rules of literature to the standards of bourgeois society, foreshadowing his own eventual destruction with the mocking image of a lover courting under eminently practical regulations. Yet he also speaks poignantly of man's urge to surrender to the comforts and peace of routine and restriction. The ambivalence is clear, and the unstable mixture explodes into the pistol shot that kills him. He tries once, openly and desperately, to violate the values of society by pleading for the murderer with whose situation he identifies, and the judge's reprimand becomes for Werther society's judgment on his own transgression, his love for the married Lotte. On a scrap of paper found among his effects was a note apparently written just after the trial: "Du bist nich zu retten, Unglücklicher! ich sehe wohl, dass wir nicht zu retten sind."[e][22] Shortly thereafter he comes to the inevitable conclusion. With bitter irony but obvious agreement he says that his love is a sin for this world, and he shall willingly punish himself for it:

> Und was ist das, dass Albert dein Mann ist? Mann! Das wäre denn für diese Welt—und für diese Welt Sünde, dass ich dich liebe, dass ich dich aus seinen Armen in die meinigen reissen möchte? Sünde? Gut, und ich strafe mich dafür.[f][23]

At that point Werther becomes a self-appointed scapegoat, and his suicide not only rids him of society but rids society of him as well. His gesture is replete with ironies: if it shows a realization of his inability to acquiesce to the social order, it also shows him performing an action—the expulsion of the scapegoat—which is one of the clearest instances of a social judgment made for the benefit of the social order. Werther took the making of that judgment upon himself, playing both judge and jury at once. He was never more a member of society than when he left it, purifying himself and society in the same act. Of course the scapegoat need not have died: society might have been satisfied if he were driven out into the desert or the wilderness beyond its confines, keeping his stains harmlessly isolated. But that was clearly more than

Werther could tolerate, and he never really considered that option. His ties to society were so tense and sure that he was left only with the choice of modes of extinction. His alternative to acquiescence was nothingness, not the brooding, disconnected wanderings of a René or a Childe Harold. Like Vigny's Chatterton, though for different reasons, Werther refused to accept the role of pariah that his position in society forced upon him. Neither of them could bear the thought of standing alone outside.

One or two further examples of those who thought they could manage by themselves should suffice to establish some contours for this problem. René, less obviously concerned with social values than Werther, but without Rousseau's clarity about the forms of the inner life, suffers from a failure of his self to supply images other than the narcissistic. He is beset by vague, free-floating anxieties that seem traceable, in part at least, to his feeling that he is in some sense sinful because different. Like Werther, René attempts to flout established public value as it appears in a visible, ceremonial form, in his case at his sister's initiation into the cloister. But he, too, arrives at a confession of public sin, defined in terms of the religious awareness he has just challenged. Eventually this guilt wears him down, though in the interim he has clearly enjoyed the company of his own unending sorrow. (René shows the same pattern of self-generating self-consumption that we saw in Werther.) For that and other reasons the ambivalence never quite resolves although, like *Die Räuber, René* ends with an ambiguous return to the fold. At the conclusion René is chastised by Father Souël because he has acted as though he needed nothing outside of himself: "Jeune présomptueux qui avez cru que l'homme se peut suffire à lui-même! La solitude est mauvaise à celui qui n'y vit pas avec Dieu."[8][24] René is accused, in effect, of the Satanic sin of self-sufficiency. The content and tone of this reprimand were predictable, given its source as well as the pressures of the institution. But the priest seems to understand more than convention requires: "elle [la solitude] redouble les puissances de

l'âme, en même temps qu'elle leur ôte tout sujet pour
s'exercer."[h][25] This is a clear acknowledgment of the powers
that consciousness can draw from solitude, of the strengths
available to subjective autonomy in the proper surroundings.
Father Souël's rebuke of René is not the moralistic attack of
a spouter of pious platitudes but, instead, the work of one
who is well aware of the nature of the contemporary loner
and particularly of his special strengths. He does not ask René
directly to dissipate "les puissances de l'âme," yielding abjectly
to God. René, though naturally withdrawn, would never have
willingly weakened himself. Rather, Souël asks René to direct
those strengths outside of himself, putting them at the service
of the community. The suggestion seems good, since it would
appear to give René the chance to become a more successful
(and more pious) Götz or Karl Moor; but in fact, since those
strengths came out of the soul in solitude, such engagement
would effectually weaken and eventually conquer René. Chateaubriand (if not Souël himself) was fully aware of the war
between isolation and engagement, and the way that war
seems always to finish. René allows the old priest's words to
go past him, even if he is troubled and humiliated by them.
Yet if he does not accept Souël's challenge he does not quite
reject it either. The story concludes without resolution and
with René passively resistant: "On dit que, pressé par lex deux
vieillards, il retourna chez son épouse, mais sans y trouver
le bonheur."[i][26] Pushed by the others, he goes so far and no
further, neither fully within the fold nor quite outside it. His
tale ends in irony and ambivalence, with all strengths acknowledged and with no obvious winners.

The ambivalence and ambiguities do not fully resolve with
Byron's Manfred either, though he, unlike René, refuses the
welcoming gesture of the institution. The ending of *Manfred*
reads like a precise and deliberate refutation of Chateaubriand, setting up a similar situation in order to turn it in
another direction. Byron's Abbot does not speak quite so
sharply to Manfred as Father Souël does to René, partly because of Manfred's rank, partly also because the French priest

is a friend and a paternal figure and is therefore familiar enough to drop all courtesies when necessary. Manfred's refusal to return to the fold (that is, if he had ever been in it) is consistent with a lineage that is very different from René's, Manfred emerging from the Satanic and René from the Rousseauistic line. That difference is made explicit in Manfred's echo of Satan's assertions and in René's reliance, throughout the story as well as at the end, on feelings, particularly melancholy, as a source of energy for day-to-day existence. (René is one of the cardinal instances of the vulgarization of Rousseau.) Manfred's welcome of death resolves some of the ambivalence—only at the moment of extinction, of course, though there quite beautifully. The deaths of Clarissa, Harley, and Chatterton, as we have seen, were the occasion of parodies of the return to the community, the welcoming of the reprobate back to the fold. Manfred's death is clearly nothing of the kind. Yet here again one finds it difficult to account for the hero's agony in terms other than those he professes to despise, the values of society. For Manfred's sin is incest—all the ponderously vague allusions in the text can be taken no other way; and, as we learn quite unequivocally in Byron's *Cain*, incest is a sin made by circumstances, by society, and not absolute in itself, for neither Cain nor Adah is guilty of it. Obviously, then, Manfred is guilty in terms of an external and relative set of values, and his remorse indicates his assent to standards of reward and punishment other than those he has created for himself. His explorations of the nature of individual mind and will, his insistence upon their autonomy, are countered and qualified by his unwitting agreement with elementary rules of the social order. The vestigial social ties remain, and (as they always seem to do) they find their way to the hero by means of the obsessive secret sin.

Society for these heroes, no matter to what degree they considered themselves unique, special, or merely different, obviously had a great deal to do with the terms under which they chose to assert themselves. The hero may insist that he makes up his own rules (and there is always some sense in which he does), but the nature of society and the structure of his personality find points of antagonism that are elements in a mutual attraction as well as a necessary repulsion. The mind is unquestionably its own place—for the romantics it could never be anything else—but it is only rarely as independent as the romantic heroes said it was. Indeed, despite the prevalent assertions of self-sufficiency it is difficult to find at this stage of literary history a passive hero who has removed himself to so extreme a distance from accepted value that he no longer, in any meaningful sense, wants to affirm it or to judge himself by it. Conversely, those heroes who feel an urge toward commitment always hold back something of themselves and what they retain is like the secret sin of the others, the flaw that does them in.

Such a flaw seems, at times, a consciously ironic reversal of the flaw in the tragic hero, which we usually define as the moral weakness in a basically well-ordered and reasonably decent man. For the romantic hero the flaw is just the opposite, the one moral or decent aspect in a nature that tried hard to be unsociable or wicked. Byron's Corsair, after all, had "a single virtue and a thousand crimes" to contend with, and that one virtue, the flaw in his piratical makeup, was sufficient to bring him down. Autonomy and even the most limited dependence may be degrees on a scale but they are also radically different states. The romantic hero is not always sure of the difference but he is unfailingly subject to the tension it causes. The resultant ambivalence makes for much of the attractiveness of the romantic hero, because the flaw in his autonomy makes him human and not merely deficient.

The ambivalence is also a sign of his ultimate incapacity in one of the imagination's most difficult jobs. Romantic heroes shared with other romantics an obsession with the order and content of consciousness. The difficulties were always the same: how can one make forms for the self-sufficient consciousness? is the imagination equal to the business of bringing such forms into being? The ambivalence proves that the imagination was not always adequate to the demands made upon it, that the gap between assertion and actuality, between the illusion of strength and the reality of vulnerability, was sometimes too painfully apparent. Such inadequacies were obvious as early as the Satanic forebear, who softened, however briefly, at the sight of bliss he could never have. The warfare of values subverting the romantic hero shows that the self is, after all, open to attack, and not only from social forces outside itself but from aspects of those forces that had never been expelled from within. The hero's autonomy was far more contextual than he realized. He shared in systems and codes that had seemed to be the exclusive property of all those others out there beyond the environs of the self. If the sentimental poet and the man of feeling were subject to unwilled discontinuities, the romantic hero—asserting his autonomy all the while— was equally the prey of unwitting continuities. It is not that he wanted to permit himself access to society but that society, quite without his knowledge, had already achieved access to him.

Once again the characters of *La Nouvelle Héloïse* helped to establish a model, and as usual with an irony that escaped most of their successors. In the early part of the novel Julie is aware (and is repeatedly told by her friends) that she and Saint-Preux are unlike most others in their society. They are separated out in a spiritual aristocracy that, in later hands, too easily became tawdry, sentimental, and (eventually) soporific. Yet it is her close ties to the values of the social order that win out and demolish their relationship. Her separation from society was never safely complete: the continuities, in the form of filial love, overwhelmed the subversive pairing and brought her back into the fold. Yet if that was where many subsequent heroes ended it was only half of Julie's experience. Rousseau's novel, replete with mutually supporting ironies, carries her into a simulacrum of society, the success of which depended upon a unique balance of subjective forces. Julie is the arch insider: we are told very often that she is the spiritual center of the ménage, that all of it exists, in an important sense, as an homage to her. The imagery of apotheosis

begins when she is still in the ménage, not after she leaves it.
Yet, as it turns out, Julie has been carrying within herself more
of the outsider than she suspected. In a precise mirror-imaging
of the events in the first part of the novel, the values of the
asocial (and unsociable) order, those which had lost out before, reach in and subvert this very special version of the social
enclosure. The totality of Rousseau's novel holds most subsequent history within itself. It reveals the major forms of
vulnerability to which the romantic hero was prone, and enfolds them in an irony whose intensity and breadth were
matched only by Stendhal, who is to the ending of the movement what Rousseau was to its beginning.

The ironies inherent in this situation blossom in Stendhal's
great figure of Julien Sorel. Detached and aloof, an admirer
of both Napoleon and Rousseau, Julien chooses to rise and
be admired in terms of the very values he despises, to make
out of hypocrisy a moral stance that would permit involvement without commitment, and thus an ironic compromise.
Julien's affairs, his assertions of autonomy, and his curious
blend of craftiness and incompetence will occupy most of a
subsequent chapter.

∾ *SEVEN* ∾

The Landscape of Desire

No one is quite as exemplary as Rousseau, which means that
we have to turn to him at nearly every stage in our study of
some of the problems of autonomy from his time to Pater's.
That is particularly so when we consider the shape of the self's
landscape, whose contours he had studied, both generally and
in detail, with elaborate care. Since that shape became a major
matter in the working out of the attendant problems, we shall
have to turn to it once again, this time as it occurs in *Emile*.

Quite near the beginning of the book the narrator warns
other preceptors not to be too zealous in what they teach their
charges about moral values. He urges them not to play the
tempter and give to the still innocent child a premature knowledge of good and evil. After all, he argues, this world had
been the place of man's first paradise, and, since it is still that
way for the child, we ought to leave him ignorant of the
forbidden fruit until he knows how to handle it.[1] This is a
version of what he calls, a few pages earlier, negative education: the most useful and important rule in education "n'est
pas de gagner du tems, c'est d'en perdre" (323).[a] Emile, it is
clear, is not only natural man, caught so early that he is pure,
unformed potentiality; he is also a version of the first man,
the preceptor's Adam, placed, as one critic puts it, "dans une
province écartée, dans un îlot d'innocence miraculeusement
préservé depuis l'âge d'or."[b] [2]

It is the preceptor's job to preserve Emile in the same way
that this landscape has been preserved. The tutor will function
as tutelary deity, so shaping the inner life of his Adam that
Emile will be protected against the possibility of a Fall. In

effect Emile will be prevented from enacting within his own life the history of the original tumble from bliss into the woes of the world of Experience. He will bypass the Fall, guided rigorously by the preceptor from a childhood Eden to a mature one. He will be forever prelapsarian, demonstrating in his natural way that the old edicts were wrong, that nothing was more unnatural than the expulsion from Paradise.

The issue comes up again toward the end of the book when Emile and Sophie are brought together and the preceptor, always thinking ahead for them, contemplates their marriage. While he and Emile are traveling to see Sophie he meditates on the initial stages of love, calling the lover's feelings "douces illusions," noting that such supreme happiness is a hundred times finer in hope than in realization. All the same he goes on to say: "fais ton paradis sur la terre en attendant l'autre" (782).ᶜ If anyone can make it work, Emile can; he has been trained for Eden since birth. Somewhat later, speaking to the lovers on their wedding day, the preceptor recapitulates this combination of confidence and cynicism, telling them that they alone seem capable of accomplishing the impossible, of prolonging the happiness of love in marriage and thereby creating a Paradise on earth (861). Indeed, the tutor's usual coolness and detached self-control give way for one of the few times in the book, and he shapes an eloquent vision of the world Emile and Sophie will build around them:

Je m'attendris en songeant combien de leur simple retraite Emile et Sophie peuvent répandre de bienfaits autour d'eux, combien ils peuvent vivifier la campagne et ranimer le zéle eteint de l'infortuné villageois. Je crois voir le peuple se multiplier, les champs se fertiliser, la terre prendre une nouvelle parure, la multitude et l'abondance transformer les travaux en fêtes, les cris de joye et les benedictions s'élever du milieu des jeux autour du couple aimable qui les a ranimés. On traitte l'age d'or de chimére, et c'en sera toujours une pour quiconque a le coeur et le goût gâtés. Il n'est pas même vrai qu'on le regrette, puisque ces regrets sont toujours vains. Que faudroit-il donc pour le faire renaitre? Une seule chose mais impossible; ce seroit de l'aimer (859).[d]

But of course the golden age does not seem impossible for the young lovers because, as the preceptor finally adds, "il semble déja renaitre autour de l'habitation de Sophie."[e] The marriage of two such beautifully nurtured beings promises fulfillment for their surroundings as well as for themselves.

The preceptor's vision is both pastoral and paradisal, foreseeing the realization of all possible desires in a landscape crammed with joy. This is not a primal Eden but an achieved one, a place to be reached and not a point of beginning. All the talk is of revivifying, refreshing, making it new by turning labor into a festival and deprivation into universal fruition. All of its inhabitants except Emile and Sophie have gone through adversity to get there. For Emile, however, the old Paradise has never really been lost. In the preceptor's vision he has only shifted roles, going from pupil to patriarch simply by maturing under the proper direction. In fact, all the years of guidance seem to have led him directly to this place. Emile's education was designed to make him autonomous and self-sustaining, with an inner life so fertile and coherent that he can depend upon himself for every sort of sustenance. He will be as complete within himself as are the gorgeous and prolific surroundings of his preceptor's golden dream. Thus, there will be an exact parity of inner and outer landscapes. The long work of the preceptor will have made his Adam as paradisal within as is this landscape of desire, which seems to be Emile's proper home.

The terrestrial Eden promised to Emile has behind it all sorts of fabulous landscapes, antique fictions that were finding new and comfortable homes at the endings of a number of eighteenth century romances. In Ann Radcliffe's *The Italian*, for example, the young lovers are led, after all their difficulties, into a pleasure ground described as "a scene of fairy-land."[3] Their marriage is celebrated with feasts and dancing, and with a joy so widespread that Vesuvius spouts up fire just to add sparkle to the occasion. Though the preceptor's vision has no such exuberant mountains, the patriarchal conditions he foresees for Emile and Sophie have precisely the same sort of lineaments. Mrs. Radcliffe's Gothic romances share with Rousseau's treatise on education a culmination in an image of Claudean harmonies. In both cases the celebration and the promise are designed as rewards for the young lovers, and in both nothing appears to the writer to be so fitting as a traditional landscape of desire, idyllic, pastoral, and fabulous, suffused by the same glow that enfolds Virgilian shepherds and the princely lovers at the ends of fairy tales. With Mrs. Radcliffe the tone and the reward are particularly appropriate. Her fictions touch on the same archetypal levels as fairy tales, and the gauntlets her lovers go through earn them all kinds of justified recompense. In the last scene of *The Italian* one of her characters stops dancing long enough to put the point unsubtly and precisely: "we had to go through purgatory before we could reach paradise."[4] With Rousseau, however, the situation is very different. Emile and Sophie are granted the same fabulous landscape as Mrs. Radcliffe's young lovers, but in their case the reward is more like a diploma than a victory medal, more a sign of having completed a course of training than of having been through a confrontation with the forces of darkness. Emile knew nothing of the purgatory that Mrs. Radcliffe's characters remembered. He skipped from Eden to Eden without tripping.

But the prize awarded to Emile does not sit comfortably with the purpose of his training. The preceptor insists from the beginning that his pupil is being brought up to find a place in society: "Emile n'est pas fait pour rester toujours solitaire; membre de la societé il en doit remplir les devoirs. Fait pour vivre avec les hommes il doit les connoitre" (654; cf. 325 and 662).[f] In fact, the point of the experiment is to take a personage who is as close to natural man as one can find and to so direct his natural inclinations that he will be a satisfied and satisfactory inhabitant of the prevailing social order. The preceptor urges his pupil to live in the country, far from all forms of urban blight, but even that choice is a direct acknowledgment of the realities of contemporary experience. Emile himself has a good idea of what the world he inhabits can do to him, of how the passions of other men can impose on his own wishes for an independent private order: "J'ai cherché dans nos voyages si je trouverois quelque coin de terre où je pusse être absolument mien; mais en quel lieu parmi les hommes ne dépend-on plus de leurs passions?" (856).⁸ Indeed, the autonomy he finally achieves has no meaning unless it is placed in the context of contemporary society, a point Rousseau had already recognized in *La Nouvelle Héloïse*: there he made Wolmar's ménage a counterpart of the greater social order, separated from the world of the cities but taking its fullest meaning from its relationship to that world. For all these reasons, then, Rousseau's resort to the context of Arcadia at the end of his treatise leaves a curious and unsettling coda, with a sense of unfinished business. The landscape predicted for Emile is finally irrelevant, the reward for winning a game he never played. The preceptor's vision concludes the book but it does not complete the argument the book had been making.

As it turned out, no one was more aware of the inconclusiveness of the ending than Rousseau himself. He pondered a continuation of the treatise in the form of an epistolary novel, and shortly after the publication of *Emile* in 1762, he wrote out two letters of a sequel entitled *Emile et Sophie, ou les Solitaires*. The point, as he saw immediately, was to put Emile to the test, subjecting the pupil and his education to intensive pressure in order to show how effective his preparation had been. The letters, addressed by Emile to his preceptor, spell out a rapidly paced series of events. Emile and Sophie, easing comfortably into their new life, have several children but suddenly lose one, an especially beloved daughter. In order to distract the inconsolable Sophie, Emile takes her to Paris, where they enter a very different style of life and another mode of fiction. Rousseau, with a surprisingly deft touch at unfolding urbane intrigue, sounds for several pages like nothing so much as a prefiguration of Laclos. Emile and Sophie are drawn into some tawdry circles and they begin, eventually, to go their separate, pleasure-seeking ways. Sophie is drugged by a jealous aristocratic slut and seduced by an accommodating friend. Emile's melodramatic reaction (which echoes the mad scenes in *Clarissa* after she has been raped) is followed by Sophie's disappearance and Emile's retreat to his old profession as a carpenter. All of this is reported within the dozen-and-a-half pages of the first letter. The startling shift in mode from a promise of Paradise to the actualities of Paris, from pastoral fable to the conditions of realistic fiction, brings Emile's story more precisely into line with his long preparation for society. If the change was disconcertingly swift, at least the point had been made. The business was no longer unfinished.

But Rousseau could not stop even there. Death and infidelity were not, it seems, quite enough to prove the strength of Emile's self-sufficiency, and Rousseau shifts modes once again, this time to the conventions of adventure romance. Emile goes on a voyage, is captured by pirates and sold into slavery, where his subjective independence, now imbued with classical stoicism, earns him the admiration of his captors. That is where the continuation, as we now have it, ends. The various accounts about Rousseau's plans for the rest of the novel agree that Emile ends up on a desert island where, according to the report of Bernardin de St. Pierre, he encounters a Crusoe-like figure who has been shipwrecked on the island with his daughter.[5] Emile marries the girl and settles down forever in this small, isolated society, ensconced on a fortunate isle, which is as paradisal a location as the one originally foreseen for him. Rousseau, the connoisseur of fictions, took his hero through an anthology of literary modes before settling him finally into a venerable form of the landscape of desire, an all-sufficing island of the sort that had turned up as far back as Homer and Hesiod. Emile is battered but the surroundings are idyllic, comfortably disengaged from the social order and no less fabulous than his preceptor's dream. At the end Rousseau has it all ways at once: Emile earns his Elysium, and the landscape he wins is as remote in locale and mode as any of the places in ancient fable.

In this struggle as in others Rousseau was an instructive model for the romantics who followed him. The shift in modes from the ending of *Emile* to the beginning of *Emile et Sophie*, the clear need to change tonality when he continued the story, point to a distinct uneasiness with the adequacy of the patriarchal conditions. Rousseau's resort to those conditions shows the kind of nostalgia for the naive that Schiller was to define with pungency and poignancy some thirty years later. But Rousseau could not carry that nostalgia beyond the ending of *Emile* because the student's experiences were not, in fact, complete, because the state of awareness Emile had reached was only a way station and not a terminus. Nostalgia is a fit feeling for a condition of frustration, for a set of irrelevant circumstances which are not fully satisfactory and cannot be improved. It is irrelevant in a state whose potential has not yet been completely explored, a point Schiller came to see at the end of his essay *Uber naive und sentimentalische Dichtung*. It is wrong to equate Emile with the savages Rousseau described in his second discourse because the savages had achieved precisely the degree of self-consciousness necessary for their minimal and easily satisfied needs. Emile had not reached the degree sufficient for himself, and it was only by dropping out of his initial paradisal situation that he could finally do so. His education had brought him to a state where he could begin to realize the autonomous selfhood that had been prepared for him; but that state was no more than a first stage of realization, and Rousseau obviously felt that the final stage would come only with the highest degree of self-consciousness. Emile thus had several more way stations to go through before he could reach the privileged condition of superior self-sufficiency, a condition in which there would be no occasion for nostalgia because the stages of the past would have been shown to be insufficient.

To put it another way, Rousseau saw that Emile's autonomy, the paradise within him so carefully built up by his preceptor, had to have a landscape outside that matched it in comfort and coherence. But there was patently something wrong with the matching of inner and outer landscapes proposed at the ending of *Emile*, a radical inadequacy in each that only a Fall could repair. The initial condition of bliss turned out to be temporary and unreliable. A landscape of desire can be secure, it seems, only if it is postlapsarian. The patriarchal landscape initially offered to Emile was not a world fallen and restored but one in which Humpty Dumpty was still sitting securely on his wall. What Rousseau wanted was a landscape in which Humpty had been put together again.

Most of Rousseau's romantic successors felt much the same way, though they added their own intricate needs to the complexities of the situation. The romantics looked on at Paradise from the perspective of the world outside the gates, their awareness of the unfallen region within informed by an irrevocable sense of distance and otherness. There was rarely any question of their finding the old renderings of that region perfectly satisfactory. If they struggled with the same temptation to nostalgia Rousseau had felt, they were as aware as he was of the insufficiency of those images that stayed put at the primary stages of human experience; and most traditional renderings of the happy places, particularly the dominant Virgilian kind, said nothing of the fallen or purgatorial stages that follow the first. The romantic artist of whatever persuasion felt that experience was characterized by the tendency of innocence to fall, not to remain static; indeed, for most that tendency was a necessity, costly beyond measure yet immeasurably beneficial as well because the Fall brought the full self-awareness the imagination needs for its highest functioning. Such an attitude had to be ambivalent: images of the unfallen were usually accompanied by a profound sense of pathos, yet the romantics recognized that the most thorough deployment of the capacities of consciousness could not take place in the constricted world of innocence described by traditional imagery. Nostalgia, however gratifying, was an impediment to the realization of the mind's necessary freedom. Thus, the romantics worried over the efficacy of tradition, concerned whether the received figures of paradisal places could be used to further the basic items of romantic business. Insofar as those images presented conditions of coherence and consonance they offered a precise external counterpart to any self that had achieved a state of harmonious wholeness; but since the romantic self, harmonious or not, was part of the postlapsarian world, those unfallen landscapes, touching as they were, would never finally do.

Blake faced these issues directly in *The Book of Thel*, which focused specifically on the difficulties of the transition from the old landscape to the new. The topography of the poem defines a world of primal innocence, with all the customary inhabitants and relationships of such a world; yet it is rendered in a tonality that, if not quite cloying, finds no place in its sweetness for even a whisper of discord. Thel herself does a bit more than whisper. She wanders through the landscape, obscurely dissatisfied and self-pitying, unable to clarify the sources of her uneasiness. The region of Arcadian desires in which she moves is clearly no longer sufficient for her. At the end the possibility of another landscape is broached, a world of Experience whose harshness and insatiate sexuality are mockingly disguised in Petrarchan imagery; but Thel (whose name comes from the Greek word for wishing or willing) does not have the courage to activate or even acknowledge her current desires, and she flees back to the cozy old land, which cannot sustain her. She is caught between old desires and new ones, and cannot commit herself to either landscape. Yet if the world of Experience is itself not a final place, it is the only place that can match up with the impulses vexing her; she is incongruous anywhere else. Thel is left, finally, in a kind of limbo, terrified and somewhat ludicrous, unable to coordinate the demands of her inner and outer worlds.

The rest of Blake's early work puts the same case with an equally precise and incisive irony. The *Songs of Innocence*

and Experience treat the traditional images of a soft, bloom-
ing, prelapsarian landscape as an inappropriate and dangerous
delusion, with no genuine relevance to the facts of our inner
life. Those images are snares because they permit us to flee
from the exigencies and crises of the fallen world, ignoring
the dark, Satanic mills that are the true external counterpart
of the desolate souls of Experience. Thel runs from the barest
hint of the tonalities of the fallen world, and the chimney
sweepers and little black boys are consoled with stories of
bright, paradisal pastures. With Blake, no wholeness and harmony of self would be possible until the fallen world was
renewed through the apocalyptic imagination; yet the renewal
could not begin until the doors of perception were cleansed
and the old images were deprived of their powers of hallu-
cination. Blake argued that those images were privileged fictions, figments of dream set off from the immediacy of things
and independent of all vicissitude. Their purpose is to allow
us to envision Paradise but not to do the hard work that is
necessary in order to live it.

Here was one of the most precise renderings of the problem.
The old figures of satisfied desire could not be avoided: their
priority was too firmly established, too tightly entwined with
all previous imagining of contentment, for them to be simply
bypassed. One answer, of course, was to do as Blake had
done, use the figures against themselves to expose their radical
inadequacies. It was Byron's way as well as Blake's, and others
followed suit. But in any case the voices of romanticism had
to be allowed to speak, and to do so through figures that had
been created for other modes of envisaging· the world. The
conditions of the challenge to the romantics were clear and
exceptionally difficult to fulfill. Time and again we hear from
romantics of very different persuasions that the old landscapes
need to be domesticated, cleansed of their remoteness, and
realized in the world of immediate experience. That, after all,
was where the self was located, and the landscape had to
come to the self and not vice versa. At the same time the self
that had attained a measure of stability and autonomy in the

contemporary world was clearly an uncommon one, privileged for what it had accomplished. Any landscape professing to be its counterpart would have to be equally privileged, claiming for itself an exceptional status. The consonance of inner and outer landscapes required no less. This meant that the landscape of desire, with all its traditional prerogatives, had somehow to be defined in postlapsarian tonalities, yet still had to keep its own special aura and conditions of being. The problem for the romantics, very simply, was how to do all that.

Blake's treatment of the issues in *Thel* and the *Songs* was more a rendering of the problem than the proffering of a solution, but it was, all the same, an obsessive issue for him. It was equally obsessive for Wordsworth, whom Blake thought of as, in many ways, his precise antithesis. In *Home at Grasmere* and the Preface to *The Excursion* Wordsworth turned out what was to be seen as a major manifesto on the usefulness of Edenic places. He mulled over these matters compulsively because they touched at his deepest understanding of who and what he was, of what he, as a modern poet, had to do to make himself heard. Even at Cambridge, Eden had been part of the contours of Wordsworth's immediate world, placed there by an enlivening vision that had found out quite early it could invest the natural world with privilege. In Book Three of *The Prelude*, describing his days at college and his concern for vocation, he tells how he turned to the earth and the sky for instruction; and he sees the earth there as "nowhere unembellished by some trace / Of that first Paradise whence man was driven."[6] At this period Wordsworth was entering into his earliest mature awareness of what he had grown to be and what his mind was able to do. He put those capacities into practice by endowing every object in his path with a moral life and seeing all of those lives as "bedded in a quickening soul" (134). Yet there were already hints of the possibility that his surroundings would not always yield themselves to the mind with such cozy geniality. He knew that context could refuse to cooperate, that it could put pressures on the mind of considerable severity. But he also knew that the stubborn exercising of his mind could mitigate those pressures: "let me dare to speak / A higher language, say that now I felt / What independent solaces were mine, / To mitigate the injurious sway of place / Or circumstance" (99-103). The point here is not in his early recognition that the mind and its context might well be at odds, but that the mind can make its own autocratic way through all the pressures of context, that it can overcome the world by turning the world into a place where Adam could walk in comfort. Wordsworth's confidence would not always be so unqualified; but then his mind had not yet encountered all the rebuttals it was going to meet. At Cambridge he was primarily interested in testing the autonomy of his consciousness (its independence from vicissitude) and the adequacy of his imagination (its ability to shape an independent world). He took his greatest pleasure in watching himself build a cosmos both self-made and self-sustaining, shared only with his own Maker: "I had a world about me— 'twas my own; / I made it, for it only lived in me, / And to the God who sees into the heart" (144-46).

The next stage in his Paradise making, that is in his testing of the potency of the imagination, came at the time of the French Revolution, when circumstances were far more urgent and more immediately compelling. The realization of Paradise called for at the time of the Revolution came out of an impulse to build Edens for all men, and it was clear that solutions such as Rousseau's fabulous island, however difficult it had been to reach, would not be finally tenable. When Wordsworth describes his enthusiasm for the French Revolution, he puts his fervor in terms of scorn for old fictions of Paradise and the welcoming of an engagement with the absolute present. As Wordsworth recalls it, lovers of liberty

> Were called upon to exercise their skill,
> Not in Utopia—subterranean fields,—
> Or some secreted island, Heaven knows where!

But in the very world, which is the world
Of all of us,—the place where, in the end,
We find our happiness, or not at all!
(*Prelude*, XI, 139-44)[7]

The key point here is immediacy, the commitment to the
shared contemporary world; and though Wordsworth changed
his mind about the bliss of the Revolution, he never swerved
from the compulsive need to find his place in the actuality of
the present. Elsewhere he pushed that passion for immediacy
to the furthest conceivable point. In the first book of *The
Prelude* he appraises a series of possibilities for an epic poem,
his choices determined initially by the kinds of subject called
for by tradition. But the themes he goes over, all occurring
in the past and in other places, are put by for something closer
to home, more in harmony with his private interests: "A tale
from my own heart, more near akin / To my own passions
and habitual thoughts" (222-23). Finally he moves from suggesting something near to his thoughts to contemplating those
thoughts themselves. All possibilities give way to an epic upon
the most immediate of subjects, the growth of the self toward
its potentially Edenic place here in the present. In these passages the operative word is "truth," as it appears in the phrase
"simplicity and self-presented truth"—that is, the truth of and
in the contemporary moment, his own truth and not a reflection of ancient dreams (I, 249). Again, the difficulty lies
in how to do it, how to bring about an Eden for the self here
when France would no longer do. How can one speak truly
of the self in its immediacy and actuality? How, in trying to
speak truly, can one learn to localize Paradise?

After his rejection of the Revolution Wordsworth concluded
that Paradise was to be a more private place, though it would
always be available for those who could learn to see it. All
of these changing pressures required of him an increasingly
more elaborate and extensive analysis of his sense of vocation,
and of the powers that made his vocation possible. He shared
with Blake the difficult understanding that the realization of

Paradise is a function of the ability to see, and that we can bring it into being only when vision has become vocation. Paradise making is therefore a proving of vocation, particularly when the green and pleasant places one moves into are not the hand-me-downs of cultural history, the "subterranean fields,— / Or some secreted island, Heaven knows where!" For Wordsworth this meant putting Paradise on his home grounds, and putting a harmonious and autonomous self within that Paradise. In 1799, with his fascination for the Revolution behind him, Wordsworth settled into Grasmere with his sister. In the early spring of 1800 he began what looked to be a definitive statement of the actualization of Eden.

The poem in question, *Home at Grasmere*, eventually became the first part of the abortive *Recluse*, though it is best known as containing, at its end, the most compelling romantic manifesto on the marriage of mind and nature, including the well-known lines on wedding the "discerning intellect of Man" to "this goodly universe."[8] The manifesto also includes a telling declaration of the need to purge the landscape of desire of its fictionality and make the "groves / Elysian [and] Fortunate Fields . . . a simple produce of the common day" (800-801; 808). Recent criticism of the poem has shown that *Home at Grasmere* is itself an intricate attempt at demystifying Eden, making it new and real in the heart of the home country.[9] That reading of the poem ought to change, in a most significant way, our reading of the manifesto at the end of it: that is, the remarks about the need to bring the Elysian groves into the world of common day have to be seen in the light of *Home at Grasmere* itself, the poem seeking to show how the revitalization of the tradition of Paradise could be accomplished. From that perspective both poem and manifesto take on a delicately ironic tinge, and their relationship assumes an intricacy of texture that makes *Home at Grasmere* one of the most complicated instances of romantic Paradise making. The complication comes about because the poem and the manifesto that ends it never quite match up. If the statement about making the Fortunate Fields present and actual is comforting in its assurance, the poem itself displays all the difficulties and uncertain success Wordsworth had with his project. Indeed, the manifesto has to be seen as one of those insufficient conclusions which are incisive and eminently quotable in themselves (witness the ending of *Resolution and Independence*) but are not nearly as conclusive about the poems they end as they claim to be. *Home at Grasmere* is, in fact, a knowing, subtle, and determined attempt to combine the privileges of the Edenic situation with a landscape that supports them and a set of inhabitants that gives them trouble. If Wordsworth was more successful at seeing the problems than at overcoming them, that is not a question of insufficient skill but of the difficulties of reconciling vision and truth.

In fact, Wordsworth's rendering of the Vale of Grasmere was an attempt at reconciling vision and possibility, what he could guess, however dimly, of the fairest world, and what he could make out of the world available to him now. The D text of the poem, the only one generally known until the publication of the earliest version, has the poet and his sister, "like two Ships at sea, / Or like two Birds" (D160-61), pushing against the resistance of the winter winds to find their way into the Vale. The B text records an event from that journey the later one omits, a visit to Hart-Leap Well and a meditation on "the hunted beast who there / Had yielded up his breath" (B242-43). In the poem he was to write about the scene, an edifice was built to commemorate the killing. Wordsworth took the crumbling of that edifice as an instance of the revenge of nature upon needless cruelty, especially the arrogance of men toward hunted innocents. The B text gives no details of the story but dwells, instead, on their reactions to it. As he and his sister stand at the "doleful place" the scene puts them into a trance, which offers them an "intimation of the milder day / Which is to come, the fairer world than this" (B238-39). And that omen of a cleaner, brighter life lights up not only their distant future but the more immediate one as well. The trance seems to promise them a refuge in "that hallowed spot to which [their] steps / Were tending" (B250-51). Grasmere was to give them, even "in the midst of these unhappy times," a foretaste of bliss, "a portion of the blessedness which love / And knowledge will, we trust, hereafter give / To all the Vales of earth and all mankind" (B253-55). In effect, what the B text shows is that in Grasmere they were sketching out a temporary Paradise, a figura for the final one, the kind of happy place they could handle now until the world was transformed into a total Eden. Emile's preceptor had told the new lovers to make a Paradise here on earth while they were waiting for the other. The vision at Hart-Leap Well is equally stereoscopic, combining present actuality and future possibility to promise a satisfying semblance of Paradise which would do until the real thing came along.

Wordsworth's task, then, was to so render his reading of the conditions at Grasmere that the reading would recall tradition but stress immediacy, making the reading at once current and perennial. Further, the Vale had to have a character that made it credible within the context of the real world yet put it distinctly apart from the debilitating pressures of that context. Everything depended on the skill with which Wordsworth articulated his vision, and particularly on his handling of the tonality of this postlapsarian foretaste of permanent bliss. That skill is often remarkable. The poem delineates the Vale as a place of prerogatives, replete with a variety of those signs that so often identify the paradisal landscape. The Vale is as self-sufficient, as complete within itself, as either of the fabulous landscapes of desire Rousseau had made for Emile. In the A text Wordsworth speaks of it as "this majestic, self-sufficing world, / This all in all of Nature" (A204-05). It is "a Whole without dependence" (D149) in which "extreme penury is ... unknown" (D363) because the place contains "all that luxurious nature could desire" (D23). Though it is not one of those "secluded islands" mocked by Wordsworth for their unreality, the Vale has a definite insularity about it. Wordsworth plays with images of enclosure and embowering throughout the poem, and these are reinforced by echoing

patterns of circularity, from the swooping and rising movements of birds to a marriage of earth and heaven through the
joining of the Vale's "huge Concave" (D44) and the "etherial
vault" (D641) of the sky. Most telling, though, is the sense
of the Vale as omphalos, the hub of the world. There is,
Wordsworth says, "something that makes this individual Spot,
/ This small Abiding-place of many Men, / A termination and
a last retreat, / A Centre, come from wheresoe'er you will"
(D145-48). The Vale has the sort of centrality that has always
characterized the places of highest privilege. In mythologies
these points of convergence are usually the site of theophanies,
consecrated and enclosed spaces where men and the gods have
come together.[10] Eden was one of those spaces. Wordsworth
so handles his rendering of the Vale of Grasmere that it has
all the aura of privilege, the autonomy, insularity, and centrality that define paradisal and other sacred enclosures.

But then of course he had to make it real, that is, to put his
Paradise into the fallen world and to put within that Paradise
his own fallen and retrieved self. Wordsworth's Grasmere is
a decidedly postlapsarian place; more precisely, a post-Rev-
olutionary one. Ambiguous comments about the cost of getting there, the qualities of courage involved, all the realities
of life which had been "more bountiful than hope, / Less timid
than desire" (D69-70)—all these are placed precisely between
an image of himself as a child, when he first saw the valley,
and himself now seeking to shape a home for the self after its
difficult wanderings. The world within the Vale has to be a
place where one can rest from fallenness, yet still acknowledge
the stiff cost of Experience. For the poet this means a dense
and complex figuration holding within itself all possible tonalities:

> Is there not
> An art, a music, and a strain of words
> That shall be life, the acknowledged voice of life?
> Shall speak of what is done among the fields,
> Done truly there, or felt, of solid good

And real evil, yet be sweet withal,
More grateful, more harmonious than the breath,
The idle breath of softest pipe attuned
To pastoral fancies?

(D401-09)

Wordsworth's compulsion for the truth, both of the self and its context, led him to reject Rousseau's kind of compromise, which could be seen as a retreat from veracity, and to strike for another kind, which would face up to the immediate facts of the fallen world. He was not, he points out, "betrayed by tenderness of mind / That feared, or wholly overlook'd the truth" (D309-10). He then goes on to face directly the contrast between the perfection of place and the imperfection of its inhabitants: the loud reiterated whoops he hears as he walks in the mountains are the sounds of shepherds calling their sheep to feed; but he has also heard those same voices making sounds that were the articulated tokens of a drunken brawl. "So be it," he says: "I came not dreaming of unruffled life, / Untainted manners" (D346-48). He knew what his hill people were like. The purity of traditional pastoral, its dissemblings in the service of artifice, had no place in his rendering of the Vale of Grasmere.

Yet there were other disturbances, some bleaker strains that run like a leaven throughout the poem, and these were not so efficiently absorbed into Wordsworth's postlapsarian consciousness. The poem is studded with images of tentativeness and death, the most striking of which is a pair of swans whom Wordsworth identifies with Dorothy and himself. The birds used to be visible "at the centre of the Lake" (D245) but they have disappeared and may be dead, quite possibly killed by someone in the Vale. This Paradise has much of the classical Edenic glow about it, but it is also a place of extinction, shot through with a brooding sense of the mortality of men and all other creatures.[11] In a less chilling vein Wordsworth recognizes that his own stay there may not be permanent. The Vale is his, he says, "perchance for life" (D56); he can find no firmer guarantee than a good possibility. (There is no such hesitation in the B text, which says straightforwardly " 'tis mine for life" [52].) All these signals come through clearly and forcefully, their import unmistakable. A Paradise grounded in the fallen world is a provisional one. Purging the landscape of desire of its fictionality means purging it of its security as well. Tenuousness is the price of realization, even for one who, like Wordsworth, knew that there was no better place for him to live. He brought the imagery of privilege into the Vale of Grasmere, but in so doing he created a subliminal uneasiness, a tension between image and context, which qualified his landscape of desire. The vision at Heart-Leap Well, with its promise of a proximate image of bliss, was only partly fulfilled.

In the B version of the text Wordsworth acknowledges these points with absolute frankness:

> Give entrance to the sober truth; avow
> That Nature to this favourite Spot of ours
> Yields no exemption, but her awful rights,
> Enforces to the utmost and exacts
> Her tribute of inevitable pain,
> And that the sting is added, man himself
> For ever busy to afflict himself.
>
> (B837-43)

He does not offer this as an admission of partial defeat or a disclosure of the Vale's inadequacy, yet it eventually comes out that way as the succeeding lines make clear. In both versions he goes on to say that there is "one sufficient hope," a trust that life in the Vale will supply them with pleasure and with food for the "insatiable mind," that there will be an abundance for knowledge and for love, that, finally, the "Inmates" of the Vale will prove "not unworthy of their home" (D647). All this is to take place because they feel

> How goodly, how exceeding fair, how pure
> From all reproach is yon etherial vault
> And this deep Vale, its earthly counterpart,

By which and under which we are enclosed
To breathe in peace.

(D640-44)

Still, these fine things might not happen after all. As if to cover every eventuality, Wordsworth foresees the possible collapse of such hopes and then comes up immediately with a consoling alternative: "And if this / Were otherwise, we have within ourselves / Enough to fill the present day with joy / And overspread the future years with hope" (D648-51). Much earlier in the poem he had pointed out that a few of the cottages in the Vale are clustered together but the rest are scattered singly, "like separated stars with clouds between" (D125). This is a perfect image of sequestration within a community, the contextual autonomy that had seemed so desirable at least since Richardson. Now, after his admission of Nature's inexorable primacy, he sees that their context might well fail them but that in their own family circle, their "beautiful and quiet home" (D652), there is sufficient to keep hope and joy alive. The effect of this gesture is to separate the family's self-sufficiency from its setting, to see their autonomy as independent of external props and therefore of their (quite possibly unstable) surroundings. It is, in fact, a rejection of the contextual and a withdrawal to an independent familial privacy which can outlast all other forms of community.

At that point, as if to chastise himself for dwelling on the possibilities of such pleasure in the Vale, Wordsworth brings up the question of duty, telling himself that "something must be done" (D665), that he must find his vocation and set himself to work at it. We have seen that, for Wordsworth, vocation and vision are inseparable, perhaps, finally, identical. Given that relationship it is clear why he then moves to an examination of his own capacities, seeing what he has within himself that can further his vocation: "but yet to me I feel / That an internal brightness is vouchsafed / That must not die, that must not pass away" (D674-76). But if that line of thought is understandable within the context, what follows has no immediate explanation. Suddenly the argument goes askew, and he begins to ponder a different set of problems. Carrying on the image of internal brightness he has just established, he throws out a series of questions that take him beyond the issue of vocation toward the radical issue of relation, his position in the family:

> Why does this inward lustre fondly seek
> And gladly blend with outward fellowship?
> Why do *They* shine around me, whom I love?
> Why do they teach me, whom I thus revere?
> Strange question, yet it answers not itself.
> That humble Roof, embowered among the trees,
> That calm fire-side—it is not even in them,
> Blest as they are, to furnish a reply
> That satisfies and ends in perfect rest.
>
> (D677-85)

And he follows this deep bemusement with an assertion revealing his knowledge of the *un*relatable, of that which can never be reached by another: "Possessions have I that are solely mine, / Something within, which yet is shared by none— / Not even the nearest to me and most dear" (D686-88).

A bit of perspective should help us with Wordsworth's very difficult argument in this part of the text. His thoughts had gone from a recognition of the Vale's possible insufficiency to an acknowledgment of what seemed to be the certain sufficiency of the family. He then remembered that his vocation had to do with more than these immediate pleasures, and he began to ponder the given qualities of his inner life, his "internal brightness." At that point, and at some profoundly subliminal level, the lingering thoughts of the family's autonomy came together with his thoughts of his subjective capacities, and he realized that there was an independent life within himself that could never be touched, even by those who matter most. This is a crucial conclusion, surely the most crucial in the entire text because it is a challenge to the insufficiencies of even the best of this world's conditions. The family itself, though it is self-contained and independent, cannot give him all that he needs. Even they cannot "furnish a reply / That satisfies and ends in perfect rest." This is, in effect, the last step in the dialectic which had been working its way through the text. That working had begun with an assertion that the Vale is a paradisal enclosure, and the next step was a countering of the assertion with a recognition of the difficulties of building a Paradise in the actualities of Grasmere. The movement within himself is the final step in the dialectic, the final countering, the final assertion: there is, after all, something in our experience that cannot be touched by the world, something that remains independent, and it is to be found in hiding places so deep that their very depth guarantees their inviolability.

This gesture has other significant consequences for the entire text. With the assertion of unassailable autonomy the structures informing *Home at Grasmere* fall into place, and their organization is seen to have a rigorous logic in which the self is both independent and contextual, part of a community yet irrevocably inviolate. The poem as a whole had begun with a look at the felicities of the entire Vale, its unity ("A blended holiness of earth and sky" [D144]), and its centrality ("A Centre, come from wheresoe'er you will" [D148]). It had moved eventually to a study of the family's felicities, its unity and its position as a centre. His brother had come there and "others whom [they] love," "Sisters of [their] hearts" and a philosopher-poet, will come at a later time (D653-60). The shape of the entire context, the shape containing all the life in Grasmere, is a perfect enclosure, the meeting of the "etherial vault" and the "deep Vale." The shape of the cottage and its immediate surroundings, the family seat, is also an enclosure, a "humble Roof embowered among the trees." The movement of the poem, then, the momentum of its perception of its world, goes from a reading of the largest shape to a reading of the next one down, from the Vale to the cottage. Within that humble place he stands with others but within himself is the unassailable center of self—the place that has turned out to be the goal of the poem's momentum because it is the focal point of all the other enclosures, the center of all the centers. From another perspective we can see that the momentum had moved irresistibly from the circumference to the center, from the hills encircling the Vale to the hearth at the heart of his being. That energy is inexorable, leading him not only to a sense of his own inner light, but finally to a recognition of the independence of that light. The profound center of self stands sovereign and free. Later on in *Home at Grasmere* Wordsworth speaks of "the individual Mind that keeps her own / Inviolate retirement, subject there / To Conscience only, and the law supreme / Of that Intelligence which governs all" (D772-75). In *The Prelude* he calls it "the last place of refuge—my own soul" (X, 415).

The aim of *Home at Grasmere*—and it seems to be the aim of all the romantic landscapes of desire—had been to find a context of and for the self. That is, not only to show the kind of place in which the self could function but also the best kind of place for it, the one that would be most consonant with its character and concerns. Now we can see that such consonance, though highly desirable, is not absolutely necessary. The matching of inner and outer landscapes obviously creates a kind of ease. In such a situation there is no tension between the Paradises within and without, no unsettling discrepancies in their content or tone. But the profoundest movement in *Home at Grasmere* had been toward an awareness of the separateness of the self and its context and an affirmation of the self's harmony with itself. The poem, it is clear, has built up a series of concentric entities: at the center of all is the self, just beyond it are the cottage and the embowering trees, beyond them is the enclosing Vale and beyond that is the world. But the self is finally immune to the world's uneasiness, unassailable even when old fictions do not quite mesh with current reality. The poem had made an attempt to realize pastoral but it also sought to define the substance of the self and its most private contours. Now we can see that the self has no need of fictions, no need of context, though it would certainly feel comfortable having one. It need not share in attempts at the realization of Paradise because it is itself already realized, a central and centering reality. It needs no fictions to give it context because it is, itself, its own context, the thoroughly self-sufficient omphalos. At this point the fullest ironies begin to emerge: those features identifying the places of highest privilege—autonomy, insularity, and centrality—are also the features of the privileged consciousness; and because it has those features, such a consciousness can get along without a counterpart, however privileged, in the world outside. A consciousness so organized transcends the need for consonance because it is self-consonant, and it is so in such a way that it can never be disturbed by man, his fictions and his inadequacies. The only laws it follows are those of Conscience and God, who will see to its radical health.

That ironic relation of the privileged place and its counterpart consciousness had appeared once before, in an equally concentric situation. It is precisely the same set of conditions, the same configuration of self and context, which Rousseau had encountered (or made) on the Ile de St. Pierre. There, the self sat at a center, which was surrounded by an island, and the island itself was set near the center of a nearly circular lake. The carefully orchestrated movement of *Home at Grasmere*, leading as it does from the circumference to the center, is an exact parallel of the movement in the *Cinquième Promenade*. In each case the result was the same, the revelation of the self as its own context. Further, from our understanding of how the landscape of desire is realized we can see precisely what went wrong in the *Nouvelle Héloïse*, why the images of the insular in that novel had such an uncertain success. Wolmar had established two versions of the landscape of desire, the most encompassing being the world of his ménage, the most compact the enclosure that was Julie's Elysium. Since the latter was centered on Julie herself, this pattern is still another version of that concentricity which seems to be the best sort of framework for the autonomous consciousness. But neither Wolmar nor Julie was able to purge these land-

scapes of desire of their delusiveness. Lulled by her embowering context, Julie did not take into account the power of
passion, its ability to outlast times and fictions by staying deep
within, sequestered and self-sustaining. (Indeed, the status of
that passion, its covert, autonomous existence, has to be seen
as a sardonic parody of the conditions of the paradisal enclosure.) Her tiny postlapsarian Eden turns out to be as fabulous,
as delusive about reality, as any of the models inspiring it.

The circumstances on the Ile de St. Pierre are clearly an
answer to these failures. Rousseau achieves the timelessness
endemic to the traditional landscapes of desire by drawing the
self into a timeless moment, the perpetual present of the *Cinquième Promenade*. He rejects both the perfect stillness, which
is an image of death, and also the sequentiality which carries
change and all sorts of termination along with it. Of course
the Paradise of the Lac de Bienne proved to be unstable, or
at least impermanent; but it was not so shown in the *Cinquième Promenade*. In the *Septième*, where he teases his own
desire for autonomous enclosures, the instability is certainly
implied. That *Promenade* was written from the perspective
of one who had seen a Paradise which was superior but temporary; the *Cinquième Promenade* was written from no perspective but out of the very center of the experience. There
is nothing quite like the latter in Wordsworth, whose *Home
at Grasmere* contains not only the exaltation of the untouchability of self but also the disturbing surroundings that led
him to exalt that untouchability. *La Nouvelle Héloïse* shows
nothing of the unassailable center of self; it does show that
the conditions the novel describes were not sufficient to make
the self unassailable because the self, in that novel, is its own
worst enemy. Julie could be protected against everything except herself. The *Rêveries* show both the optimum conditions
and the unassailability, but taken as a whole, they provide a
gentle yet unmistakable hint that the conditions are quite possibly tentative. *Home at Grasmere* renders the whole process,
from the initial optimism to the awareness of tenuousness and
a final assertion that the self is obliged only to itself and the

laws of its God. That poem and Rousseau's *Rêveries* go deep toward the center of romantic experience.

Yet there is still an essential distinction between the two works, and as a result of it they shape different modalities of Paradise. The old images of desire are covert in the *Rêveries*, rather than matters of visible organization. Their presence is felt because they dictate the qualities of the experience at the Lac de Bienne, its insularity and centrality; but the rendering of that experience shows no direct borrowing from its Arcadian predecessors, no echoes of the sort that had appeared in Rousseau's earlier work. The move from *Emile* and its abortive successor to *Julie* and then to the *Rêveries* reveals a purification and submergence of the Arcadian materials, leading to their eventual subliminal informing of Rousseau's most intricate statement about the autonomy of consciousness. In *Home at Grasmere* the images are overt, beginning with the introductory lines about the boy who looked down at the Vale "with paradise before him" (D14), leading through all the traditional paradisal paraphernalia, ending with the programmatic lines about realizing the Fortunate Fields in England's green and pleasant land.

This distinction is more than a matter of spelling out one's ties to the past. For one thing, it means that the considerable complexities of *Home at Grasmere* come forth most dramatically when the poem is seen from varying perspectives. Looked at in comparison with the *Rêveries* it is a subtle concatenation of potential frustration and certain triumph; looked at in relation to *Emile* and its continuation the poem is an unsettling admission of the difficulties of putting Paradise into the world where one has to live. If we see one movement in the poem when placing it next to the *Rêveries*, the other perspective brings out more strikingly how the practice of autonomy came to be seen as a question of vocation, of what the self-sustaining consciousness ought to be doing with the powers it has. "Here or nowhere is our heaven": so Thoreau was to put it nearly half a century later.[12] The duty of establishing it here was one that Wordsworth could not, and did not want to, evade. But *Home at Grasmere* shows him trying to fulfill that duty by adapting the given fictions of Eden and ending with no signal—or at least no satisfying—success. In Wordworth's own work the poem finds its most precise counterpart in *Peele Castle*, which also speaks of the failure of the antique images of Eden to match up to present actualities, particularly the distressing, humanizing presence of death. The Rousseau of *Emile et Sophie* was far more successful at turning passé Edens into usable ones.

Home at Grasmere shows men in a finer situation than the world usually offers, indeed one of the best the world can offer; but that Eden is still not good enough, still an unstable one precisely because it is fused with the uncertainties of immediate experience. Wordsworth sought in Grasmere a kind of compromise which has a profound kinship with that of Rousseau: both preferred sequestration, the enfolding surroundings which help to define the paradisal enclosure; but Wordsworth wanted a scene grounded in immediacy, linked to the contours of present, credible experience, and that left him with an uneasy mixture which could never quite settle into place. The patriarchal vision of Emile's preceptor failed because it did not take the dictates of immediacy into consideration. The secluded island in *Emile et Sophie* succeeded because its inhabitants had passed through the world of experience, paid their obeisance to it, and no longer needed to face its demands directly. Rousseau and Wordsworth (as most romantics) agree on at least one point: sequestration is acceptable with or after the experience of the fallen world, but is never acceptable without it.

What then of new life for the fabulous, turning the stuff of ancient dreams into contemporary textures? Wordsworth implicitly contrasted the Grasmere drovers, with their occasional drunken whoops, to the immaculate shepherds of traditional pastoral. He was clearly resisting the fabulous, but in so doing he brought the knowledge of death into his way of imagining Grasmere. Such knowledge unsettled him as much as it did Adam, who had brought that particular woe into the world.

Rousseau gave in to the fabulous at the end of *Emile*, countered the fabulous with its opposite in *Emile et Sophie* and then welcomed it once again (or planned to do so) at the end of that abortive work. He wanted to bring his battered hero to an apparently enchanted island after all the adjustments to experience had been made and the self could be finally, unequivocally, autonomous. Rousseau could be satisfied with images of the incredible because he had established his own and his hero's credibility. The island was not a place of tentativeness and departure because it was a place of reward. It was not a place where one faced up to the contradictions of experience but the place one got to after all the encounters had been made. He has put all tenuousness behind him.

Rousseau's courage was revealed in the writing of *Emile* and particularly in the Savoyard vicar's professions of faith. The Paradise he finally makes for his hero is not part of his struggle but its aftermath, when the need for courage was over. That was the point when one could slip comfortably into old fictions. Wordsworth's was a different kind of courage, revealed in his effort to ground his finest dreams in a place that had difficulty sustaining them. His Paradise was no aftermath but the very place of struggle itself, the locale where courage had to be demonstrated. Old fictions were not something one slipped into but the adversary one fought with and dragged, against its will, into the contemporary world. Wordsworth knew that the making of a modern Paradise is an act of the mind. He felt that only the mind which keeps tenuousness before it knows the truth about Paradise.

The permutations of these alternatives were explored all through romanticism and the rotting of romanticism in the decadents. Indeed, the circumstances explored by Rousseau and Wordsworth pinpoint some of the essential dilemmas of the romantic self as it went about in search of a paradisal context. The conditions established in *Emile et Sophie* were echoed in figures like Shelley, who ended *Epipsychidion* with a retreat to a secluded Mediterranean island that has all the accoutrements of the Fortunate Isles. Wordsworth's conditions carried on in figures like Byron, who brought Don Juan and Haidée together on a Mediterranean island which looks like all the old insular Edens but is in fact the home of death, which catches up with their comfortable forgetfulness. Keats, who could accept neither alternative, could not come up with a sufficient instance of his own. He looked on at the cold pastorals playing around the side of the Grecian urn with a full awareness of their separateness from time and therefore their ultimate irrelevance to his compulsion for climaxes; but he was as aware as Milton and Wordsworth that the warmth of any pastorals he could engender would end in the ultimate climax of death. Ahead were the instances of Stendhal, who put his heroes into paradisal prisons, and the late instance of Wallace Stevens, who found that the deathless world of traditional Paradise was not only irrelevant to the needs of a Sunday morning but that the old modes were dull, their sensuality made insipid by their inability to offer change. The results, whatever the choice, were always tinged with ambiguity. It was not so much a souring of the apples of Paradise as a recognition that the process of making it new required a mutual adaptation of vision and context, and however fortunate the result the adaptations were never without cost. The possibilities for the landscape of desire were finally the possibilities for the self in the world romanticism had made.

Parity and Proportion

Rousseau's exemplary conditions were among the finest instances of adequacy, of what it was possible to do when what one wanted, and what one could have, matched in full comfort. His autonomy fit so snugly into its enclosure, and the enclosure offered so precisely what that autonomy required, that all the possibilities of privilege—at least as Rousseau would define them—were thoroughly realized. With him it was rarely a matter of mastering the self in order to achieve these possibilities. Rather, it was a question of context, and though he managed to manipulate context more often and more successfully than most, he mastered it completely only once.

The models we have been following worked over these problems obsessively. The confluence of desire and capability had always been the most difficult aim of the autonomous consciousness; it was also the most necessary one. Quixote was definitive there too, setting up the problems for those who were to follow. He rarely noticed any disproportion between what he thought he was doing and what he did, though it was always apparent to his observers and victims. This meant that Quixote was generally at home in the world, though he had to spend much of his time getting that world to straighten itself out. However one evaluates Quixote's activities his imagination was so adequate to the demands made upon it, so cunningly protected from the imagination's usual enemies, that it could ensure the stability and autonomy of consciousness. All attacks upon that autonomy, all denials of it, were the work of jealous magicians who tried to create the illusion that his perceptions were illusory. His value system therefore remained intact and unassailable. It was privileged because he could find objects to satisfy his desires wherever he went.

The equivalence of desire and capability, which autonomy needs in order to exercise its privilege, took a different sort of turn in Milton's Satan. Satan's assertion that his mind can make a sufficient place for itself is both false and, bitterly, true in a way for which he had not planned. As he stands outside Eden peeking at its inhabitants he sees that he is forever excluded from participating in this paradisal enclosure. That is, he can never find outside of and parallel to himself that image which, more than any other, stands for the most satisfying kind of correlative landscape. Of course Satan had already argued that the mind could so manipulate reality that it could make out of reality whatever correlative it wishes. From this we could assume that Satan can create a parity that, whatever its components, is entirely self-generated and fully successful. That, it turns out, is only partly true. If paradisal parities were not within his grasp—an incapacity he all but admitted as he stood outside of Eden—that discrepancy soon resolved into a proportionateness so ironic that the literature that followed could never shake it off. "Myself am Hell" puts all the balances back, with the equilibrium of inner and outer he had desired and claimed he could reach, but with a more limited set of components than he had foreseen. His autonomy went that far and no further; it was enough only for agony.

In Sterne's case there was rarely any question of proportionateness, a predictable circumstance given what he saw as the nature of consciousness and the world with which it had to deal. Autonomy was forced upon Sterne's characters, though only Tristram knew what could be done with it. If the self was not quite a prison-house that was because feeling had visitation rights it occasionally exercised. Consciousness could not know very much about the world or do very much with it. When it dealt with the world it could only make plans and act as though contingency could be overcome, as though the world outside were not nearly as independent and unreachable as lucidity would lead one to believe. For the unlucid self only the engendering of children was ultimately fruitful. For the lucid self the obligatory independence of consciousness had another sort of fruitfulness: it exercised its self-subsistence through the instrument of its self-expression, the study of its own life. In both cases there was a final, chilling parity: the difficulty of access to individual selves was balanced by the unknowableness of the world in which the self had to function. That parity is too close to Satan's final one for absolute comfort; but then Satan never wrote down his own story and learned thereby that there was a privileged sort of play available to the autonomous imagination.

Schiller's sentimental poet found possibilities of play in the art forms through which he expressed his inadequacy. That too was close to Satan's last parity but it was as privileged a condition as Tristram's; the sentimental poet, though, would hardly think of it as such. He was haunted by discrepancy, by what he could not have or do until a brighter and more encompassing equilibrium came along. Like the man of sensibility he knew far more than he could put into practice, though in the practice that he did accomplish he found a form of relief, an equilibrium that would suffice. He was enough like Werther to be prey to self-consuming energies, but he did what Werther could not finally do: find a shape to control them. The sentimental poet's tentative proportionateness was definitive for his kind (there are clear echoes of it in Hölderlin, Coleridge, and Shelley) though it was not useful for Manfred's or Obermann's kind who saw, well ahead of Wallace Stevens, "nothing that is not there and the nothing that is." Wordsworth, who was never (except in his brief Godwinian depression) so bleak, found the naturalizing of tradition in the Vale of Grasmere to be a way of attempting equivalence, though even there the burdens of actuality made the balance distinctly uneasy. But what worked for Schiller and Wordsworth would not necessarily work for others, especially those who sought ways to beat the *mal du siècle*. If Schiller's compromise and

Wordsworth's withdrawal were equally unacceptable, if Byronic passivity seemed possible only to aristocrats, then other ways would have to be found. The self obsessed by its desire for autonomy had no choice but to continue seeking a context.

The difficulty was to accomplish that seeking with something more than the success Quixote achieved—which from one point of view is no success at all. Better, one ought to be able to accomplish it with Quixote's kind of success, that is, with a full internal freedom the world could never breach, and also with an effect upon reality of the sort Quixote thought he was having but could never really have. For the successors of Rousseau, Schiller, and Wordsworth there seemed to be several major ways of achieving the support and sustenance of privilege. Possibilities that had been inherent in attempts at autonomy since the early eighteenth century worked themselves out with fervor, frustration, irony, and all sorts of ambiguous success in the postromantic nineteenth century. The protagonists of Stendhal, Poe, Huysmans, and Wilde sought enclosures for the privileged consciousness, and each, in his way, got what he wanted, at least for a while. At the same time the movement from Richardson to Wilde made its way to an end that, if not quite inevitable, had certainly been foreseeable from the initial stirrings of the movement. There were ivory towers and dark ones, and it was not always possible to separate the two precisely.

For Julien Sorel the ivory and the dark came out to be the same, though it took the gift of his life to make that happen. For much of his life, though, he had sought neither the ornate isolation of the one nor the opaque temptations of the other: Julien was neither Vigny nor Childe Harold. Instead, he looked for engagement with the world and also a kind of bright, spartan luxury, though the latter was not his primary aim. Julien did not seek the things of privilege but, rather, the rights pertaining to it. He was more interested in the capacity to possess things than in the actual possession of them. Julien was as little of a materialist as the Rousseau of the *Confessions* who, in Julien's selective reading of the book, became one of his models. He shared with Rousseau the radical understanding that, to keep one's self-possession safe and intact, being able to do what one wanted was more important than actually doing it all the time. Of course the ability Rousseau cherished when he was away from society was not the same as that Julien wanted when he was in it; but we shall see that what Julien wanted included, in its totality, Rousseau's kind of adequacy as well.

How then, to make all that happen? How to reach the resolution of desire, that is, the attainment of absolute adequacy, and still allow one's self-possession to survive that struggle and function freely? The headnote to chapter 22 of part one of *Le rouge et le noir* quotes a Jesuit named Malagrida as saying that "la parole a été donnée à l'homme pour cacher sa pensée."[a][1] Several pages into the chapter Stendhal compliments Julien on his ability to handle words because words have become the major tools for making things happen: "Julien atteignit à un tel degré de perfection dans ce genre d'éloquence, qui a remplacé la rapidité d'action de l'Empire, qu'il finit par s'ennuyer lui-même par le son de ses paroles"(346).[b] Julien has turned into a master of indirection: action is immediate, language mediating; language can describe the patterns of actions but actions are the embodiment of those patterns; language cannot be or embody what it describes unless it describes itself. Rhetoric, in Stendhal's definition, is different from ordinary language, that which tries, however tenuously, to talk of reality. Rhetoric of the sort that Stendhal praises in Julien is a false semblance of ordinary language. If the latter is an uneasy but genuine attempt to find words for reality, the former is an attempt to render the opposite of reality. Julien's rhetoric seeks to create a mask, one which hides what ordinary language has discovered. The language through which Julien interprets reality for himself, the language of his private thoughts, is therefore concealed under the rhetoric he uses on others. The words with which he meets the world are not the words he speaks to himself. The latter seek to uncover, the former to cover up. Thus, Julien's rhetoric is the contrary of ordinary language, its ironic, parodic opposite. It is also duplicitous (doubling) in several senses: it is a deliberate attempt to deceive; it is twice-removed from reality because it is an attempt to falsify an interpretation of that reality. Julien has learned to live by and with such doubleness, aware always of the structure in which the exterior perceived by the world is separated by several levels from the place where one's being moves.

What Julien did with the relations of language and reality he also did with the order of personality. His purpose was twofold, based on two kinds of privilege, and thus again it was variously duplicitous. He chose to build layers of personality, all of which serve to hide and protect the pristine place where his self lies—that place where the crass worlds of Verrières and Paris were never to be allowed to approach, the place to which, at very rare moments, he could withdraw and be only himself. The uppermost layer is that aspect of personality with which he meets the world, the layer whose demeanor is priestly and whose weapon is rhetoric. It is the only one everyone sees. The stratum beneath that, concealed by the duplicities of the external, is his sense of himself as a warrior, and it infuses with secret aggressiveness the clerical layer above it. Much of the more obvious comedy in the novel comes from the interplay between these strata, especially Julien's sublimation of the energies of the one into the delicacies of the other. His stance as soldier is apparent to very few, primarily to Mathilde de la Mole, who is as devoted as Julien is to living an anachronism.

If this structure of personality were to function with complete efficiency, Julien could partake of two kinds of privilege. The priest could (and eventually did) seek out and use the prerogatives associated with those classes whom Julien had often heard of and finally comes to meet. His conquest of Mathilde brings him, briefly, the capacity to have whatever that kind of prerogative can ask for. Desire and capability come together, for once, in the purest of harmonic proportions. At the same time Julien wants to exercise the privilege owned by the autonomous and untouchable self, that which can look on at the practices of the other privilege, smirk at them, admire them, but insist upon its own irrevocable uniqueness, its independence, and its private aims. Obviously these two modes of privilege are completely different. Obviously, too, they are completely incompatible, which no one knew better than Julien. His multilayered and variously duplicitous order of personality was built precisely to afford him access to both modes at once.

That order had another, related purpose: it was designed to permit Julien to control the ambivalence that had destroyed a series of romantic heroes. We have seen how the old ties to social value were not to be snipped so easily as the heroes had claimed, that vestigial connections caused René and his kind to twist and turn and eventually strangle themselves on the links that remained. Werther and Manfred could not reconcile this menacing dilemma; indeed, it finally destroyed them. There was never any chance of their reaching an equilibrium among differing orders of value. Rather, they were still at the stage of recognition, still coming to see that there was, in fact, a warfare of contradictory forces and that the opponents could not possibly come to terms with each other. The heroes had imagined themselves to be partisans, clear supporters of one side of the dilemma. In the end they were shown to be adherents of both.

Julien, their immediate and cannier successor, knew better than to try to choose sides; moreover, he saw no need to do so. He recognized that there were irreconcilable modes of value at play, and he not only refused to ignore the social or disclaim his ties to it, but also tried to make use of those ties to build a structure of self that could stand free anywhere. If the problem had to do with differing value systems, and if he wanted to take part in both, then he needed to bring them into each other's vicinity and yet manage to keep them apart; that is, to put them within the same overall framework but make certain that they never had to meet. However, this intricate juggling, this sleight of self, does not imply that Julien gave equal respect to the differing systems: as I indicated in an earlier chapter he had only contempt for the values he adopted in order to succeed. Yet there was never any question of his repudiating those values; he disdained their corruptness but not their efficacy. In him the ideal, which had magnetized the sentimental poet, became not only terrestrial but social and cynical as well. The naturalizing of the imagination exemplified in Wordsworth became, in Stendhal's hero, a socializing impulse.[2] The need to adapt the imagination to the earth became a need to adapt it to society, to find free play for the autonomous consciousness by creating sociable forms through which it could express itself and still survive. The adequacy Julien demanded of his imagination was of the same sort and had the same purpose as that of the romantic heroes and their immediate predecessors. But where they were painfully uncertain of how to take (or accept) the values of society, Julien was perfectly clear on that issue. He was equally clear on the difficulties of the balancing act he had undertaken and on the need to keep his audience from realizing that he was doing any juggling at all. His amazing history shows him eminently, if only tenuously, successful at that enterprise.

Still, if Julien thought he could be Rousseau and Napoleon at once, we can see that he was also reliving the situation of Clarissa. He sought the same counterpoint of accommodation and sequestration that Clarissa tried to establish; he sought, that is, a contextual autonomy for the self. Like Clarissa, he wanted to partake and hold back, both at once. Yet there were essential distinctions between the two figures, differences in the quality of the selves that they were seeking to enclose. Julien had Rousseau behind him, helping to make him what he became, and Clarissa had Milton. The self Julien cherished and sought to protect was therefore of a very different order than any that Clarissa could imagine or understand. Its qualities are revealed by the tears Julien often has to hold back, by his sentimental and sensuous reaction to religious pomp (echoed later in Emma Bovary), by all those needlings of compassion that had always identified the man of feeling. Julien, after all, is not one of Clarissa's kind of elect. He is much closer in kind to Julie, so close, indeed, that the parallelism of names is very likely a clue to one of Stendhal's profoundest ironies.

Julien succeeds, then, in isolating the self by enclosing it. The most difficult question about his personality has to do with the relation of that aspect of self to the other strata of his personality: in particular, does that part of him he most wants to protect supply the energy that informs the other strata? Is it the source of his ambition? Put another way, in which of these strata do we find Julien's capacity to be touched by the silencing of prisoners in a country jail? He is sitting at dinner in the house of M. Valenod:

> Julien, déjà fort mal disposé, vint à penser que, de l'autre côté du mur de la salle à manger, se trouvaient de pauvres détenus, sur la portion de viande desquels on avait peut-être *grivelé* pour acheter tout ce luxe de mauvais goût dont on voulait l'étourdir (347-48).[c]

The prisoners sing a vulgar popular song, and are silenced. Julien, touched to a degree he cannot control, sheds a single large tear. That is all he does about the event. Somewhat earlier in his history he had a different sort of clash with the class to which he is aspiring. Just after he has had his initial success with Mme. de Renal, Julien approaches her with pleasure and eagerness, deeply taken by her charms. She reacts with what seems like a profound chill. His immediate response to that gesture is part humiliation, part hurt, part anger; but then he catches himself:

> Il n'y a qu'un sot, se dit-il, qui soit en colère contre les autres: une pierre tombe parce qu'elle est pesante. Serais-je toujours un enfant? quand donc aurais-je contracté le bonne habitude de donner de mon âme à ces gens-là juste pour leur argent? Si je veux être estimé et d'eux et de moi-même, il faut leur montrer que c'est ma pauvreté qui est en commerce avec leur richesse, mais que mon coeur est à mille

lieues de leur insolence, et placé dans une sphère trop haute pour être atteint par leurs petites marques de dédain ou de faveur (282).[d]

In the first quotation, describing Julien's discomfort over the prisoners, the deep center permits (or is compelled to permit) an overt but restrained play to the feelings impelling it. That one tear, however, is the only outlet those feelings have. We can hardly conceive of Julien berating M. Valenod for his cruelty; he does, however, go on to berate himself for what he might choose to do were he in M. Valenod's place. With the single but crucial exception of the tear, the energies of feeling are thoroughly internalized. The scene with Mme. de Renal is only superficially similar. There is no tear through which to externalize his complicated reaction to Mme.'s chilliness. Instead, Julien says that, one, he will barter just enough of his soul to balance the money they give him; and, two, his heart is a thousand leagues away from their insolence, so they cannot get near that part of him. How are we to distinguish between *âme* ("soul") and *coeur* ("heart") in this passage? The former can be traded off to varying degrees while the latter, he says, cannot be approached at all. However muddy Julien's thinking, it is clear that *âme* is part of the uppermost reaches of personality and therefore available to the world, while *coeur* is at, or is the same as, the deep center of self. Julien is wrong, of course, when he says that they cannot reach his *coeur*: it was reached in M. Valenod's dining room, for example. Still, we can see that there is one aspect of self, his *âme*, whose energies he allows to have egress, while there is another, *coeur*, whose energies are given egress only against his extraordinary will, and then only briefly and with no effect upon the world. In fact, *coeur*, according to Julien, wants nothing to do with the world. It is ensconced in its own faraway place, concerned only with itself, self-sufficient in a way that no other stratum of personality can match. Except for the rare, unwilled breakthrough, its energies are kept only within itself. Its sole ambition is to stay where it is, continuing to be what it is.

Here, precisely, are the glory and risk of the autonomous center, the source of its opportunities for grace and also of its potential for incarceration or extinction. The history we have been tracing since Richardson indicates unequivocally that for many figures, and perhaps for all, *coeur* has to find means for the egress of its bourgeoning energies or the protective enclosure may well give way, causing the whole edifice to collapse. Clarissa, raped, found release in envisioning heaven and preparing for it. Rousseau was profoundly uncomfortable with a deep center that was totally unaware of any sounds from outside. The collapse very nearly happened to Julie, who thought her passions could be tucked comfortably away, and it did happen to Werther, who could find no referent outside the self through which the self could discharge its energies. Julien finds what appears to be a solution, with *âme* releasing the pressures of subjectivity while *coeur* remains safely secluded within. There were, of course, other possibilities, some not nearly so promising. Among them was the chance that the self would find the walls of its (once protective) enclosure so impermeable that there would appear to be no exit. Saint-Preux, we remember, was struck by the disappearance of the door once he had entered Julie's garden:

A peine fus-je au dedans que la porte étant masquée par des aulnes et des coudriers qui ne laissent que deux étroits passages sur les côtés, je ne vis plus en me retournant par où j'étois entré, et n'appercevant point de porte, je me trouvai là comme tombé des nues.[c][3]

The line from Richardson through Stendhal to Pater is long but direct, and its development is based to a great degree on such alternatives. We shall be inspecting the latter part of that development for the rest of this book.

Julien's encounter with the apparent indifference of Mme. de Renal came on a morning when he was about to set out on a trip. The journey would give him the opportunity both

to exult and to wind down after some tense affairs: he had
succeeded so well in manipulating his employer's vanity that
he had gotten a rather large raise out of that tight-fisted bourgeois. Julien sets out to a distant valley to see a friend, the
timber merchant Fouqué, and on the way he climbs a considerable mountain leading to a spectacular view. Even he, for
whom nature means nothing at all, is touched: "Quelque in-
sensible que l'âme de ce jeune ambitieux fût à ce genre de
beauté, il ne pouvait s'empêcher de s'arrêter de temps à autre
pour regarder un spectacle si vaste et si imposant" (284).[f] At
the top of the mountain Julien takes up a position of pure
defensiveness: "Caché comme un oiseau de proie, au milieu
des roches nues qui couronnent la grande montagne, il pouvait
apercevoir de bien loin tout homme qui se serait approché de
lui" (284).[g] Circumstances and images exactly like these had
appeared a few pages earlier in the novel, and in precisely the
same sort of natural context. Just after he maneuvered his
employer into granting him the raise, Julien went out into the
woods to ease his excitement. In fact, he was so highly charged
that "il fut *presque* sensible *un moment* à la beauté ravissante
des bois au milieu desquels il marchait" (276; my italics).[h]
Slowly, with pauses for rest, he starts to climb the mountain
and stops at a place where he is both superior and isolated:
"il se trouva debout sur un roc immense et bien sûr d'être
séparé de tous les hommes. Cette position physique le fit sou-
rire, elle lui peignait la position qu'il brûlait d'atteindre au
moral" (276).[i] Below him he can see "vingt lieues de pays."[j]
Above he sees a sparrow hawk circling and looking for prey.
He envies its energy and isolation, and thinks of Napoleon.

In the later event it is Julien who is the sparrow hawk,
"caché comme un oiseau de proie" (284).[k] Yet there, para-
doxically, his defensiveness is even more pronounced. That
event adds a cave to the basic scenery, and he immediately
takes advantage of its shape and depth: "Ici . . . les hommes
ne sauraient me faire de mal" (284).[l] Julien pulls the cave
tightly around himself. He turns it into a warm and encompassing container where, astonishingly but with perfect logic,

he takes apart the edifice of self. There "au milieu de cette obscurité immense" (285)[m] he lets himself go, writing down all that he thinks about things, pondering his future and the heroism that is waiting for him. There he is happier than he has ever been because, for the first time, he is totally liberated. His sudden ease shows how the self had been a prisoner in its own house, free to function only within the limits imposed by the edifice. Now it can be itself in complete openness, at liberty in a situation without peer or precedent in Julien's experience. And that is both its glory and its irony. Julien is released only in this unparalleled place, with its deep seclusion and vast darkness (*obscurité immense*). That happens because the cave, with its embowering somberness, offers what nothing else has been able to grant, an effective correlative for Julien's core, that (heretofore) hidden center that had seemed never to need such a partner. He can operate openly only in this dark enclosure, but he can do so with the ease that comes from having a perfect external affiliation. The necessary isolation of the self is mirrored in its isolating counterpart. Julien has found absolute parity.

This is the epitome of the separateness he spoke of when he saw the sparrow hawk and thought of Napoleon. But there was another factor mentioned at that time, energy. That factor, as Julien employs it, is clearly centrifugal, just as the isolating impulse is centripetal. Julien's meditations in the cave were dreams about energy and what he would do with it; that is, he has chosen shelter and an openness of self but he uses them to meditate on their opposite, acknowledging, in effect, that he still wants it all, that he can be content with no less than the satisfaction of every impulse. Thus, when the night grows fully dark (that is, when the world outside is, most enticingly, the full correlative of the dark center), Julien recollects himself, burns his comments, and sets out on the last leagues to Fouqué's house.

The cave had offered Julien an immediate release and an impossible temptation. At Fouqué's he is tendered a more acceptable one, a partnership with the timber merchant, which would involve sharing a house with him in this isolated valley. Julien considers the offer briefly, including the possibility that "solitaire dans cette montagne" $(286)^n$ he will rid himself of the frightening ignorance that impedes his way in the world. He ponders Fouqué's loneliness and then realizes that he cannot deceive his friend, that the "feu sacré" and "énergie sublime" impelling him will not tolerate that temptation.° He returns, therefore, to his state of mind on top of the mountain where he found an external referent not in the darkness of the cave but in the energetic isolation of the hawk. These two scenes set up an interplay of eminence (in several senses) and recess. Eminence won out because it seemed to offer satisfaction for all of Julien's primary impulses, that is, for the total edifice of self.

The remainder of Julien's career works that interplay out, and it does so with a tidiness and logical symmetry that show him coming full circle. The bullets aimed at Mme. de Renal (at whom he was not able to shoot until she had nearly disappeared under her shawl) are intended as instruments of revenge, that is, as the precise opposite of a reward. Their results, however, are both vengeful and eventually gratifying in a way that none of the participants could have foreseen, but which is consistent with the orderliness of Julien's development. Mme. de Renal is distressed at her survival: to die thus would have been no sin, however much she wished it to happen, and to die through Julien would have been ecstatic. As for Julien he is redoing Werther's pistol shot, though it is not immediately self-directed (it is, of course, ultimately a replay of Werther's suicide). Werther had used the bullets to blow his way out of an entrapment, a subjection to a corrosiveness of self that seemed to have no end. It is a release of energies that otherwise would have generated and consumed themselves in an intolerable cycle. Although Julien's pistol shots are intended to do otherwise, they create, for both himself and Mme. de Renal, exactly the same effect they had created for Werther: that is, they ease extraordinary pressures. If the result is not instantaneous—Julien spends some time imagining the posthumous figure he will cut—the release brings him a completeness and self-sufficiency such as few of his heroic predecessors had known.

Once, when he had won an especially important victory over Mathilde, the hero exulted: "Julien ne pouvait contenir sa joie. Il fut obligé de descendre au jardin. Sa chambre, où il s'était enfermé à clef, lui semblait trop étroite pour y respirer" (525).ᴾ Energy and its effects make Julien and his room inequitable. The room is too tight for his private celebration; only the breadth of the garden will do. Energy, we remember, is centrifugal, fleeing the enclosed center as though it were frightened of the hearth of self, of its warm and encompassing darkness. The sparrow hawk looks for bright openness because it needs to fly freely as it seeks out its sustenance; energy looks for that openness too, and for much the same reason. Energy and isolation are, it seems, antagonists, though they live together in the personalities of the hero and the hawk. Julien wanted them together in his own personality and for a long time he succeeded in having them so. But at the end— and when he ran into the garden he was very close to the end—Julien turns away from openness. At the end, in the cell, there is neither the need nor the possibility of energy, no room out of which he can hasten himself, no garden for expansion; nor, most importantly, is there any desire to have one. The isolation, which had been broached, used, and put by when he was in the cave, is now accepted (enforced). And it is pure isolation, with no rival impulse seeking to mix with it and counter its centripetal drive. Julien is content with and within his confines, thinking mainly of his son-to-be and Mme. de Renal.

Victor Brombert has written eloquently on the ambiguities of the prison in Stendhal, finding in it Stendhal's finest paradox, the achievement of the epitome of freedom within the most constricting confinements.[4] In our terms Julien has reached an absolute parity of self and context. As his ambitions have been taken from him, so has he stripped away all those aspects of the edifice of self that had protected the dark

218 ◆ *Parity and Proportion*

center. Like Jean-Jacques at the shore of the lake, he dispenses
with everything except the irreducible, that beyond which
there is nothing. Of course Julien's limits are not Jean-
Jacques': we could not expect the wary seminarian to be interested in, or even to know about, the fine essence of consciousness Rousseau sought to reach in such circumstances.
But for both Julien and Jean-Jacques those moments offered
the ultimate of satisfied desire, bringing together in one place
all that they needed or wanted. Like Julie, Julien had been too
confident about the passions that had been pushed below the
socializing surface. Julie's order of self was, as we have seen,
accretive. So was Julien's, and in both figures the autonomous
passions at the core of self came through with a vengeance,
seeking vengeance. But where Julie's garden of the self threatened to turn into a prison-house, Julien found in a literal
prison the place for his passions to blossom. Unlike Werther
he had blown his way *into* entrapment; but in so doing he
forced himself into a satisfaction whose fullness was rare in
the previous quests for autonomy and without precedent in
his own life.

Of course Stendhal cannot allow history to be chastened
so easily. Julien's subdued ecstasy lasts to the end, which
comes with just enough delay for him to appreciate all that
he has. His enclosure, as paradisal as any, is more fleeting
than most. Keats, who slips into the dark embowering center
when he seeks out the home of the nightingale, knows that
dying is the only possible climax to his ecstasy, that here and
now the act would be richer than ever. Julien's ecstasy comes
from the perfect congruence that only his ending was able to
bring him. He was never as self-knowing as Keats but he saw
that what he had at his dying was, in every possible way, his
culmination.

The journey from Verrières to Paris and back is a process
of expansion and then, to a remarkable degree, condensation.
The initial center of Julien's life had been at Verrières, whose
values he scorns and whose possessors he cannily manipulates.
His life expands to encompass another center, Paris, the hub

not only of culture but of nearly all conceivable ambitions. Each of these places is a value center and also a point in Julien's itinerary. The curve back begins immediately after two related acts of revelation, Mathilde's announcement of her pregnancy and Mme. de Renal's letter to M. de la Mole. From the moment of the pistol shot Julien's world begins a process of purification, of condensation to a refined residue in which he is left with the tiniest center of all. The cell, like the other centers, is a framework for value and in this case Julien lives out the values completely, with no reservations and no set held in abeyance. Now, finally, the center of self can emerge and remain in full openness. There had never been a context so congenial to its needs. The words of the preceptor to Emile—"fais ton paradis sur la terre en attendant l'autre"— had never been acted on with such a combination of irony, sensibility, and satisfaction. Clarissa had acted on her own version of that charge, in varying ways and with differing degrees of success, but she had never fulfilled it in Julien's manner. It took his special kind of competence to accomplish that special performance. In these matters Stendhal is impressively, movingly unique.

But this peerlessness had its own kind of problems. Stendhal's solution to the problem of autonomy in the modern world was, literally, a dead end. If it is more satisfying to its protagonist than the end of *Manfred* was to Byron's hero, who also has to die but chooses to do so on his own terms, the result is equally conclusive. Stendhal's reading of all these quests is ultimate—no one could go further with such success—but it was also a signal that the cost of achieved autonomy was going up, and that the walls were closing in.

܀܀܀ NINE ܀܀܀

Centers of Nostalgia

Poe's characters are creatures of enclosure, observers of walls, edges, encircling mountains, all manner of palpable boundaries. In every case the enclosure is a center of value or disvalue: a room decorated with bizarre eclecticism, a maelstrom engulfing the flotsam on the sea, a paradisal valley repeating all the paraphernalia of tradition. His people are within those centers but they are also, fundamentally, the centers themselves, because all of the enclosures are finally images of the self and what can happen to it. His stories are studies of the self's relation to experience, of how the world within the walls tries to endure and prosper, and of how the world outside of the walls puts every kind of pressure on those boundaries. Curiously, though, that outside world has no life other than in its relation to self. Every Poe setting, natural or to the highest degree artificial, is an emblematic instrument, designed to reflect on human life and particularly on the special types who people his world. Poe's entire work is a pondering on how to survive within the enclosure of self and, when survival seems possible, on how to make the enclosure strong and self-sufficient. There runs through his work a radical fable, a grand underlying parable about survival and sufficiency, which has enough potency in it to put even the clumsiest aspects of his work in an enlivening context. The best aspects gain substantial life from that context.

Poe's fable begins with a Fall; or, more precisely, with the act of falling, usually described through recollection though occasionally as a present and immediate situation. A version of the latter is seen in *The Island of the Fay,* a short, rich meditation: it is a commentary on solitude, a sketch of a pantheistic cosmology, and a narrative (though that may be too active a word for this observer's passivity) of a delicate, sentimental revery. There is nothing in it of the fiery inwardness of *Usher* or some of the other familiar tales but it is equally involved with the essentials of Poe. Arguing with Marmontel on whether music is best appreciated in solitude, the speaker asserts that its highest order ought to be experienced in that condition but that "there is one pleasure still within the reach of fallen mortality—and perhaps only one—which owes even more than does music to the accessory sentiment of seclusion."[1] That is the pleasure in looking at nature. To this observer all scenery is "but the colossal members of one vast animate and sentient whole" which includes not only man but all "life within life, the less within the greater, and all within the Spirit Divine" (194-95). If we seem to be alone then, we are not absolutely so; we share Being with the clods of the valley as well as with every other spirit in this vastness.

All of this is prelude to the observer's description of a revery, where he had it and how he got there. The structure of the cosmos Poe describes at the end of the prelude—"cycle within cycle without end—yet all revolving around one far-distant centre which is the Godhead"—is echoed in the shape of a landscape through which the observer once wandered: "a far-distant region of mountain locked within mountain, and sad rivers and melancholy tarns writhing or sleeping within all" (195-96). Deep inside of this landscape he discovers a rivulet and an island. The area where he stops to rest is nearly encircled: "On all sides—save to the west, where the sun was about sinking—arose the verdant walls of the forest" (196). The rivulet disappears within the encircled area, turning sharply until it is lost to sight. It "seemed to have no exit from its prison but to be absorbed by the green foliage of the trees to the east." Near the center ("about midway") of the valley "one small circular island, profusely verdured, reposed upon the stream." This is the classic round paradisal island, centered in its place and replete with all the flora it can pack in. Versions of this island turn up frequently in Poe, though never with so much signifying detail as is given in this sketch. What Poe adds to the old image is a kind of deep centering, which is one of the essential ordering principles of his imagination. Several readers of Poe have remarked how his enclosures have to be worked into, usually through a kind of mazy path that follows winding valleys or heavy shrubbery, corridors, catacombs, and the like.[2] At the deep center lies, very often, an aspect of creativity, a version of the self. In this sketch the observer, half-dozing with half-shut eyes, permits his mind to wander into fantasy. The island is oddly, though richly, endowed. At its western end is a "radiant harem of garden beauties," the trees "of eastern figure and foliage" (197). All is rich, dense, with "a deep sense of life and joy." At the eastern end everything stands dark, solemn, and beautiful, redolent of "mortal sorrow and untimely death"; and that is a clue to some of the essential actions in the sketch. Shade covered the eastern end of the island because the sun was setting, which explains the chiaroscuro but not the relish with which the observer turns the western end into an image of the Levant, complete with harems of flowers and eastern trees. The eastern end, in its turn, holds all the somberness our traditions sum up in "going west." What we see here is the observer's consciousness at play, willfully upsetting stock responses by turning the givens of the island into images of their geographical contraries. All tensions relaxed, consciousness has no need to tie itself to things it must report about with exact information. Borne into a center echoing all paradises, consciousness can make out of Eden what it wills. Milton's Satan was never so free: making Hell into Heaven would have been difficult enough but not quite so tricky as making the points of the compass turn out to be, simultaneously, themselves and their opposites.

What consciousness finally chooses to do with this place is as striking as what it made out of the chiaroscuro, and its actions are based precisely on that patterning. The encroaching darkness leads the observer to think of burial and, from that, to fancying the island as "the haunt of the few gentle Fays who remain from the wreck of the race" (198). At this point the place has been peopled, and the shifting tonality of the side-by-side darkness and light suggests a narrative, the most basic story of all. Floating flakes of sycamore bark, which "a quick imagination might have converted into anything it pleased," trigger a vision. The form of a Fay "in a singularly fragile canoe . . . with the mere phantom of an oar" moves out of the western light into the eastern darkness. She rounds the island, returning to the light, and goes about "the circuit of the island" repeatedly until, at sunset, she disappears into the darkness. "And that she issued thence at all I cannot say,— for darkness fell over all things, and I beheld her magical figure no more" (199).

The order of this intricately designed sketch is based on a series of centerings. Encompassing all, as I have indicated, is the cosmos, the concentric structure of which is reflected in the system of mountain within mountain of the landscape. Deep within the landscape is the enclosed valley, near its center lies the circular island, and orbiting the island in movements echoing the "cycle within cycle" of the cosmos is the Fay on her boat. All these homologous shapes and movements mirror each other in a patterning that continues through the last lines of the sketch. In essence the sketch balances off two parallel centers, the place in the cosmos where Godhead stays, and the island in the middle of the valley. But the inhabitants of the centers are clearly not parallel. Godhead is, to all indications, alive and thriving, while the end of this Fay and the end of her race appear to be happening together. The observer has come into the valley at a crucial point in its history.

Of course he made up that history himself, and that fact lends further intricacies to the sketch. If the Fay's placement at her center repeats the position of God at His, the observer, "musing, with half-shut eyes" at the center of the valley, du- plicates God's creativity. The observer peopled his landscape precisely as God had filled the cosmos (the repletion of which was emphasized in the cosmological passage), and each did so in free, autonomous activity. In both landscape and cosmos, desire and capacity are one. The observer and God are each fully sufficient to the demands put upon his creativity. Of course the observer is not fully the master of his own enclosure. The landscape is God's: "In truth, the man who would behold aright the glory of God upon earth must in solitude behold that glory" (194). Thus, while the observer and the Fay are each, in their way, parallel to the Godhead, the Fay is to the observer as the latter is to the being whose center is at the core of the cosmos and everywhere else as well. *The Island of the Fay* accepts the hierarchical system of the Great Chain of Being, with all its plenitude and demarcations. Poe brings about the interplay of forces with consummate skill.

Several questions, unstated but insistent, push themselves forward at this point. At the beginning the observer has said that "to me, at least, the presence—not of human life only—but of life in any other form than that of the green things which grow upon the soil and are voiceless—is a stain upon the landscape—is at war with the genius of the scene" (194). Why, then, did he people the landscape? Surely for the pleasure of exercising his inventiveness. But at the end the Fay disappears, and he admits that he cannot say whether she will go round again, whether these were her final cycles. He has come into a Paradise instinct with death, a pleasant place with overtones of incarceration within it: not only is the Fay locked into her cycles but the rivulet "seemed to have no exit from its prison" (196). In the most basic sense the observer found in the valley what he brought to it. He put death and imprisonment there along with the Fay, and all in the same gesture. In effect that is his reading of Paradise, and it is a radically ambivalent one. The observer rendered Eden at a point of decline—not of the place, surely, but of its current possessors. But if his imagination is so free and fine, why can't he repeople Paradise and, while he is at it, make up a place with no uneasy overtones? *The Island of the Fay* turns out to be a parable of mind, a dense and disturbing meditation on its capacities. Though the sketch depicts declines, it also ponders cycles and creativity. At the end it raises, with subtle insistence, the difficult matter of redemption.

The questions posed in this piece are by no means isolated. I have said that Poe's work as a whole embodies a radical parable beginning with a Fall. In this master scenario the Fall is succeeded, first, by a series of attempts to accommodate the mind to its postlapsarian condition, and then by a set of efforts to redeem the mind, bringing it to at least a semblance of ancient conditions. Since it is the mind that has fallen as well as the mind that seeks to redeem, Poe's scenario shows the mind's exercises in self-salvation. Those are not the product of solipsism (the world outside is, if anything, too palpably real), but of a recognition that such redemption can come from nowhere else. Most of the familiar Poe, which includes most of his best work, covers the second of these stages, in which the mind seeks to adapt to an alien and menacing context. *The Island of the Fay* is obviously part of the first, but of the first at its point of decline, when the second stage is clearly looming and ready to begin. In fact, no work by Poe shows a pure prelapsarian state, that is, one that remains as it is with no rumblings of what is to come. He was as aware as Rousseau and Wordsworth of the insufficiencies of Eden and of what they meant to the imagination, which was forever testing out its adequacy.

Other pieces by Poe serve to fill out this image of a some-what inept Eden, and its relation to mind. *Eleonora,* published the year after *The Island of the Fay,* puts it even more incisively than did its predecessor. The protagonist points out in the first line that he comes "of a race noted for vigor of fancy and ardor of passion" (236). Though he is quite possibly mad, he argues that there are two states within him, a lucid one "belonging to the memory of events forming the first epoch of my life" and a second, foggier one relating to the "second great era of my being" (236-37). The remainder of the story shows him exploring both areas of the past. He describes a tropical paradisal place, the "Valley of the Many-Colored Grass," whose placement and makeup are classical and familiar. "Far away among a range of giant hills," it is exceedingly difficult of access, an "encircled domain" watered by a winding river and made lush by a rich and beautiful grass speckled with a wild coloration of flowers. When he and his cousin Eleonora fall in love, the whole valley is enlivened. "Life arose in [their] paths," the colors deepened and a crimson and gold cloud settled down over them "until its edges rested upon the tops of the mountains, turning all their dimness into magnificence, and shutting us up, as if forever, within a magic prison-house of grandeur and of glory" (239). With the arising of life, which comes simultaneously with the arousal of passion, time enters the valley and the lovers speak of death. (Poe had read his Keats with care.) Eleonora dies, "life departed from [their] paths," and the foggy stage of his existence begins. Before she died he had promised Eleonora that he would never seek another woman, and that if he did he would suffer a curse; but his lusts are too much for him. Still longing for love—the emotion is now free-floating, separated from its old object—he leaves the valley for the world, a strange city, and, eventually, a new lover.

Eleanora, like *The Island of the Fay,* is in part a tale of mind, and though it seeks to end more conclusively than the *Fay,* it leaves some of the same questions unanswered and begs a number of others. The speaker boasts from the beginning about his "vigor of fancy and ardor of passion," and there can be no doubt of the creativity of those subjective energies when they are aroused: "The passions which had for centuries distinguished our race, came thronging with the fancies for which they had been equally noted, and together breathed a delirious bliss over the Valley of the Many-Colored Grass" (239). Poe is being Keatsian once again. In the letter to Benjamin Bailey of 22 November 1817 Keats made the point with marvelous concision: "for I have the same Idea of all our Passions as of Love they are all in their sublime, creative of essential Beauty."[3] The passions of Eleonora and her lover had enlivened the valley but it was a cyclical life and loveliness that they created, not a beauty of perennial essence. Thus, it was not the Miltonic sin of arrogance but the glories of love and the imagination that brought death into the world of the grassy valley. The tie of the passions to a life creative of death is a radically (though not exclusively) romantic phenomenon, which was picked up near the end of the line by Wallace Stevens. Putting romantic ambivalence behind him, Stevens argued, in *Sunday Morning,* for precisely that Paradise instinct with death ("Is there no change of death in Paradise?") Poe had difficulty managing with his imagination. Stevens shifts the order of ideas slightly but the result is the same. "Death is the mother of beauty" and therefore of lust. Because of death his maidens "stray impassioned in the littering leaves." It is the same passion that drives Poe's protagonist out of his valley. His center shifts from pastoral to courtly, his nostalgia for the love in the old enclosure is outflanked by "burning thoughts" and "terrible temptations," and then the uneasiness inseparable from nostalgia disappears with his new consummation. Or at least it does for the protagonist. Poe still has the old promise to Eleonora to take care of. At the end he brings her back and her sweet voice announces: "Sleep in peace!—for the Spirit of Love reigneth and ruleth, and, in taking to thy passionate heart her who is Ermengarde, thou art absolved, for reasons which shall be made known to thee in Heaven, of thy vows unto Eleonora" (244).

This ending is oddly unsatisfactory, not simply because it seems tacked on as an afterthought but because it has no place in the speaker's postlapsarian life. "I wedded," he says, "nor dreaded the curse I had invoked; and its bitterness was not visited upon me." Since he felt neither guilt nor fear, what was the point of introducing this sentimental absolution with its vague promise of a future explanation? After all, his life had rounded itself out, and the promise leaves a large and (apparently) unnecessary knot untied. The answer, I think, has to do with what happened to the qualities of the protagonist's inner life after Eleonora dies, and especially with Poe's reaction to those qualities. The speaker leaves the valley only at the urging of passion. He says nothing about his previous emphatic coupling of fancy and passion (twice asserted), either after Eleonora dies or while he is involved with Ermengarde. His imagination succumbs to his feelings, which take over and master his personality from the time of Eleonora's death.

But if his imagination has gone, and Eleonora too, there are still strange lingerings in the valley. Just before her death she promised to make her spiritual presence known through winds and perfumes, and even though the valley loses its bloom, she comes back to him often through touches and odors. Though he has lost his former wholeness (the wholeness of self because he has lost his imagination, the wholeness of love because he has lost Eleonora), her spirit seeks to remind him of past unity by stirring a combination of his senses. In recalling his completeness she at least keeps alive in memory the time when all his creative energies had objects through which they could realize themselves. But the distinction between sensuousness and sensuality becomes absolute at this point. Though these contacts ease him somewhat he still can think only of his cravings, of the need for another object of love. The memories turn to pain and he leaves the valley. In fact, though, he was finally leaving Eleonora as well. At the high point of their love she had come to be identified with their paradisal home: "No guile disguised the fervor of love which animated her heart, and she examined with me its inmost recesses as we walked together in the Valley of the Many-Colored Grass, and discoursed of the mighty changes which had lately taken place therein" (240). The last word is wonderfully ambiguous: it reverberates back not only to the valley but also to her heart, for the "inmost recesses" of both had undergone "mighty changes." Thus, leaving the valley means giving up memory for immediacy, nostalgia for lust, though for a while he is still able to sense the presence of Eleonora "in the silent hours of the night."

With the curious, unexpected conclusion Poe shows that he was more troubled by nostalgia than his hero was, that even though the latter had finally gone beyond the past with complete impunity ("and [the curse's] bitterness was not visited upon me"), Poe still felt the need to account for nostalgia. The hero had disposed of his own version of nostalgia in a fully effective way, a recognition (not necessarily self-serving) that his new love transcended the old: "What indeed was my passion for the young girl of the valley in comparison with the fervor, and the delirium, and the spirit-lifting ecstacy of adoration with which I poured out my whole soul in tears at the feet of the ethereal Ermengarde?" (243). Eleonora's spirit had accepted that judgment, as her comments indicate. But it was clearly not enough for Poe. Though the last words of the story were extraneous for the hero, they were not so for the author.

Finally, however, Poe's gesture at the end of *Eleonora* has to be understood not only in terms of the easing of nostalgia but of the combination of nostalgia, the imagination, and the paradisal place and of the intricate relations among these elements. In this story the relations are implicit but murky, and Poe does not work on them enough to clarify their deep-seated complexities. The result is sentimentality. Elsewhere those elements are shown to be obsessive, driving Poe to explore their relations with a fierceness that does much to define the tonality of his writing. Indeed, in the radical myth informing his work that exploration is one of the primary sources of postlapsarian creative energy.

The identification of the beloved with a paradisal place (so that the loss of the one is coincident with the loss of the other) is explicitly stated in other of Poe's works, for example, the first stanza of the poem "To One in Paradise":

> Thou wast that all to me, love,
>   For which my soul did pine—
> A green isle in the sea, love,
>   A fountain and a shrine,
> All wreathed with fairy fruits and flowers,
>   And all the flowers were mine.[4]

The loss, it is clear, is the sign and result of a Fall. Thus, the act of remembering (reuniting the members) is not only nostalgic but restorative, for it returns Paradise, however briefly, to the one who remembers. Further, since the loss is double, restoration, to be fully successful, has somehow to bring both back together. An act so obviously difficult could lead to the imagination's despair, but in fact the conditions of Poe's fable help to ease the difficulties somewhat. Since place and beloved are united, recalling either—thinking of the love one has lost or of the place where one has lost it—can lead to a double recall. This means that remembering, if accomplished with sufficient skill, can make the remarkable happen. It can become rejuvenation, because it restores a lost youth, and it can become reintegration, because it restores a lost unity.

Poe does other surprising things with nostalgia:

TO F—
Beloved! amid the earnest woes
   That crowd around my earthly path—
(Drear path, alas! where grows
Not even one lonely rose)—
   My soul at least a solace hath
In dreams of thee, and therein knows
An Eden of bland repose.

And thus thy memory is to me
   Like some enchanted far-off isle
In some tumultuous sea—
Some ocean throbbing far and free
   With storms—but where meanwhile
Serenest skies continually
Just o'er that one bright island smile.[5]

Here is a subtle, suggestive, and important change in the pattern of identification. It is not the beloved who is directly likened to Eden but, rather, the recollections, the memories themselves. His soul knows Eden in dreams of her; his memory of her is "like some enchanted far-off isle." She and Eden arrive together because thinking of her is, in itself, a paradisal experience. Thus, this is not only an act of restoration but of making, of the creation of a new paradisal context by a mind that is now part of the fallen world. The difference between the two poems is of enormous significance in Poe's informing myth. "To F—" does not deny that the lost beloved is identified with Eden—indeed, we can assume that identification routinely in Poe—but it does assert that the mind is a Paradise maker. If there is an old Eden in the past, there is a new one in the present, and the two are not precisely alike. That in the past is the place remembered, that in the present is the result of the act of remembering.

It is apparent that Poe had been contemplating, with care and obsessiveness, the conditions of creativity in the fallen world. He saw that the imagination could not be loosened from its context since the possibilities of its achievement, indeed the very strength with which it works, are determined to a considerable extent by the conditions in which it must function. Of course this is to say that the pressures of context qualify all assertions of autonomy; but it also means that those pressures can make the imagination fiercely assertive, since it may be compelled to demonstrate its capacities in the most formidable circumstances. In fact, it may be forced to fight for its survival in an environment that appears to be unalterably alien. That is precisely what happens in Poe, where the intensity of struggle seeks to match the countervailing intensity of an adverse context. That context originated with a primeval split, a dismembering or, in Poe's own language, a decentering. *Eureka* puts it in neat if garish cosmological terms. The universe had begun with the irradiation of atoms from a center, a "primordial and irrelative *One*."[6] Poe calls this decentering "a diffusion from Unity" that "involves a tendency to return into Unity—a tendency ineradicable until satisfied" (503). The state of unity is the normal one (by *normal* Poe means little more than *former and still desired*), and every effort the separated atoms make has the return to unity as an ultimate object:

Nothing like *location* was conceived as their origin. Their source lies in the principle, *Unity. This* is their lost parent. *This* they seek always—immediately—in all directions— wherever it is even partially to be found; thus appeasing, in some measure, the ineradicable tendency, while on the way to its absolute satisfaction in the end. (513)

The atoms seek to make clusters because these satisfy their compulsion for unity. The clusters are, in fact, temporary means of gratification, an "appeasing" as Poe calls it in this passage. We shall see that the life of fallen man is made up in great part of such momentary satisfactions.

In *The Colloquy of Monos and Una* the Fall occurs in more commonplace terms. Poets, who were "living and perishing amid the scorn of the 'utilitarians' . . . pondered piningly, yet not unwisely, upon the ancient days when our wants were not more simple than our enjoyments were keen."[7] Then the Arts "arose supreme, and, once enthroned, cast chains upon the intellect which had elevated them to power" (203). The result was system and abstraction, the dark deities which led to priesthood in Blake and democracy in Poe. This amalgam of Rousseau, Bentham, and journalistic romanticism culminates in a vision of the ending of days when the earth, purified of its "rectangular obscenities," is reclothed in "the verdure and the mountain-slopes and the smiling waters of Paradise" (205). Intellect will be exalted, freed from the poison of knowl- edge and, one gathers, from angularities.

But that is all yet to come, and we are now, as "The Haunted Palace" argues, wanderers in a once-happy valley, which used to be the greenest of all in "the monarch Thought's domin- ion."[8] It has become the home of fallen, abstract, systematic, angular mind. Yet we have seen that our minds can be Paradise makers, that their remembering is recreative of the old and inventive of the new. Poets are the most obvious instances, authoritative shapers of a green world within:

If, indeed, there be any one circle of thought distinctly and palpably marked out from amid the jarring and tumultuous chaos of human intelligence, it is that evergreen and radiant

Paradise which the true poet knows, and knows alone, as the limited realm of his authority—as the circumscribed Eden of his dreams.[9]

But poets are not, in fact, the only creators in this chaos. Poe's major stories show that the fallen mind is compulsively creative, seeking to build again, in versions ranging from reproduction to hellish parody, those enclosures that had once sheltered ideal unity.

Take, for example, *The Masque of the Red Death*. Prince Prospero sought to establish a totally protective and comforting situation, one which would keep the Red Death out and a world of ornate gaiety within. He and his party "retired to the deep seclusion of one of his castellated abbeys"—not simply into isolation, a movement away from the deadly context outside, but into a deep retreat, an ensconcing far within.[10] "Deep" prepares us for the intricate topography of the world inside the abbey. To seal out externality the courtiers welded the bolts of the iron gates that were fastened into the walls encircling the abbey. Within the walls is a full store of supplies for the senses: the Prince has ensured their self-sufficiency by arranging for ample provisions as well as "all the appliances of pleasure." Thus, desire and capability are perfectly matched. They did precisely what they wanted to do and, thanks to the Prince, they did it to perfection. Only his wealth could have purchased such an arrangement. They owned a contextual autonomy without peer, a paragon to be envied in that time of sharp pains and sudden death.

The Prince's gesture was a response to threat. In shaping the circumstances of their withdrawal he does the precise opposite of what the protagonist in *Eleonora* did. The latter left his declining Eden "for ever for the vanities and turbulent triumphs of the world," while the Prince puts that world outside by retiring into his protective enclosure: "The external world could take care of itself. . . . Without was the 'Red Death' " (251). The Prince's gesture is an act of nostalgia. It is a recreation of the unfallen place, the bounded, self-sustaining shelter, walled off from the turbulence of experience. This is very like a ritual reenactment, those acts of imitation by which shamans and magicians ward off evil. By reproducing the form and conditions of the paradisal enclosure the Prince instinctively recreates prelapsarian circumstances, seeking to make anew the place that had existed before death came into the world. How better to ward off death than to live in the image of a place which, in its pristine glory, knew nothing of the threat of decay? To guarantee that no Fall can end their seclusion the Prince has the courtiers seal themselves in: "They resolved to leave means neither of ingress or egress to the sudden impulses of despair or of frenzy from within" (251). This is clearly a place one has to come to, not a place one departs from. That is, it has all the virtues of the initial Paradise plus the advantage of having grown out of the world of experience. In a universe that has long been decentered and discontinuous the Prince has made a new center. This is, in effect, an ingathering of the exiles.

What the Prince does, then, is the best that one can do in the face of the Red Death. But Poe, with masterful canniness, has the last word even while he is having the first one. His initial paragraph describes the disease itself, its symptoms and rapid effects. In some ways the most appalling of the latter is not physical but moral: "The scarlet stains upon the body and especially upon the face of the victim, were the pest ban which shut him out from the aid and from the sympathy of his fellow-men" (250). Here is a sardonic prediction of the effect of the Prince's self-imposed incarceration. As the victim of the Red Death is trapped within his disease, where no man can or will help him, so are the Prince and his retinue trapped within the shelter they have set up to protect themselves from the disease. By sealing themselves in they become the prisoners of their own gesture. And of course they shut the enemy up along with them: the inmost chambers of the abbey are drawn in the scarlet color of the disease and the black of death. In seeking to escape the Red Death they shaped a precise correlative to the condition of one of its victims.

In sum, they tried to make an enclosure reminiscent of Paradise but succeeded only with a hellish one, a gross and deadly parody of the paradisal, which had all the paradisal lineaments but none of its life-enhancing qualities. The result is a lesson in the effectiveness of nostalgia. Though one seeks to reproduce the old figure of the enclosure, the repetition has to happen in the fallen world, and for that reason the impersonation can never be exact, however much it shares in shape. If there is a doubling in one way, there is a distinguishing in another, emphasizing, at once, both likeness and difference. The likeness is linking, copulative: the unfallen world and its fallen successor are joined, not only in simple sequence but because the configuration at the center of the one can be repeated at the center of the other. But that linking is bitter as well as comforting. It is ironic because of the recurrence of shapes, agonizing because the shapes are in very different worlds, have different contents, and therefore very different meanings. In his attempt to echo the old world Poe's hero succeeds mainly in showing how far he actually is from it.

Thus, what had appeared to be an incongruence of inner and outer, disease outside and partying within, turns out to be a congruence so precise that the walls are shown to be ineffectual. It is Satan's old mistake all over again. Their minds are incapable of creating a heaven in the spaces within. Autonomy, however arrogantly trumpeted (and perhaps in part because it is so asserted), has no way of countering the pressures of the hell out there and the sickness of self within. It has sealed out salvation and tucked the enemy comfortably inside. At this stage of Poe's fable the Satanic model is stronger than the Rousseauistic because most of Poe's heroes, like Satan, are notoriously self-deluding about the effectiveness of mind, the degree of its self-sufficiency, its ability to execute its desires, its capacity to withstand pressures. Whatever the cleverness of the hero or the variations in the pattern, delusion seems inescapable. For example, the speaker in *The Black Cat* tries to close off the evidence and the enemy, both at once. So does the protagonist of *The Tell-Tale Heart*. Ordinarily one walls in what one loves in order to separate it, and oneself, from the uncertainties of experience. But if that protective gesture is a postlapsarian imitation of the making of Paradise, *The Black Cat* and *The Tell-Tale Heart* carry the creation one step further, turning the protectiveness inside out and making the enclosure hellish. In those stones the hero walls *in* what he fears and hates, separating it from himself as effectively as, in the ordinary pattern, one walls the enemy *out*. He succeeds, finally, in building an impediment to the enemy though their places in the radical structure have been exchanged. But Poe cannot let this parody rest. The reversal is, and is not, a departure from the expected relationship. The nemesis is, and is not, walled in. In *The Black Cat* and *The Tell-Tale Heart* the protagonists have submerged their guilt and disgust within themselves as well as on the other side of the barrier, and all those enemies thump and howl until the walls come tumbling down. The barricades are as ineffectual as those of the Prince's abbey and for precisely the same reason: there is no distinction between walling in and walling out because all enclosures, the paradisal or their hellish counterparts, are enclosures of the self. Packing away one's adversary means packing him inside as well; shutting out one's nemesis does no more than invite him in. The concealment is a revelation, the creation a de-creation, the walling in a dissolution.

There is still another distinction in Poe's fallen world which turns out to contain as much likeness as difference. The willful actions of the protagonists in these stories succeed only in putting them in the same situation as that of the passive, will-less protagonists of *The Premature Burial, MS. Found in A Bottle* and *A Descent into the Maelström*. In the latter story the protagonist is trapped within an enclosure, the funnel of the whirlpool, whose walls are as firm and impregnable as those of any Paradise: "the belt of surf is considerably lower than the general bed of the ocean, and this latter now towered above us, a high, black, mountainous ridge."[11] Of course he is not willingly within it but the result is no different from what happens to most of those figures who seek deliberately to wall up part of their experience. The enclosure is, or is revealed to be, malevolent. The postlapsarian mind is dangerously prone to entrapment, whatever the degree of its will and autonomy.

In the context of these developments there is a significant, revelatory exception, *The Cask of Amontillado*. That story has the same walling-in of the nemesis, who is feared and hated as much as any of those who took post-mortem revenge upon their gravediggers. In *Amontillado* the murderer is touched by the needle of conscience only once, at the very end: "There came forth in return only a jingling of the bells. My heart grew sick; it was the dampness of the catacombs that made it so."[12] But that is not enough to keep him from positioning the final stone. Unlike the other protagonists who pack away their enemies, this one succeeds in keeping that death from vexing his soul and compelling it into self-revelation. "*In pace requiescat,*" the last words of the story, may be directed as much toward his own soul as toward that of his victim. But fifty years of success are a good indication that if there were any grumbles of guilt, they had been quite ineffectual. As the opening lines show, the story is a confession; but since the events are fifty years old, we can assume that this is a deathbed revelation or its equivalent. The murderer has gotten away with it. In a story which is in part about the meaning of impunity this protagonist, unlike his counterparts elsewhere in Poe, finally wins out.

Of course this is Satanic autonomy, and a more successful instance than most others in Poe or elsewhere. It has nothing in it of the eventual self-entrapment that had seemed inevitable with such assertions, at least since Satan. This time the talent for decreation does not turn on its possessor and make him an ironic double of his victim, subject to the same nullifying powers. Decreation exults in the imagination's prowess as much as creation does, and in this story its exultation is complete, earned by a signal instance of success. But this success comes from a complicity with the malevolence inherent in the fallen world, and that—aside from the obvious moral issues—

is why this story has no precise duplicate elsewhere in Poe. Because *Amontillado* images such a victory, it runs counter to some of the deepest patterns in Poe's fable, particularly the self-devouring that is endemic in his work. If it stands as an odd (awed) instance of one thing that could happen, those patterns were simply too compelling for *Amontillado* to serve as anything more than a momentary triumph of malice.

The nearest parallel to *Amontillado* is *Ligeia*, in which a nearly autonomous will destroys the image of its successor, and with no hint of what happens to the destroyer. Nostalgia in *Ligeia* takes a more overt form than it does in *Amontillado*. The protagonist seeks out an English domain and abbey to which are attached "many melancholy and time-honored memories," that is, a mood and context which "had much in unison with the feeling of utter abandonment which had driven [him] into that remote and unsocial region of the country."[13] This balance of inner and outer does not appease his nostalgia. In fact, it seems obvious that he does not want to ease it but to enrich it, give it depth. Why else seek out this place? If he cannot cool his nostalgia by finding an object of the sort it craves, he can at least find places that are themselves images of nostalgia. If he cannot objectify the lost beloved, he can at least objectify his craving, and there is clearly some pleasure in that. The need to enact nostalgia even to that interim degree is obsessive in Poe. It is better to give some form to nostalgia than to leave it without objectification. In a more direct and destructive way nostalgia drives *Ligeia* as well. As the protagonist tells us, she was his superior in intellect and attainments, and as the tale shows, she is also more effective in the realization of nostalgia. Nostalgia is a kind of recall, and in order to give form to it, to literally enliven the past, Ligeia has to literally supplant the present. But her will, it appears, cannot do this entirely alone. It was extraordinary when it was in life but it is now faced with its most difficult job. It is not self-sufficient enough to bridge the gap between the quick and the dead with no help. It must use an already established bridge as a way back to her lover. That bridge is the lover's nostalgia, the "passionate waking visions of Ligeia," which move him as he watches beside the corpse of Rowena. Each time he succumbs to those dreams the body gives a start of life. Ligeia pulls her way back to life by using his nostalgia (now, for the first time, fruitful) to give form to her own. Of course she does so with that same talent for decreation owned by all of Poe's successful destroyers. She literally unmakes Rowena, taking her apart and replacing her with her unmaker. Ligeia has supplanted Rowena but, at another remove, she has supplanted her old self as well. Still, this is not the full narrative of success that *Amontillado* was because there is a vast mystery after the ending. The aftermath of these events is literally unimaginable. There is a gap of time between the ending and the beginning, the long-distant event and the recollection of it, which we cannot fill and which Poe chooses not to. In fact, much of the horror in the story lies in our pondering of those spaces between the ending and the beginning, our wonder at what could have filled them. It is an additional horror but not a gratuitous one, since, once we have absorbed the shock of the ending, the story invites us to contemplate the sequel to this self-recreation.

In any case this is a triumph, however tentative, for the fallen will. *Ligeia* points out with as much literalness as anything in Poe that such a victory may well involve an unmaking, and that in such a case the will is necessarily malevolent. If the malevolence is not always personal—Ligeia is clearly indifferent to her victim as a person—it is always eminently successful, achieving its main object. Lethal volition gets what it wants, though, as we shall see, it generally gets more than it wants as well. It is the fallen world's parody of paradisal self-sufficiency. Indeed, from the perspective of Paradises past and to come the kind of autonomy Ligeia possesses, however qualified, is dark and hellish, the tonal opposite of the self-sufficiency associated with pre- and postlapsarian worlds. *Amontillado* has that same dark tonality, and those values color an unqualified triumph. In that story we are shown how the perpetrator succeeds absolutely, with no cost exacted from him. It is a pinnacle of postlapsarian achievement, an evil that became, for its inhumane exponent, an absolute good.

In Poe's cosmos the great nemesis of man's humanity is "fallen-ness"; more precisely, the malevolence inherent in the fallen world. The antithesis of that malevolence, indeed its only serious antagonist, is the imagination's capacity for viable creativity, that is, the sort that is not only life-enhancing but also able to create that which can function actively in and for itself.[14] It is clear from Poe (there are hints of this in Blake, who helps us to gloss Poe) that malevolence can infect the imagination and spin off a dark double of it, the strengths of which are not viable but lethal. The result is the decreating to which I have referred. The purpose of the viable imagination is to counter the malevolence in the fallen world, the purpose of the lethal one is to serve as the instrument of malevolence. The lethal is a making to destroy, the bitter twin of that Paradise making of which the mind, in Poe (and Rousseau and Wordsworth) is seen to be capable. Despite all its demonstrable inadequacies and capacities for self-delusion, the viable imagination is the only certain way to offset the decline of man. There is nothing else in Poe's world that comes forward as an instrument of redemption but there is much that, as *Amontillado* shows, seeks eagerly to bring men down. In that story the lethal imagination is seen at its most potent and successful. Toward the end of the story the victim goes into a decline, losing his distinctiveness as a person and eventually his fullness of self. Only a few sounds come from him, some low moaning cries, the shaking of chains and then "a succession of loud and shrill screams" (174). When Montresor flashes a light into the recess he sees only "the figure within," "the chained form"—an object making noises. There is a brief resuscitation of the victim's humanity but we know only through his voice that he is there and even then the protagonist "had difficulty in recognizing [it] as that of the noble Fortunato" (175). Finally the voice subsides and "there came forth in return only a jingling of the bells." That is the point at which Montresor's heart grew sick for an instant. It was the penultimate stage of the reduction of Fortunato, that sinking of man to which all the energies of the fallen world seem devoted.

As *Amontillado* shows, the lethal imagination seeks to dehumanize. It abides with malevolence, working with it to usurp the territory the viable imagination considers as its own. Poe's world is radically man-centered, and the fable which defines its meaning is derived from myriad versions of the fall of man, all of which speculate upon his potential redemption. In these conditions dehumanization is predictable, indeed inevitable: it has to be the enemy's strongest weapon. It counters the thrust toward unity, the impulse to join and coalesce, which in *Eureka* is seen as the primary and redeeming instinct of the decentered world. Dehumanization separates man from himself and turns him into a thing which jingles. It pries human centers apart, showing them in their essential weakness, their inability to face up to the potency and ferocity of the fallen world's malevolence. But that malevolence has one more trick, and it is usually a final one. It makes men into self-devourers, creators of their own engorgement. Malevolence is so nasty that it turns its partners upon themselves. Its success can be considered complete only when that lethal imagination, which is the major instrument of malevolence, becomes its own victim. But *Amontillado* shows that sometimes the lethal imagination beats the game, getting its prey and preserving itself. In his efforts to make a full world and flesh out his fable, Poe had to consider all possibilities, even that rare one. *Amontillado* exists because it had to be shown that this dark double of the viable imagination was not always self-consuming.

There is still another mode of imagination in Poe, a curious amalgam which is cousin to both the viable and lethal modes though not quite to be identified with either. In *The Murders in the Rue Morgue*, Poe inspects the characteristics and techniques of a mode he calls, variously, the analytical or the resolvent. It disentangles arcane complexities, seeks to identify itself with that which it examines, bases its activities on a shrewd understanding of process and method: "The necessary knowedge is that of *what* to observe."[15] It is opposed to the "constructive or combining power, by which ingenuity is usually manifested" because even near-idiots can possess the constructive power while a considerable intelligence is required for the analytical (149). The latter is, in a sense, deconstructive, not only because it takes its opponents apart but because, in order to do so, it must unravel the opponents' thinking and understand the preconceptions, sometimes unconscious, on which that thinking is based. The opponent of the analytic imagination is not, finally, any individual but the mystery the individual embodies. Its activities are therefore demystifying ones.

This mode of imagination is insidious because it seeks to subdue its adversary and destroy his position. It is not, as a rule, malevolent, the lethality need not be literal, and its possessor is unlikely to become his own victim. But since the mystery is generally personified in a figure, in one way or another that figure loses out. The ape in *Rue Morgue* is put in a zoo, the thief in *The Purloined Letter* is put in a position where he will bring himself down. Someone suffers, someone gains. In fact, in the instances examined by Poe, society is a major beneficiary. The analytic imagination is shown to be viable in the sense that it performs a social function by working out the mysteries of some unsociable action. That service, however, is only a secondary product, a gratifying result but not its primary aim. The analytic imagination is, to its possessor, "a source of the liveliest enjoyment. As the strong man exults in his physical ability, delighting in such exercises as call his muscles into action, so glories the analyst in that moral activity which *disentangles*" (146). Dupin finds "an eager delight in its exercise—if not exactly in its display" (152). He has less compulsion to show it off than to use it for its own sake, for the freedom and for the pleasure involved in the freedom. He exercises his capacities mainly to find a joy he cannot share with others, though others may benefit from the results of that exercise.

The powers of the analytic imagination are as self-contained as its joy. Few modes of the imagination could be as autonomous as this, and none could ever be so unfailingly accurate. It is a model of self-sufficiency, as rare and precious in its way as Schiller's naive imagination, though quite possibly not as healthy as Schiller's unsentimental sort. Dupin's power, the narrator says, "was merely the result of an excited, or perhaps of a diseased intelligence" (152). That may be why Dupin is extraordinarily self-conscious about his abilities, as the naive is not, and why, unlike the naive, he is hardly in harmony with his environment. When the narrator goes to live with him, they furnish their place "in a style which suited the rather fantastic gloom of our common temper" (151). Packed away from the world in perfect seclusion Dupin exercises "the wild fervor, and the vivid freshness of his imagination" in darkness, in a house that admits no light (150-51). Whenever possible he travels only at night. Bizarre but not malicious, withdrawn but willing to serve society (though he is most of all serving himself), Dupin the analyst is a paragon of effective autonomy. But he is not, perhaps, all that the fallen world needs for its ultimate interests.

There are, it seems, several kinds of success to which the fallen imagination can aspire. *Amontillado* shows one kind, a rare instance of a totally prosperous complicity with malevolence. The stories of Dupin show another, one that has a curious neutrality about it. It is deconstructive without being dehumanizing; or if it does sink some men, there is general agreement that they deserve it, that the taking apart has a constructive effect. Dupin's is not an actively nostalgic imagination, the kind that seeks to mimic the enclosures of the innocent world, the kind parodied in *The Black Cat* and sardonically imitated in *Amontillado*. Still, if it does not create new enclosures, his mind is unquestionably touched by vestiges of nostalgia: Dupin and the narrator lived in a dark, closed-off place, in perfect seclusion, existing within themselves alone. He seems to have sensed a need for such a place in which to do his thinking. But that was not enough nostalgia for Poe's fable. The overall thrust of the fable is teleological, geared toward an end that would recall the beginning but from a more exalted situation than even the glories of the beginning could realize. That thrust affects the fallen world too because the world not only remembers the original places but seeks desperately to recreate their protecting forms. Thus, the fable was responding to a Poesque paraphrase of the impulse generated in Emile by his preceptor: "fais ton paradis sur la terre en attendant l'autre." The exhortation rebounds through all the echoing enclosures in Poe's fallen world, often with an ironic snicker, but compulsively all the same. Dupin's imagination, though it can help society out of some difficulties, cannot help Poe's fable to enact that remaking.

The problems involved in building the one place while waiting for the other are obvious and nearly overwhelming. A successful remaking, however tentative, should try to overcome the irony and the agony in the nostalgia, that doubling of the old that is also a distinguishing of the old and the new. It should counter the dehumanization basic to the lethal imagination and should do so with all the energetic productivity of the analytic. In the decentered world it should conspire with the impulses spelled out in *Eureka* and try to make new and viable centers, clusters of humanized experience. Above all it should seek for a congruence of contexts, Paradises outside whose existence guarantees that there are Paradises within, tentative as each may be. The imagination should be able to make stopping places as predictive as they are nostalgic, fulfilling completely Poe's version of the preceptor's edict.

In a series of three interlocking sketches begun in 1842 Poe sought to give form to his conception of the temporary shelters, that is, to his reading of the possibilities of redemption. The set is concerned with the art of landscape gardening, to which Poe turned in an effort to show what the mind can do to counter the ancient collapse of Paradise. His purpose, clearly, was to show how the mind's abilities could be mapped out on the face of the earth, working in the most direct and literal way with the fallen world. The series started with *The Landscape Garden*, which became, with minor revisions, the first part of *The Domain of Arnheim*, published in 1847. *Landor's Cottage* completes the series. Both *The Landscape Garden* and *The Domain of Arnheim* begin with stanza forty-two of Giles Fletcher's *Christ's Victory on Earth*:

> The garden like a lady fair was cut,
>   That lay as if she slumbered in delight,
> And to the open skies her eyes did shut.
>   The azure fields of Heaven were 'sembled right
>   In a large round set with the flowers of light.
> The flowers de luce and the round sparks of dew
> That hung upon their azure leaves did shew
> Like twinkling stars that sparkle in the evening blue.[16]

We are hearing some familiar signals. The identification of the garden with a woman echoes those identifications of the beloved with a paradisal place that, elsewhere in Poe, denote the activation of nostalgia. The sketch that follows is to be a proving of nostalgia under circumstances so lush that, as Poe is to explain, they require sublime expenditures to bring that beauty about. The lushness is forecast in the rich texture of Fletcher's earthly flowers of light (flowers de luce, fleurs-de-lis, irises) as well as the flowers of light in Heaven. Fletcher sets Heaven's large fields in the classical paradisal round. The echoing of the heavenly flowers in the earthly, as well as the presence of azure in each, reveals a microcosmic reflecting of the Heavenly Paradise in the earthly grounds. The realms are linked through beauty and the harmony of form and content. This is, indeed, a very arty place, predictive of the sort of earthly Paradise that Ellison was to make.

To the narrator the career of Ellison is a refutation of original sin, not only of the conception of radical human evil but also of the doctrine that the Fall is irreparable without help from outside. The saving of man is to come from within man himself; the laws that have been violated are "a few simple laws of humanity," and therefore "man, the individual, under certain unusual and highly fortuitous conditions, may be happy" (176-77). In the *Marginalia* Poe had spoken about such conditions in regard to another kind of happiness. There he referred to ecstatic fancies, which particularly moved him and which had once been totally beyond his control. He learned, however, to induce them "when all circumstances are favorable"; but those circumstances are rare "else had I compelled already the Heaven into the Earth."[17] Yet such compulsion is precisely what Ellison wants, and in his case the "unusual and fortuitous conditions" necessary to stimulate human happiness have actually fallen together. He has the necessary will and unimaginable wealth. Further, he can limit the extent of his enterprise, leaving aside grandiose universal schemes because he has no faith in "the possibility of any improvement, properly so called, being effected by man himself in the general condition of man" (180). What he does he does on his own and for himself, with his own inner and outer resources. Clarissa too had hoped to lean on her independence of mind and fortune; but the difference between her bourgeois longing and Ellison's opulent aestheticism speaks of two hundred years of literary meditation on the autonomy of the self.

Ellison's interests are involved with the history of taste, particularly with landscape gardens and the picturesque, but his attitude toward the capacities of the mind forecasts the future more than it recalls the past. Even the loveliest of natural landscapes cannot compete with what a man can make: "No such paradises are to be found in reality as have glowed on the canvass of Claude" (182). In a passage added in *The Domain of Arnheim* the narrator puzzles over the decline from "the primitive intention of nature [which] would have so arranged the earth's surface as to have fulfilled at all points man's sense of perfection in the beautiful, the sublime, or the picturesque" (184). The decline came about through "known geological disturbances—disturbances of form and color-grouping, in the correction or allaying of which lies the soul of art" (184). Ellison explains the decline as forecasting death, a change from the original intention of keeping man immortal. We are not told why death was brought into the world, though we can guess, but we do know that death and inharmonious form came into the world together. The differences between Ellison and Stevens's meditating heroine for whom "death is the mother of beauty" speak of other strange entanglements of literary history. Ellison's emphasis is aesthetic, not ethical; taste and the moral sense are kept apart, precisely as Poe suggested they should be in *The Poetic Principle*. In a curious but important qualification Ellison admits that our alterations of nature might be exaltations only from our own point of view, that we might actually be spoiling it. There could be, he says, "a class of beings, human once, but now invisible to humanity, to whom, from afar, our disorder may seem order—our unpicturesqueness picturesque" (184-85). These odd beings—he calls them "earth-angels"—would be humanity transformed. Ellison adds that the garden that is the world might well have been made for their "death-refined appreciation of the beautiful" (185). This completes his paradox: if death and disharmony came jointly into the world, death could make possible an exalted appreciation of nature's actual beauty.

But for now Ellison has palpable and present men to deal with, and it seems that nature, even from the perspective of living men, has a special relationship to the human. He argues that the touch of art in a garden gives it a beauty beyond the natural, a beauty whose strengths come from associations with the life of man: "The slightest exhibition of art is an evidence of care and human interest" (185-86). Of course this is a countervoice to the lethal imagination, whose activities are radically dehumanizing, lowering man at least to the level of the rest of nature. But Ellison does not stop there. In a deft argument resulting in a remarkable act of compromise, he exalts the human and transcends it, both at once. There may be a condition that, while keeping the necessary awareness of man's touch, "would lend a charm to the landscape-garden far surpassing that which a sense of merely human interest could bestow" (187). The "merely" is neatly put: man is important but there is more. Even in the wilderness one senses the art of a Creator, though it does not strike to the feelings but only to reflection. An ideal landscape would occupy a middle ground between man and the divine: "Now let us suppose this sense of the Almighty design to be *one step de-pressed*—to be brought into something like harmony or consistency with the sense of human art—to form an intermedium between the two" (187). One would see in it the concerns of "beings superior, yet akin to humanity," possibly the earth-angels. The result would be "an intermediate or secondary nature—a nature which is not God, nor an emanation from God, but which still is nature in the sense of the handiwork of the angels that hover between man and God" (188).

Ellison is not in a contest with God but doing the best that a man can do in circumstances so extraordinary that only Ellison, with his unmatchable resources, can even think of them. There is neither intellectual nor spiritual arrogance here but, rather, an effort to shape the face of the world so that it would be something more than fallen nature but less than nature spiritualized. The requisite touch of artifice which elevates nature does not take it beyond terrestrial bounds. It is an interim landscape, the sort one would expect from intermediate beings who are neither God nor man. In fact, the landscape Ellison has in mind would be the precise mirror image of the one envisioned at the end of *The Island of the Fay*. That sketch had shown a prelapsarian world at its point of decline, fading into the next stage of mortal experience. Ellison's landscape would show a postlapsarian world easing toward apotheosis but not nearly there because the world still has its mortal weight. To that degree his landscape would be a place of foretaste, of prefiguration. Of course Ellison is canny enough to have it all ways at once, that is, to transcend ordinary nature but still keep his natural humility before God.

The finest achievement to which the independent imagination can aspire will have about it a sense of semblance and compromise. That achievement will look like an imitation of life, but it will be higher than life has been made to be. Arnheim's viable imagination is, to begin with, a humanizing one; but it culminates in a vision that fuses the human with more than it could have expected, given the conditions in which the human now has to function.

The Landscape Garden carried the argument only to this point. *The Domain of Arnheim* continues with an application of Ellison's aesthetics, but there might have been an interim stage between the two sketches. In April 1844, a year and a half after *The Landscape Garden* appeared, Poe published *A Tale of the Ragged Mountains*. Its hero is a parody of the Byronic hero who has most of that figure's characteristics but not his good looks. In this elaborate narrative the protagonist works his way through a ravine into a bizarre area deep within the mountains and finds there an exotic city, an illustrated weekly's conception of a Near Eastern or Indian metropolis. The result is disaster, the living out of another's death in that city, a metempsychosis occasioned by an extreme case of magnetic relations. It is likely that this tale had much to do with the latter half of *The Domain of Arnheim*. Poe's decision to continue Ellison's story and put his ideas into practice came out of an awareness that to leave the ideas at the level of deliberation was to leave unrealized an unusual chance to resuscitate the fallen imagination. *A Tale of the Ragged Mountains* seems to have helped him to think the problem out. Its exotic city centered within hitherto inaccessible confines was associated with the poisonousness of the world within, while the hypnotist's magnetic powers were an unwitting but efficient extension of the lethal imagination. In *The Domain of Arnheim* the city appears again, but this time as the product of an imagination so viable, and so careful of what it is about, that the tonality of the way in and of the place at the center has been entirely changed. It is as though Poe were deliberately crafting twin tales, which would be precise mirror images of each other, structurally identical but with varying resonances and opposing conclusions. *A Tale of the Ragged Mountains* is an ironic, malignant prefiguration of Poe's most complicated attempt to raise the tumbled mind.

Ellison begins by working out precisely what he needs, as well as inspecting that which is good for others but not, finally, for himself. He rejects the predictable Pacific island because, though it would be sufficiently secluded to offer the necessary "difficulty of ingress and egress" it would not be close enough to a crowded city (189). He wants Wolmar's kind of proximate autonomy with all the intricacy of access that had characterized the most effective images of the sequestered self. Ellison also turns down an elevated plateau with a gorgeous panorama because the view is, for long-term association, too broad: "in the constant view the most objectionable phase of grandeur is that of extent" (190). He wants, that is, to be walled in, to stare up at the edges of the confining site, to have at his control the kind and modality of his repose, to exchange it for extension and association as he wishes. Restriction must be nearly complete; community must be available though not evident.

The result not only filled this bill precisely but turned the energies that had elsewhere consumed the self into those which gave it independent, creative, nostalgic life. One got to Arnheim's domain by way of the river, the surroundings of which changed gradually from the civilized to the pastoral and then from retirement to solitude. The windings (we are within Poe's familiar image) become more and more intricate while the walls gradually rise and close in. The move toward the interior is a carefully designed displacement of the ordinary:

> The thought of nature still remained, but her character seemed to have undergone modification: there was a weird symmetry, a thrilling uniformity, a wizard propriety in these her works. Not a dead branch—not a withered leaf—not a stray pebble—not a patch of the brown earth was anywhere visible. The crystal water welled up against the clean

granite, or the unblemished moss, with a sharpness of outline that delighted while it bewildered the eye. (191-92)

After flowing through these manicured grounds, which give
no hint of physical decay or of the sod they will become, the
stream flows into a circular basin, which is walled-in except
for narrow entrance and exit points. The sloping sides of the
chasm are rich with gorgeous flowers, but there is hardly a
touch of green. The "unblemished moss" has given way to
exotic profusion in which the brown of earth has completely
gone and green, the other main color of natural life, has nearly
disappeared. With this unusual lushness Poe hints at a special
rebirth: "a miraculous extremeness of culture . . . suggested
dreams of a new race of fairies, laborious, tasteful, magnificent
and fastidious" (192). Poe is quietly paying off an old debt,
as well as playing off Ellison's ascent from nature against the
recollection of a former submission to it. The decline pictured
in *The Isle of the Fay* is being countered by an art seeking to
ease out all recollection of nature's radical earthiness. In fact,
the gardener goes even further, imaging luxurious things that
do not grow in luxurious things that do: "it became, indeed,
difficult not to fancy a panoramic cataract of rubies, sapphires,
opals and golden onyxes, rolling silently out of the sky" (192-
93). After this the traveler steps into a self-propelled ivory
canoe, which begins to move on accompanied by melancholy
music that seems to have no source. (Thus does Shelley's
Alastor slip into the matter of mid-century aestheticism.) The
canoe glides through exquisitely clean grounds and past "grass
of a texture resembling nothing so much as velvet, and of a
brilliancy of green which would bear comparison with the tint
of the purest emerald" (194). Nature, after all, is not put away
but is brought up to a level of spotless opulence where the
metaphors that best fit with it have nothing to do with organic
growth. This is a green and pleasant place but not quite in
any of the traditional senses. Finally the canoe descends into
an enormous amphitheatre surrounded by purple mountains.
Inside it is the Paradise of Arnheim. Out of the midst of a

lavish amalgam of exotic vegetation rises "a mass of semi-Gothic, semi-Saracenic architecture, sustaining itself as if by miracle in mid-air" (196). It is a dream compounded of Beckford and Byron and all the popular Levantism of the previous century. At the heart of Paradise lies a conglomerate artifice. Nature has been sifted, transformed but not extinguished, made into what it would be if it had no dark memories of its recent past. Arnheim's Paradise is a world without nightmares. It looks back to the very old and forward to what could be if the hands of angels were to reach down into the world.

In *The Colloquy of Monos and Una,* which preceded *The Landscape Garden* by less than a year, Poe speculated briefly on what a regenerated earth would look like. Its topography is traditional ("the verdure and the mountain-slopes and the smiling waters of Paradise") and in the "exalted intellect" of men "there should be poison in knowledge no more."[18] Man would be redeemed and immortal but still material, earthly but no longer subject to the varieties of decay that natural time brings about. In the *Colloquy* Poe had put forth some thinned-out Rousseauisms on the decline of culture through Art, meaning, most likely, those aspects of intellect that make cities and the life that goes on in them. *The Domain of Arnheim* takes a very different attitude toward cities, nature, nostalgia, and artifice, prefiguring the literary history to come more than that which had long been absorbed. Nature, in Poe, had always been emblematic, at the service of the human much as it is in Emerson's *Nature* but with no provision made for a transparent eyeball. In the major stories nature is the place in which human events occur, and sometimes an apt correlative for the meaning of those events. Poe had no interest in nature's self-subsistence; he was concerned, most of all, with how man could, in nature, shape out his own autonomy. Toward the end of his life Poe came to feel that nature as it was could not help out with the most crucial postlapsarian issue, the mind's need to make its private place and time in a world seeking to rot it and send it to hell. Stendhal had come to similar conclusions, though in a very different mo-

dality. Julien's cave, ensconced in the forest, was only a stopping place on the way to a salon and a cell. For Julien, however,
it took the promise of death to create the conditions in which
his life became most satisfying. There was no such paradox
in Poe. Ellison wanted a consummately independent life without the browns and ordinary greens signaling the treachery
of time as well as the muddiness of experience. Thus he made
a nature such as angels might make, stable and swept clean,
neither fleeting nor sticky with dirt. It is, one assumes, the
precise correlative of the angelic mind that would make such
a place. Ellison realized his nostalgia by imitating the thoughts
and the mentality of that which he was not. There is—this
point bears repeating—no hybris about his gestures, nothing
of Tate's angelic imagination.[19] Indeed, his gestures take their
final significance from their character as gestures, and they
are fully realized to be such. They are the best that the most
independent mortal mind can fashion. Arnheim's domain is
a raised place in a fallen world, no more than that but at least
that much. Poe's remarks on the aesthetics of landscape were
warmer news in eighteenth-century Europe than in America
of the 1840s. But if his imagination could do little more at
this point than put together some cultural commonplaces, if
all he could do in realizing an earthly Eden was to make this
gaudy product of scissors and paste, *Arnheim* does show his
final awareness of the full meaning of his fable as well as his
sense of what a humanized landscape can signify. Nostalgia
is predictive as well as regressive, and there are, it turns out,
alternatives to the tendency of nostalgic enclosures to become
hellish. If the price is a scrubbed-up nature, if the vegetation
must come from a hothouse, that might, after all, be the most
appropriate context for the mind which is making its own
place in the mid-nineteenth century.

Though *Arnheim* was the culmination of Poe's scrutiny of
his fable, he worked on some subsidiary issues until his death.
In *Mellonta Tauta,* published two years after *Arnheim,* the
sanctimonious explorer he created as his protagonist gave Poe
an opportunity for the sort of self-parody he relished and

seemed to need for perspective. All sorts of old ideas about democracy and cosmology turn up again, and in the entry of 8 April the balloonist receives news about the building of "a new fountain at Paradise, the emperor's principal pleasure garden."[20] The balloonist goes on to explain that "Paradise, it appears, has been, literally speaking, an island time out of mind," an unexceptionable comment until it turns out that he is speaking of Manhattan (never named as such), whose civilization had been obliterated by an earthquake in 2050. This amalgam of old tropes, Coleridgean decor, and a slap at contemporary feminine fashion ("the women, too, it appears, were oddly deformed by a natural protuberance of the region just below the small of the back") works with neat and pleasant blatancy. Poe, it is clear, can step back, however slightly, from his ongoing obsessions. A more complicated continuation of these concerns appears in the very late *Landor's Cottage,* which is subtitled "A Pendant to 'The Domain of Arnheim' " but can also be seen as an adjustment of that story. As in *Arnheim* the only narrative progress involved is in getting to the paradisal place, and the only other significant action is in the activity of seeing. All the familiar apparatus appears, from the undulating path in (there is only one pass, and it serves as both entrance and exit) to the contours of the paradisal valley. Arnheim's grass shows up again: it "looked more like green Genoese velvet than anything else."[21] The path is a model of picturesque organization as is the vegetation surrounding the oval lake sitting in the amphitheatre of the valley. If Poe had not read Rousseau's *Cinquième Promenade,* he fashioned by instinct what Rousseau came upon and concluded to be an elegant gift of nature to the autonomous spirit: "At the *turn,* the stream, sweeping backwards, made an almost circular *loop,* so as to form a peninsula which was *very* nearly an island, and which included about the sixteenth of an acre. On this peninsula stood a dwelling-house" (264). In the house the observer is greeted by a young woman whom he thinks of as "the perfection of natural, in contradistinction from artificial *grace."* And that, with his emphasis upon the careful simplicity of the cottage, makes Poe's point. *Landor's Cottage* is a qualification of *Arnheim*, offering an alternative, which, from some points of view, is a corrective. Though it is equally picturesque, and to a considerable (though not equal) degree the result of the mind's manipulation, Landor's domain is in the classical paradisal valley. Its center is not a mishmash of exotic architecture but a tastefully fashioned version of the standard cottage in such pastorals. The sketch is not a step backward but a presentation of another way, associating artifice not with angels but with deeply engrained cultural tradition. Poe wanted to show that this too was a possibility; or, alternatively, that he could do it this way as well as the other, tuning in to familiar harmonies as well as angelic ones. But this is, after all, a pendant. *Arnheim* is the main place, the central postulate, the best way if not the only one. Even had Poe lived longer it is doubtful whether he would have gone further.

ᏧᏧᏧ TEN ᏧᏧᏧ

Nocuous Nourishment

The major activities of Poe's characters, what we see them actually doing or suffering, are designs to ensure survival. The differences between Ellison of *The Domain of Arnheim* and the unnamed protagonist of *A Descent into the Maelstrom* are those between willed and unwilled experience, active and passive engagement, spiritual and literal confrontation; but their involvements have the same radical motivation, survival at any cost. That element of cost is one of the reasons for Poe's emphasis on Ellison's extraordinary wealth. The description of the extent of Ellison's resources is another instance of Poe's literalness; it shows how much may be needed to survive exceptionally well. What is the going price for survival? Whatever it takes, apparently; or so it would seem from the choices Poe's characters make. In fact, it appears that any cost is acceptable, because the result, if achieved, is an unparalleled good for the characters involved. The subjective equivalent of Ellison's wealth is the enormous cunning, the fund of craftiness, with which the lethal imaginers lead their opponents toward dismemberment or entombment. They expend the energy of the self to such an extent that its depletion can lead to spiritual exhaustion and, very often, to their own entrapment: witness the endings of *The Tell-Tale Heart* and *The Black Cat*. The entrapment means that there is a kind of risk in lethal imagining, that is, the literal risking of one's freedom and life in a confrontation with experience, to which Ellison is not personally subject. Since these characters see their own survival at stake, they feel no hesitation in assuming the risk, even when they are aware of the full extent of the danger. Thus, it appears that there are two levels of possible cost for the lethal imagination: the expense of spirit; and the potential (and generally fulfilled) sacrifice of oneself. But if Ellison is not desperate or subject to threat, he is no less compelled to put all he has into his own exercise of self-sufficient creativity. To do less than the utmost possible would risk involving him in another kind of cost, enslavement to a world and to a level of nature in which the sinking of man is a regular occurrence. It was not his life that was challenged but the integrity of his spirit, the quality and independence of its existence if not the existence itself. Further, we do not have to read Baudelaire on Poe to see Ellison as a figure for the poet who is not so much *maudit* as averse to full affiliation with the social order. We remember his preference for qualified isolation, for a contextual autonomy that would permit selective association. To frustrate that desire would involve still another kind of cost, not spelled out in *The Domain of Arnheim* but fully comprehensible from Poe's attack on the vulgarity of bourgeois taste in *The Philosophy of Furniture*. At the least, an enforced association would disturb Ellison's acuteness of perception. That was one more contributing if not sufficient reason for creating the domain.

It is in this kind of context, with these questions of cost, craving, and survival, that the ironies in Stendhal come out for their richest display. Julien finds a more complete success at the end of his life than at any other time in it, and the degree of satisfaction in that period of unwilled achievement is hardly to be matched by any of his predecessors. If the degree of cost was the only element in the picture exceeding the degree of satisfaction, Stendhal did his best to make up for that. He knew that a parity between desire and capacity was the rarely mastered goal of Julien's predecessors, the only unequivocal good. Generous to every fault, he gave his hero a version of what he wanted. Though Julien cannot survive this perfection, he will at least have had it. At this point we encounter Stendhal's obsession with mirror images. That obsession is rendered not only in the relations among his characters, who are often paired with an opposite but equivalent figure (Mathilde and Mme. de Renal, or the various father images), but also in the events climaxing and ending Julien's career. When Julien was at liberty he was deeply beholden to his desires and the roles he assumed in order to enact them. But, as Victor Brombert has shown, when he was incarcerated he was most free. In our terms, then, he became, at the end, comfortably autonomous, beholden to nothing because all that he needed was there, given to him as a matter of justice. He was in debt, of course, owing his life as the price for his present independence; but he had the self-sufficiency, however temporary, and that time of parity was entirely without parallel. This was not the performance of a role but, in effect, the claiming of a place in history. Rousseau's most promising successor becomes as self-sufficient as his model, but only when there are no more promises to be made and just one more, the guarantee of his death, to be kept. Thus, each of Julien's extreme positions, the moment of glory before the fall from the heights and the moment of satisfaction before the fall of the axe, are mirror image opposites. Each is a moment of achieved desire, but the conditions could not be more different. One has cost persistent vigilance and the affection of M. de la Mole, a man he could not help but admire; the other gives him the love of a woman he had rejected and asks of him no more than his life. The situations are identical in form, but the relationships within them are precisely reversed. As for self-sufficiency, the autonomy which was the goal of the desire for parity, it comes with the wealth and position handed to Julien before his tumble; but an even purer kind comes with the dispossession and disgrace of his trial and incarceration. In the history we have been tracing up to Stendhal, the pleasant place threatened to turn into a trap, and it frequently did so. In Stendhal the opposite occurred: the trap turned into a place of unparalleled pleasure. Only Poe among the writers of his time could match Stendhal in his treatment of these complexities, and Poe's ironies had a very different tonality.

Stendhal might have been arguing that the early-nineteenth-century self could not succeed as comfortably as that of the mid-eighteenth century because his own was an age of different ambitions. Julien's mix of Rousseau and Napoleon was as unworkable historically as it was untidy in tone. Stendhal did side with Rousseau in seeing that some kinds of good could never be for the greatest number (Rousseau's practices were not for everyone), but some versions of that good appeared to be obtainable, at Stendhal's late date, only at the greatest price. Poe's world was more blatantly overwhelmed by cost than Stendhal's. Concomitantly, it was also more overt and urgent about ways to overcome the cost. If nostalgia for an encompassing enclosure for the self runs as a subdued but efficient stratum through both of Stendhal's major novels, it is not only more aggressive and demanding in Poe but also a sovereign structuring principle in his work. Finally and ironically it is Poe's only hope for the mortal self. His speculation in Gothic Orientalism (*Arnheim*) and the safer investment in a descendant of classical pastoral (*Landor's Cottage*) are the imagination's attempt to purchase a secure place for itself with no mortal cost. Neither Ellison nor Landor has to give up his own life (as Clarissa did) or that of a loved one (as Emile did) or pay the less drastic but terribly exacting price of Sterne's claustrophobic cosmos. Through artifice they avoid such ultimates and realize their autonomy.

But life, it seems, has to be involved somehow, somewhere, in the sacrifices one makes for the self's protection. If it is not life itself that has to go, then it is the feel of life. Poe's need, clearly, was to give the impression of transcending the pull of mortality so that the self, fooling itself, could imagine the surroundings of a transcendent Paradise. As Poe saw, the spoiler was organic nature, which was both the life and death of the party. His decision to offer an expurgated semblance of nature was not the promulgation of a lie—nobody was fooled—but the establishment of a necessary delusion. If one is so impatient as to want such a place here and now, then the natural context has to be incomplete, without earth colors. Poe's stress on the absence of those colors shows that he knew what had to be put aside. His decision to supplement *The Domain of Arnheim* with *Landor's Cottage* can be taken as a sign of uneasiness over these maneuvers; the later sketch is deliberately less drastic in what it removes from organic experience. Poe's is a borderline romanticism, with traces of a guilty conscience about that status. Still, we should not over-estimate his uneasiness about tampering with organic nature. The abysses of guilt in his work have far more to do with human nature than with the organic, and his protodecadence is so hungry an instinct that the qualms apparent in the appearance of *Landor's Cottage* after *The Domain of Arnheim* could only be slight and temporary. The costs of the quest for autonomy make up much of Poe's rendering of experience. His mind was so attuned to those costs that he could not speculate on the triumphs of the imagination without worrying, however briefly, that he might have gone too far.

Others worried about those costs as much as he did, though in different proportions and with different emphases. Among his American contemporaries these concerns about the price of the self's autonomy were frequently obsessive. Consciousness, nature, conscience, the cost to the self—how relations among the first two can affect the third and effect the fourth—are profound issues in American romanticism, particularly the kind that was uneasy with Transcendentalism and all related assertions about the mind's immense strength. *Moby Dick* is a harvest of conjectures on these matters. Melville knew all about the intricacies of romantic consciousness, not only the various Promethean possibilities of imposition (both Ahab and the Ancient Mariner try to force their will on the natural order) but also the Transcendental-Emersonian forms as well, including the classic version of the wreck of those forms in Coleridge's *Dejection*. Out of his rich awareness of the relationships among the various forms of the imposing consciousness, Melville makes Ahab both Promethean and Emersonian at once. In doing so he shows in the figure of Ahab how each can lead into an order of self with no exits. And all the evidence of unmistakable allusion indicates that Melville knew that the

Emersonian had already been present in Coleridge, particularly in the person of the speaker of *Dejection*. Ahab's Prometheanism needs no analysis. But there are times when the same character speaks in precise and carefully orchestrated echoes of the language of *Dejection*:

> Dry heat upon my brow? Oh! time was, when as the sunrise nobly spurred me, so the sunset soothed. No more. This lovely light, it lights not me; all loveliness is anguish to me, since I can ne'er enjoy. Gifted with the high perception, I lack the low, enjoying power; damned, most subtly and most malignantly! damned in the midst of Paradise![1]

> Would now St. Paul would come along that way, and to my breezelessness bring his breeze! O Nature, and O soul of man! how far beyond all utterance are your linked analogies! not the smallest atom stirs or lives in matter, but has its cunning duplicate in mind. (264)

In the first quotation Ahab is both Coleridgean and Satanic: "damned in the midst of Paradise." The second quotation is a skillful blend of Coleridge and Emerson. One of Melville's points, for those who can hear the voice of Coleridgean suffocation, is that the Transcendental analogy-hunter has his own kinds of egoism and therefore a special potential for barrenness and frustration. Melville knew about the prison-house of the self: "How can the prisoner reach outside except by thrusting through the wall? To me, the white whale is that wall, shoved near to me. Sometimes I think there's naught beyond" (144). He also knew that self-subsistence has an appealing quality of independence: in "The Grand Armada" Ahab, the sun, and the whaling ship are compared for their self-sufficiency: "[The sun] needs no sustenance but what's in himself. So Ahab" (319). But even in late-romantic, mid-century America, self-consciousness and self-sufficiency were as prone as they always were to becoming the content of a prison-house in which self-consumption was the only occupation left. In one of his more incisive ironies, Melville uses the imagery

of the new world's wildness to body forth the difficult autonomy of one kind of old and new world consciousness:

> And as when Spring and Summer had departed, that wild
> Logan of the woods, burying himself in the hollow of a
> tree, lived out the winter there, sucking his own paws; so,
> in his inclement, howling old age, Ahab's soul, shut up in
> the caved trunk of his body, there fed upon the sullen paws
> of its gloom! (134)

Another series of points—the same ones Melville had been
making since *Typee*—argues that the relations of consciousness and nature can be grotesque and cacophonous as well
as fluent and supple, that there can be hellish enclosures as
well as paradisal ones, and that when the enclosure is of one
moral kind, its surroundings may well be of another. Ahab
had pitted his private hell against the Paradise outside. But
in *Moby Dick* there are still other variations of the conflict
of the enclosure and its surroundings, examples which, along
with those echoing Coleridge, form a running criticism of the
more sanguine Transcendental forms of analogy. In the chapter "Brit," on the sea's savagery not only toward man but
toward its own offspring, Melville speaks of an inner Paradise
whose peace mocks the horrors outside:

> Consider all this; and then turn to this green, gentle, and
> most docile earth; consider them both, the sea and the land;
> and do you not find a strange analogy to something in
> yourself? For as this appalling ocean surrounds the verdant
> land, so in the soul of man there lies an insular Tahiti, full
> of peace and joy, but encompassed by all the horrors of the
> half known life. God keep thee! Push not off from that isle,
> thou canst never return! (236)

And in "The Grand Armada," when the becalmed boat, stuck
fast to a whale, runs into a whole school of them, the boatmen
stare into a quiet nursery deep in the center of the revolving
school:

But even so, amid the tornadoed Atlantic of my being, do I myself still for ever centrally disport in mute calm; and while ponderous planets of unwaning woe revolve round me, deep down and deep inland there I still bathe me in eternal mildness of joy. (326)

These are exactly the inverse of Ahab's experience, for they put all the hellish wildness outside of the center of experience, but the contrast and cacophony of inner and outer are the same. The resultant ambivalence blends not only with the other ambiguities in the world of Melville's imagination but also with the whole romantic experience with the *locus amoenus* of the self, the garden that can die into a desert. In Melville savagery abuts peace while sterility looks out on Eden.

There are similar contiguities in Hawthorne. In *Rappaccini's Daughter* he meditates on the speculations about self-sufficiency of the previous hundred years, and he maneuvers them into a commentary on the costs of the arrogance of consciousness. In fact, the situation in Rappaccini's garden is, like so many others of its time, strongly reminiscent of Julie's paradigmatic Elysium, though with some neatly ironic twists. The feelingful young man who came upon it in the midst of Padua "rejoiced that, in the heart of the barren city, he had the privilege of overlooking this spot of lovely and luxuriant vegetation. It would serve, he said to himself, as a symbolic language, to keep him in communion with Nature."[2] This is a fertile island in the insipid sea of the city, the precise opposite of the machine in the garden because it is a garden in the midst of the urbanized world. Such juxtapositions can be treated at a number of levels, and Hawthorne does exactly that, taking on several at once. Giovanni's perception of the place makes it an ideal of journalistic romanticism, an anachronistic one, of course, but no more so than its equivalents in the best Gothic fiction, which placed eighteenth-century sensibilities into sixteenth-century situations. The banality of Giovanni's comments reveals the limitations of his previous

experience and the kind of understanding with which he encounters the garden and its inhabitants. Early in the text Hawthorne speaks of "the tendency to heart-break natural to a
young man for the first time out of his native sphere" (93);
but this is less a universal predilection than a predictable one
in the kind of character Hawthorne is developing. Giovanni's
sentimentality, however commonplace, cannot be easily
thwarted. He comes out with his observation about the garden
as isolated and idyllic even after he has seen Rappaccini,
sensed a curious insecurity about him (Giovanni can guess
much from gestures and expressions), and wondered if this
place was "the Eden of the present world?—and this man,
with such a perception of harm in what his own hands caused
to grow, was he the Adam?" (96). So subtle an observation
ought to have made him somewhat uneasy about considering
the garden as a place of communion, yet he managed to do
so despite what he saw. His *Bildung* has begun, but it needs
the full set of events to take effect. Through these maneuvers
Hawthorne accomplishes several tasks at once. Not only does
he quickly give his protagonist a personality and point of view
but he also succeeds in making the garden both romantic and
traditional, contrasting it to the city in an accepted fashion,
and allying it, however sardonically, to Eden. The language
is familiar, indeed conventional, and deliberately so. We are
to see that the place is a paradisal enclosure, an old trope with
a number of intricate recent implications; but it is a special
version, imbued with a malignancy that is foreign to its romantic forebears.

Hawthorne's touch in these matters is admirable. He deftly
weaves Rappaccini's garden into traditions both distant and
immediate, sinking it securely into some of the imagination's
most comfortable habits. Yet with one or two gestures he
gives the garden an unsettling uniqueness, a difference that
disturbs because of this soothing and familiar context. The
garden is, of course, enclosed, separate, and independent. Further, it is as difficult of access as Julie's Elysium had been, but
old Lisabetta, the landlady who becomes a procuress, informs

Giovanni of "a private entrance into the garden" (108). She leads him to it, and Giovanni, "forcing himself through the entanglement of a shrub that wreathed its tendrils over the hidden entrance . . . stood beneath his own window, in the open area of Dr. Rappaccini's garden" (109). Here the sexuality of the entrance and entering is far more blatant than it is in Rousseau. As Lisabetta puts it, "many a young man in Padua would give gold to be admitted among those flowers" (108). The entrance leads to Beatrice, and Giovanni has found the way.[3] Still, it is not Beatrice's garden but her father's, a difference on which Hawthorne builds in order to subvert the tradition. The garden is the product of a lifetime of studies. As Beatrice says, it is her father's world (111). Giovanni had wondered whether Rappaccini was an Adam but he is, in fact, the lord of the microcosm, the father of Beatrice (who is the true Adam of this Eden) and the creator of the milieu. As for Beatrice herself, she is presented at one point as the classic ingenue whose isolation is broken into by a visitor from the greater world:

> The tinge of passion that had colored Beatrice's manner vanished; she became gay, and appeared to derive a pure delight from her communion with the youth, not unlike what the maiden of a lonely island might have felt, conversing with a voyager from the civilized world. Evidently her experience of life had been confined within the limits of that garden. (112)

Her insularity pushes their situation back to the model of Odysseus and Nausicaä but also forward to Byron: it recalls Don Juan's dealings on the island where Haidée lived with Lambro, her piratical father. This variant of the tradition was always ominous, and Hawthorne draws on that opportunity too.

Rappaccini, like Lambro, works closely with the threat of death, courting disaster for the sake of unusual profit. He is a master creator, a manipulator of nature's givens who carries nature beyond its normal confines, making it more beneficial than it is by making it more deadly. The paradoxes are harsh, almost crude: Rappaccini feels that nature's vegetable poisons can be turned into instruments of life, and, building on this natural duplicity, he produces "new varieties of poison, more horribly deleterious than Nature, without the assistance of this learned person, would ever have plagued the world withal" (100). His new poisons are the product of his new vegetable creations, the latter described not only in terms of artifice but of forbidden lusts:

> Several, also, would have shocked a delicate instinct by an appearance of artificialness, indicating that there had been such commixture, and, as it were, adultery of various vegetable species, that the production was no longer of God's making, but the monstrous offspring of man's depraved fancy, glowing with only an evil mockery of beauty. (110)

Rappaccini is even more of a pander than Lisabetta because he actually causes unnatural matings. This goes far beyond the sort of cooperation with nature, the improving of it, Julie practiced in the making of her garden of the self. All of Elysium bore her imprint, but it was composed of plants still fully themselves, though trained to satisfy their gardener. Rappaccini's plants are the product of perverse collusions between mind and the most dangerous practices of nature. The unnaturalness of their appearance objectifies his flagrant transgressions.

Rappaccini's is the free mind at play without hindrance, making a tonic out of that which seeks to destroy life. That kind of mind, committed to turning contraries into doubles (poisons into medicines, the threat of death into the support of life), would find its fullest stretch in turning heaven into hell and hell into heaven. Such radical reversals of value can be accomplished only by a mind of the utmost strength and freedom, bound to no other obligations than the exercise of that autonomy and the admiration of its own products. "Evil be thou my good" becomes, in Rappaccini's hands, "Poison be thou our health." A mind capable of accomplishing those turnings is too virile to be beholden to anything else; it has to be self-beholden. But if Rappaccini seems a dark parody of Julie and a subdued mimicry of Satan, he is also, in other ways, close to Hölderlin's Empedokles. Like the latter, Rappaccini turns nature into a tool, surely for the benefit of mankind (that point is never disputed, even by Baglioni, Rappaccini's enemy) but also as a device that makes its manipulator even more grandly self-sufficient. As he puts it to Beatrice: "Dost thou deem it misery to be endowed with marvelous gifts, against which no power nor strength could avail an enemy? Misery, to be able to quell the mightiest with a breath? Misery, to be as terrible as thou art beautiful?" (127). Rappaccini's perverted self has created a noxious garden and beneficent poisons, the benefits of which are for himself as well as others. Most of all, though, they are for his daughter, whose terrible beauty is a pure double of this garden of the self, this enclosure of unnatural practices. Poe's viable and lethal imaginations become, in Hawthorne's story, indistinguishable from each other.

Most discussions of *Rappaccini's Daughter* put it into the tradition of antiscientism, making of it a monitory tale about the dangers of fooling with Mother Nature. Of course it is that, a masterpiece in the *Frankenstein* mode. But the story is so extraordinarily complex, and the characterization so charged with ambiguity (only Beatrice emerges unscathed from Hawthorne's treatment) that to consider it as no more than a cautionary statement about laboratory hybris is to thin it out unnecessarily. *Rappaccini's Daughter* stands at a crucial juncture in the nineteenth century imagination; it is a landmark whose purpose is to pick up echoes and reverberations from all over the literary landscape. Hawthorne sensed the venomous potential implicit in some forms of self-sufficiency. Hints of malice had appeared in works such as Blake's "A Poison Tree," where the fertility of the paradisal garden is used by its owner for vengeance, not for love. But there are some especially telling ties to the past in Hawthorne's story, events and conditions that give it a formidable place in the tradition. Some of these we have seen, others are less patent but equally significant. For example, Rappaccini's attempt to find a suitable mate for his offspring echoes and parodies a conventional romantic situation, the uniting of young disciples by a wise old man, a figure who turns up in Hölderlin, Novalis, and Shelley among others. For our purposes the most pertinent version of that situation is the tutor's fostering of Sophie to be a fit partner for the mature Emile. We are aware of Rousseau's own uneasiness with the apparently blissful condition to which Emile had been brought, and his eventual realization that Emile's learning was not nearly over. But there is nothing in Rousseau comparable to Hawthorne's sense of the rankness of human nature, his uneasiness at the tampering with organic structures, and, most of all, his overwhelming awareness of cost. Emile finally gets his independence and an appropriate kind of peace. Rappaccini gets only the bitter fruits as the garden of poisonous children of his mind isolates and makes deadly the poisonous child of his body. Beatrice dies from an antidote designed to counter her poisons and conceal her isolation. The fact that she is vulnerable to health is Hawthorne's most incisive point.

The cost of autonomy had been suggested since Rousseau, usually in the form of suffocation or entrapment; but it is clear from the time of Stendhal, that is, from the beginnings of a self-criticism that was both attracted to the tradition and put off by it, that the matter of cost had come to be dominant. Indeed, it seems to have become obsessive. Stendhal, Poe, Hawthorne, and Melville had enough space between themselves and the past to take the quest for granted, seeing its full contours and possibilities. By their time all the possibilities had been exploited, and if they had seen the tentative successes, they had also seen the insufficiencies, the deaths of Julie and Werther, the dessication of Coleridge, the duplicity of Napoleon. Hawthorne crammed his story with ironic echoes because he saw the full history of what had been done and he decided to play with that history to the advantage of his theme. Of course he was somewhat unfair to the past: the magnificent paradoxical moments had taken place, there had been extraordinary works written about and under the pressure of the self's desire for flexible freedom. But Hawthorne, pushed by his own impulses, was compelled to see only the worst. His sense of radical evil mated with his reading of tradition to produce a fierce indictment of the manipulation of nature, a work which delineates and undercuts a masterpiece of arrogant autonomy. Poe's few twinges of uneasiness about the restructuring of nature were part of an extremely complex system in which the desire to build enclosed worlds of the self was seen to be potentially (and usually) deadly, but with a few suggestive exceptions. In the end Poe's exceptions spoke louder than Hawthorne's story: what Ellison did was what the decadents who succeeded Poe found most attractive and fruitful. But Hawthorne should not be counted out. Many of the fruits of Poe's successors turned out to be as fragrant and noxious as Rappaccini's plants, and the cost was equally as dear.

It is generally argued that decadent antinaturalism stems from Baudelaire's disgust with "de stupides céréales"[a] and, along with that, his love of an artifice which found its most delicate employment in the shadings of *maquillage*. In fact, though, Baudelaire's attitude emerges from a complex if subsidiary romantic line that goes back to Blake, touches on Novalis and Hoffmann among others, and peaks, before Baudelaire, in Poe's *Domain of Arnheim* (which Baudelaire translated as part of a group including *Landor's Cottage* and *The Philosophy of Furniture*). Blake's myth, which covers spaces as vast as those in *Paradise Lost*, is also like Milton's in needing established islands in the vastness, points where he can locate the action of his narrative. Beulah, his myth's version of the earthly paradise, is a comfortable but potentially seductive place of repose made for man's ease by the mercy of the Lamb.[4] One goes there for protection from the struggles of the World of Generation and the wars of Eternity, finding there all the pleasures of perfect cohabitation. At one point in Blake's myth Beulah functions as an echo of the Biblical Eden in which Vala and the Eternal Man mate ecstatically. Heaven, as a result, built a golden wall around Beulah. Naturally, man liked the whole business: "There he reveld in delight among the Flowers."[5] Beulah is an aspect of personality as well as a condition of being, that aspect objectified in a great deal of traditional pastoral and similar cozy tropes. Its lush and languid characteristics should not disguise the fact that Beulah is a way station, no more than that, between the fallen world and eternity.

Blake thickens his myth by drawing on the traditional pastoral contrast of city and country places and by giving Beulah an urban contrary in Golgonooza. Dante's *Commedia* had made the paradisal Garden a stop on the journey to the City of God, much as Beulah is on the way to Blake's fourfold Eden. Golgonooza is not, however, a terminus but one more stopping place, the city "nam'd Art & Manufacture by mortal men."[6] Fashioned by Los, Blake's high artificer, it is a walled-in citadel of art surrounded by a spiritual chaos it is forever struggling to keep out: "Around Golgonooza lies the land of death eternal; a Land / Of pain and misery and despair and ever brooding melancholy."[7] Golgonooza is an alternate state of the soul, that condition of being exemplifying the triumph of artifice over the encroachments of a raucous and quite possibly malevolent Nature. Of course Beulah is, from a Wordsworthian perspective, as much an instance of artifice as Golgonooza; but that is a perspective whose standpoint is outside the framework of conventional pastoral, and Blake is very deeply ensconced, however ironically, within that framework. (The confusion of these perspectives muddies naive readings of pastoral.) In one of its aspects Golgonooza is the human body. Generally, though, it represents all embodied form, that which is shaped by the imagination as a protection against the chaos of the fallen world. The city is very precisely placed within the limits of that world, in Blake's terms between Adam and Satan.[8]

The further complications of the myth need not concern us

here. What is important for our purposes is the way in which Blake's enclosed city compares to related places such as the paradisal clearing at the end of *Faust*. Blake's passionate antinaturalism makes the form Los carved out of chaos a very different place from Faust's image of the embattled consciousness, not only because one is urban and the other is not but because the contexts in which these enclosures of the self have to establish their contextual autonomy are radically different. In Faust's uneasy Eden man is forever busy with a universe that will always be nibbling at the dikes he has raised against chaos. His alertness has to be permanent, his repair work persistent. Blake's vision of the universe is ultimately anthropomorphic, and therefore he sees the triumph of imaginative artifice in Golgonooza as a prefiguration of the inevitable victory of the Human Form Divine.

The line of artifice we have begun with Blake takes in the magic gardens of *Klingsor's Märchen* (the emblematic center of Novalis's *Heinrich von Ofterdingen*) and E. T. A. Hoffmann's *Der Goldene Topf*. The local vegetation in both of those gardens has nothing to do with organic nature. Indeed, the selves the gardens render find in metallic and crystalline shrubbery a precise counterpart of the mind's modes of creativity. These places of transcendent pleasure touch, in one direction, on the embattled Paradise in *Kubla Khan*, whose pleasure dome reverberates to the distant rumors of impending violence. In another direction they touch on *The Domain of Arnheim* through the exaltation of human making. In a third they touch on Rappaccini's deadly manipulation of nature, serving as artful prefigurations of Rappaccini's rejection of conventional bounds. The first and third of these directions go into different aspects of romanticism; the second is part of the line leading to Baudelaire. The line also has to include, on the one hand, Charles Lamb's lavish praise of cities and his uneasiness with the country and, on the other, the morose antinaturalism of Vigny and Leopardi. All of these instances, however diverse, offer an impressive cluster of common concerns, most of all a compulsion to pit the capacities of the

mind's creativity against the very different energies of nature.
Baudelaire fused many of the facets of this subsidiary tradition
into a defining model and, in so doing, led to one of the
lovelier ironies of the time. Blake's antinaturalism set a precedent for poets whose ways, for all sorts of reasons, he could
never have condoned. Yet there is good historical sense in the
conjunction reached when someone like Swinburne, to whom
Baudelaire meant very much indeed, was also heavily involved
with a British artist, unknown to Baudelaire, who drew artifice
up into a moral and cosmic principle. Swinburne, the touchy
Victorian, was responding with a sound instinct to the radical
areas of agreement in his very different predecessors. The
ghost of Blake reappears, though surely with considerable
nervousness, in the art criticism of Baudelaire:

> Un éclectique ignore que la premiere affaire d'un artiste
> est de substituer l'homme à la nature et de protester contre
> elle. Cette protestation ne se fait pas de parti pris, froide-
> ment, comme un code ou une rhétorique; elle est emportée
> et naive, comme le vice, comme la passion, comme l'appétit.[b] [9]

Baudelaire's emphasis in this passage (it is Blake's emphasis
as well) is on what man can do naturally in competition with
nature, that is, the intrinsic superiority of his creative effects
over nature's irregular vegetables. The concern with inherent
capacities stresses the natural adequacy of the imagination,
particularly as it competes with induced capacities, which
may, quite possibly, be crippling. Baudelaire is the arch extoller of artifice, but his contempt for nature has to be inter-
preted in relation to its corollary, the exaltation of man's
innate, natural creativity. It is only when we consider creativity
that we perceive the finest shadings in his counterbalancing
of nature and artifice. They come out with particular clarity
in *Les Paradis artificiels*.[10] There is, he argues, an exceptional
visionary state that is abnormal, but no more so than any
other spontaneous condition of grace. To seek to will that
state into being through artificial means (*pharmacie*) is an act
of madness, replacing actuality with stage properties (439).

The purpose of the act is to create those equivalencies that have always tantalized man but seem to be especially urgent from the time of Rousseau: that is, the matching of desire and capability, the equalizing of the imagination's hungers and its ability to appease them. But artificial inducement is external inducement, bringing in from outside what ought to be generated from within. Baudelaire speaks of a man who has continued to seek "à la confiture maudite l'excitation qu'il faut trouver en soi-même" (451).[c] This is not only an abdication of the will (474) but a relinquishing of the imagination's autonomy, a denial of its self-sufficiency. In the state of pharmaceutical beatitude one is no longer one's own master (461). As a result, that felicitous transformation of reality, which is an essential task of the imagination (it is spoken of frequently in the *Salons*), is not triggered by the imagination's built-in stimulants but by foreign ones. That is not the kind of artifice Baudelaire cherishes.

It seems, thus, that the garden of the self comes in several styles and with varying costs. Vigilance is the price one pays for autonomy but the reward is a Baudelairean version of the *schöne Seele*: "Qu'est-ce qu'un paradis qu'on achète au prix de son salut éternel? . . . par l'exercice assidu de la volonté et la noblesse permanente de l'intention, nous avons créé à notre usage un jardin de vraie beauté" (477).[d] Hawthorne had sensed that Rappaccini's playing with poisons was not only contranatural but, despite Rappaccini's interest in curatives, ultimately antagonistic to man. Baudelaire did not share Hawthorne's worry about tampering with nature—they were at opposite ends in that regard—but he did see how such poisons could be inimical to much that was best in man. Perhaps he cherished the best because he knew the worst as well as anyone. At any rate he saw that the self-generated products of the imagination were precious, in great part, because they were the natural offspring of man's natural independence. Our autonomy is good not only for what it can do but for what it is: it is an indispensable aspect of the human. To tamper with that, whether through arrogance or an understandable desire for exaltation, is to risk a cost for which no achievement can compensate.

In the introduction to his text Baudelaire eases himself, with a well-placed echo, into line with history: "Tu verras dans ce tableau un promeneur sombre et solitaire, plongé dans le flot mouvant des multitudes" (436).ᵉ This is not simply an ironic allusion to Rousseau's *Rêveries d'un promeneur solitaire*; it is an implied identification of the roles of the *promeneurs* though with the obvious differences implied in "sombre" and "multitude." Rousseau was never really somber in his text, and the only multitudes he encountered on his walks were floral. Baudelaire offers himself as a contemporary, urbane Rousseau, in part a double and brother who also sought to make paradises for the self, in part a contrary whose botanizing catalogued a very different kind of flowers. But where Rousseau was at home in the locale of his walks (because all sorts of linkages of self and landscape were possible) Baudelaire found himself in a land of unlikeness. Outside his subjective landscape there is either the city, swarming and vulgar, or a nature with which he could find little in common. At the very least these conditions disclose a split between the most admirable qualities of the self and the crassness (urban and natural) of all that is out there. This means that there is no given externality to which the internal can comfortably conform, and that such conformity can come about only when the outer is deliberately shaped to match the inner. That is the place where artifice and the sufficiency of the imagination come in, just as they had done for Poe's Ellison. Baudelaire gives the mind a number of different jobs to do, and he is generally confident that it can do them.

But the split has some ominous implications. If conformity is imperfect, that is, if there are aspects of the self with which the shaped world cannot match, then the self is likely to end up feeding off itself rather than off a productive relationship of inner and outer. We have already seen such self-ingestion in *Werther*. Baudelaire's continuation of history was profound at this point. Indeed, his many-faceted function as a link between past and present was especially active here. His introductory remarks to the *Paradis artificiels*, in which he likens himself to Rousseau, are dedicated to J. G. F. His poem "L'Héautontimorouménos" is also so dedicated. The works have more in common than the dedicatee. The self-devourer of the poem ("je suis de mon coeur le vampire") sustains himself by living off himself, parodying the autonomy the author of the *Paradis artificiels* finds indispensable for the sustenance of the soul.[f] Baudelaire was a master of the sardonic harmonies that exist between these two works. Those who followed him found themselves sounding the same harmonies through characters who did not know that they were ingesting themselves until there was almost nothing left.

From the time of Julie's Elysium, the enclosure had implied a complex grouping of qualities, involving the shape and organization of the enclosure, the conditions of selfhood, and the wholeness and energy of nature. The relationships among the members of this triad were necessarily tense, and for a number of reasons: for example, the enclosure could not always satisfactorily image the self (Wordsworth); nature's capacities to create and destroy were equally potent (Goethe); the self could envision a situation where neither nature nor the conventional enclosure could keep up with its activities (Rousseau). This means that the relationships among the elements could be tenuous, difficult, and painful; yet when the relationships meshed the result was magnificent. We have seen it at its best. Two points are especially useful here. First, each of the elements of the triad is, or tries to be, self-sufficient, a quality frequently described through contained shapes of one sort or another, from the enclosed garden to the cycles of nature. Second, however autonomous the individual elements are, the group can achieve the result it seeks only when its components work together as a group. This does not mean that other combinations could not work or even that one element could not be left out. Stendhal is no romantic naturalist, but he shaped one of the finest instances of success that we have. Poe, in one of his phases, sets up an image that cuts out the central energy of nature, though that image is not developed enough for us to test its potential for success under pressure. The point is that this particular triad, working together, creates the dominant romantic version of the autonomous enclosure of the self. The line of artifice, which we have sketched out, and another line including Vigny and Leopardi are characterized (indeed, defined) by their antagonism to the romantic triad; but they are consciously going against the grain, and that is what makes these subsidiary lines so significant in the development of nineteenth-century literary history.

When the fervent contranaturalism of the decadents moves into its own position in history it establishes a more complicated and willfully ironic relationship to the romantic triad. One of the ways in which the decadents sought to establish their own meaning and character was by spoofing the romantic group, mocking not only nature but the kinds of creativity of which the romantic self was most proud. We seek to establish what we are by pitting ourselves against that which is strong and makes us uneasy. The flagrant teasing of nature had begun in Baudelaire (though there are hints of it as far back as Blake), and it takes its most sardonic (and desperate) form in Baudelaire's admirer, Huysmans. We have long acknowledged Baudelaire's understanding of his relationship to his immediate predecessors but we should give credit for a refined awareness of history to his decadent successors as well. They knew exactly what they were about when they drew the self in behind unnatural walls and sought the comforts of stasis. They saw that the enemy was not simply nature but *natura naturans*, whose compulsive forward thrust is the counterpart of the romantic artist's creativity and one of the major impulses behind it. The dominant tendencies of romanticism had sought to give form to the meeting of *natura naturans* and a consciousness that is zealously, necessarily struggling with it. Whatever the context of the deep stare at self, romantic consciousness is generally engaged (in a rela-

tionship that can range from love to profound uneasiness to
the most intense hatred) with *natura naturans*. However var-
iable in scope and penetration, however intense the impulse
to go elsewhere other than where nature may be driving, such
a grounding can give needed dimension to a self-awareness
that seems permanently threatened by the stasis of solipsism.
The decadents reacted to that centrality of *natura naturans*
with profound uneasiness. We can gather some of the reasons
for their attitude from Baudelaire's well-known letter to Des-
noyers on "les vegetaux," which hints at some of the deeper
strata in the anxiety over natural vitality: "J'ai meme toujours
pensé qu'il y avait dans *la Nature*, florissante et rajeunie,
quelque chose d'impudent et d'affligeant."[g][11] The issue is
made even more precise in Wilde's *The Decay of Lying*:

> Egotism itself, which is so necessary to a proper sense of
> human dignity, is entirely the result of indoor life. Out of
> doors one becomes abstract and impersonal. One's individ-
> uality absolutely leaves one. And then Nature is so indif-
> ferent, so unappreciative. Whenever I am walking in the
> park here I always feel that I am no more to her than the
> cattle that browse on the slope, or the burdock that blooms
> in the ditch. Nothing is more evident than that Nature hates
> Mind.[12]

What offended them, what was so vexing and impudent, was
nature's indifference—not merely its cruelty, the recognition
of which had long been a commonplace, but that overbear-
ingly cool aloofness, which seemed to come from its absolute
independence. And the fact that it was *natura naturans*, busy
in a world for which one had little sympathy, was all the more
exasperating. To reject it was easy enough. But Wilde, Huysmans, and others wanted more, for their impulse was to
counter the self-sufficient creativity of nature with their own.
Wilde makes that desire quite evident, and he indicates, in a
general way, how it can be activated. Just before the passage
quoted he makes a point about our need to complete the
imperfect productions of nature, an idea that is, in fact, the

same as that Poe's Ellison had pondered in the speculative
sections of the landscape pieces. Mind is, simply, superior to
nature, more gracious, less crude, with better taste. What is
new here is the emphasis on the elegance of mind; the confidence in its capacities is an old romantic tale. But the other
remarks, those about the loss of individuality and the indifference of nature, coupled with the Baudelairean-Wildean
awareness of nature's lavish creativity, are very different in
implication. They hint at some of the underlying sources of
uneasiness in Baudelaire and Wilde. Nature gives most pain
because it is the purest and most obvious image of that self-
sufficiency men ought to have, and the screws are turned even
tighter because nature is indifferent to the cravings for independence of its individual creations and to their own urges
toward creativity. Nature offends us because it is, as Baudelaire puts it, alive and arrogantly burgeoning; and, as Wilde
puts it, because in its aloofness it lumps us together with weeds
and beasts. We need not probe far into decadence to find a
hot and bitter envy of what nature can do and what it (re-
pugnantly) is.

The primary decadent weapon in this war was parody, lend-
ing a tonality that was very different from that in romantic
contranaturalism. Compare, for example, the tonal qualities
of *The Domain of Arnheim* with those of *The Decay of Lying*,
that is, Poe's confident assertiveness and Wilde's reiterated
impudence. Poe saw no need for smugness or parody, though
nature's dynamism was clearly a threat to Ellison's stability
and desire for stasis. Wilde did see the need and so did Huysmans, whose mockery of *natura naturans* and the creativity
associated with it is perhaps the most incisive, gross, and (yet)
subtle of the period. In the eighth chapter of *A Rebours* Des
Esseintes recalls how he had once preferred the most elaborate
imitations of flowers over the flowers themselves, in accord
with his instinctive preference for what man can make over
what nature can make. But that was too easy and also not
sufficiently insulting. Prefiguring Wilde's remarks about life
catching up with art, he turns to the productions of the hot-

house and seeks out genuine flowers that seem to be imitating artifice. In an impulse he empties his wallet, purchasing cart-loads of natural oddities. Some look as though made out of glossy cloth, others of metals like copper. One mimics the form of an iron spike. The masterpiece, "le chef-d'oeuvre du factice," imitates "un morceau de tuyau de poêle, decoupé en fer de pique, par un fumiste."[h] [13] But the flowers do more than copy reproductions. The most repellent resemble bits of or-ganic creatures, with appendages that recall the corkscrew of a pig's tail, a human tongue, or the remnant of a severed limb. These mockeries of the organic—nature imitating itself—are inferior, says Des Esseintes, and they appear only when nature can do no better: "Quand elle n'avait pu imiter l'oeuvre hu-maine, elle avait été réduite à recopier les membranes intérieures des animaux, à emprunter les vivaces teintes de leurs chairs en pourriture, les magnifiques hideurs de leurs gangrènes" (129).[i] Still, there is more to his attitude than an exaltation of artifice. Des Esseintes' purpose is not simply to play man up—he had done that already with his preference for artificial flora—but to knock nature down; most of all, to embarrass his antagonist by exposing its scandals. These oddities are the products of *natura naturans*, nature in its compulsive creativ-ity, man's only serious rival. This, Des Esseintes argues, is my enemy. Its tastelessness is clear, its folly obvious. It is creative, densely so, but it is ugly and vulgar. Driven by the need to produce, nature is so much the clumsy clown that it carries its exuberance to the point of creating anything, even aber-rations.

Des Esseintes' irony extends not only to displaying the shame of *natura naturans* but to mocking the essential mo-dalities of romantic creativity. Underlying the contranatu-ralism of the novel is an awareness that the classical order of romantic experience was based on a series of linking entities, each of which was (or ought to have been) whole and unified. The series itself, by its existence, gave an overriding unity to experience, which meant that the elements within the series could take part in a wonderfully coherent structure. Most of the elements are present in the following from *Werther*: "Ach könntest du das wieder ausdrücken, könntest du dem Papiere das einhauchen, was so voll, so warm in dir lebt, dass es würde der Spiegel deiner Seele, wie deine Seele ist der Spiegel des unendlichen Gottes!"ʲ ¹⁴ Of course nature's organicism is left out here, but it is an essential element everywhere in Goethe's text and can be assumed to finish out the sequence. The quotation shows how the components within the series can serve as similitudes of each other, with man's soul reflecting God and man's art reflecting his soul. In *Werther* the radical energies of the soul echo (and participate in) the energies of natural experience; thus, Werther can liken the poet to a raging river, with results more ironically accurate than he foresaw. Further, we know from Coleridge and many others that the art object— the poem, but in fact all created work—is also an active imitator of nature's wholeness and life. All of these mutually reflecting orders constitute the frame the artist works within, the sources that compel him to work, the elements his creativity shapes, and, finally, the totality his ordering has to forever assert. It is obvious that the basis of romantic art is analogy, as Werther's remarks imply. To create is to make similitudes. Romantic art is necessarily figurative, symbolic of the elements that make up romantic experience as well as the grand structure organizing it.

With these patterns in mind we can see the full extent of Des Esseintes' slyness. The plants he brings into his home, those offspring of *natura naturans*, are all similitudes of one object or another. He seeks to show nature as foul and stupid by showing it performing what *Werther* presents as an essential task of romantic creativity, the making of analogues. If nature is gross and vulgar there, in so basic a practice, then grossness and vulgarity must be basic to it. Des Esseintes knows what his nemesis stands for and where it ought to be hit. His insight is remarkable, his insult outrageous and brilliant.

In the war against nature's vitality these efforts of Des Esseintes are a major episode. He knows what he is about because, as the novel indicates from the beginning, he has a profound if selective knowledge of history. Yet there are curious factors in this masterpiece of parody that reveal that he doesn't know all he ought to know about his encounter with nature. The most difficult factors are not concerned with the quality of the parody but with the position of the parodist in relation to his victim. His intent is to show up nature, to make it play the fool for those who can appreciate such subtleties. But who is this show for? Des Esseintes is alone and remains so. Or, more precisely, he is alone with nature, a situation that repeats countless romantic instances, from the cheeriest to the bleakest, the most comforting to the frankly terrifying. At this point we need not dwell on the irony that finds Huysmans' decadent hero echoing romantic stances. The question now is whether the show of which he is the entrepreneur is for himself alone or for himself and nature. If nature is included in the audience, then Des Esseintes is guilty of anthropomorphizing, a sin he could hardly have forgiven in a poem like *Le Lac*, not to speak of an abundance of cruder cases. And if nature is not included, then Des Esseintes is talking to himself, his gestures solipsistic. Only he would be there to appreciate his spite. In fact, that seems to be the case. There is no direct address here as there is in *Le Lac*, none of the intricacies of relationship, the contacts made largely through the assertiveness of language, that are worked out with extraordinary subtlety in Lamartine's poem. Des Esseintes brings nature into the house with him, but he never gets through to it, never succeeds in making it the witness of its own shame. To make it a witness would make it a creature that could comprehend his jibes, and that would have made Des Esseintes a party to a kind of romantic pathos he could never condone. The show, it appears, is for himself alone, though he never really understands that point. Its purpose is to convince him of that which he already believes: that nature is a gross buffoon. There is nobody else to convince, nobody else listening—least of all nature itself. Des Esseintes' joke turns out to be self-directed. Its result is to reveal the degree of his isolation, a separateness from nature and other men that is partly willed but largely enforced by all that he is and chooses to be. From one point of view his actions are muddled, their direction not fully clear; from another they hint at a profound distress. We should not underestimate Des Esseintes' shrewdness—his parade of the flowers is remarkably clever—but we ought also to see the uneasiness that underlies his parodies. His is the wisdom of desperation, the knowledge of a man who is haunted (and hunted) by the energies of experience.

When Des Esseintes took himself out of society, he put himself into a cloistered situation whose contours, given the history culminating in him, were predictable. He scorned what Baudelaire scorned, but he refused to look for the solace that Baudelaire would sometimes find in the streets of Paris. Des Esseintes' place is a third term, beyond nature and the urban, drawing what it chooses from each as it stands apart from both. He builds an insularity shot through with hysteria, an Eden without innocence, higher or otherwise. He seeks an especially privileged Eden, one that is less like the Adamic version than the final one, the heavenly Jerusalem whose streets are paved with rubies and gold, though even that ultimate place might have been too busy for Des Esseintes. At some levels his enclosure of the self is as nostalgic as every other one of its kind; remembering is probably inescapable. Though this is more than a memorial of ancient selves, it does seek out many of the old privileges. For example, within his hermetic world he fashions instances of the few things that interest him, so that he need not go outside. He looks for as complete an independence as he can have, compatible with the need to be fed. He creates mockeries—that is, mock-ups— of a well-stocked ship's cabin and a monk's cell. The cell, of course, is the symbol of a willed imprisonment in stark self-sufficiency. As such it is a quietly sardonic parody (imitating monkish simplicity with the richest of stuffs) by this masterly novelist who never accepted a simple answer for anything. Within Des Esseintes' home stands the ship's cabin, like a refuge on an island: "Ainsi que ces boîtes du Japon qui entrent les unes dans les autres, cette pièce était insérée dans une pièce plus grande, qui était la véritable salle à manger bâtie par l'architecte" (48).ᵏ Des Esseintes sits like a bull's-eye at the center of images of insularity, in a room within a room within a house. Like Rousseau on Saint-Pierre, he sits at the point of concentricity, the purest image of contextual autonomy. But unlike Rousseau, he has not fallen into this situation by chance. Des Esseintes' world is self-created, parthenogenetic, the product of his money and his will. He alone has made it all that it is, which means that the degree of his success is a precise indicator of the effectiveness of his imagination. His autonomy is assumed, but the question for him, as for those before him, is whether his creativity can produce adequate structures to house and protect the autonomous self. Huysmans' novel is a testing of hermeticism, the most concentrated decadent proving of its desires and capacities.

Huysmans created a hero whose main activity is such testing. Des Esseintes probes the aptitudes of his selfhood and his chosen mode by a fierce assertion of privilege. He knows that being and doing are inseparable, that if he and the world are what he says they are, then he ought to be able to do with the world precisely as he pleases. The delicacy of his touch is perfectly compatible with the arrogance of his consciousness. This combination of the effete and the imperious is characteristic of certain modes of decadence, particularly those associated with Moreau, Huysmans, and Wilde. (Pater takes a somewhat different tack.) In Des Esseintes' case the situation is complicated by a special set of requirements. Above all he wants to circumvent immediacy, to make certain that he has as little direct contact with the reality of nature and of other people as he can manage. Most other people are gross, and the nature that made them is both gross and threatening. The need to distance oneself is obvious and insistent. Yet this does not mean that one has to give up the delights of experiencing. However desirable the state of stasis (desirable in part because it is unnatural, because *natura naturans* abhors stasis), one has to act in some way, if only to demonstrate what one is.

(Again we run into the inseparability of being and doing.) Action, it is clear, must be both distancing and direct: that is, action should not involve us immediately with nature or with others, yet it must be highly intense or we will lose all sense of the present actuality of our being.

There is one element in our experience that can satisfy this odd combination of requirements, and that is figurative language. Our similes, metaphors, and symbols have an unusually vivid life of their own, direct and immediately available, and at the same time they are mediating instruments, representing reality through indirection. They are not only analogies of experience but also objects of experience, conduits of reality, which can keep us from touching it and which yet offer us the reality of their own fascinating, mediating existence. If we were able to do a large part of our experiencing figuratively— that is, through similitudes—then we could exercise an unusual control over our lives. We could keep in contact with the world yet keep it off. We could take pleasure in the very modes that give us those mediated contacts. We could, finally, assert the strength, the self-sufficiency, the validity of our imaginations, the creators of those marvelous figures. Des Esseintes grasped the possibilities and advantages of figuration, particularly when taken to this level. That is what leads him to practice the highest privilege of all, living through analogy. Only thus could he show all that he is and all that he wants.

When Des Esseintes moves into his house at Fontenay he arranges for his servants to contact him through signals on a bell. Their world and his are to touch only through the mediation of the bell; he could not tolerate anything more direct. What is more, to avoid seeing the commonplace demeanor of the servant woman who has to pass by the front of the house on occasion, he has her dress in a vaguely religious fashion, something like a Beguine. That is, he wants her to be a semblance of someone else, another kind and quality of personality. Huysmans' touch is impressively subtle at this point. Des Esseintes moves from one level of indirection to another, from the bell to the costume, from the literal to the figurative. The purpose of the bell is single and practical: to permit his household to function without his having to see his functionaries. Part of the purpose of the costume is similar: to keep him from seeing the servant, yet to permit her to go about her business. In that aspect, it is as functional as the bell. Yet there is another aspect that is unique to the costume: through it he can experience the tone of a cloister without actually being in one: "L'ombre de cette coiffe passant devant lui, dans le crépuscule, lui donnait la sensation d'un cloître, lui rappelait ces muets et dévots villages, ces quartiers morts, enfermés et enfouis dans le coin d'une active et vivante ville" (47).[1] Figuration has made possible for him a vicarious experience of contextual autonomy; at this early stage in his experiment he feels that he needs all the support he can get. The difference between the costume and the bell is that the former is an analogy, enlarging the possibilities of his experience, and the latter is no more than itself, a useful mode of keeping the world away. The costume permits him to experience a distant part of life through the effect a similitude of that part has on his imagination. The bell does not act for the imagination but for what Des Esseintes' romantic forebears would have called the understanding, that which makes it possible for us to get on in the world. This passage, only two short paragraphs, offers an intricate lesson in the possibilities of consciousness and shows how it covers a range from coping with everyday business to expanding the scope of the imagination. In both cases he shows how the mind can so maneuver experience that we are able to live elaborately and yet not stain ourselves with the touch of life. *Natura naturans*, the maker of life, could never perform such intricate tricks.

Des Esseintes' passion for living through figuration extends into every ramification of his experience. His *orgue à bouche* ("mouth organ") is a synesthetic instrument in which the tastes of various liquors are combined to affect him with "des sensations analogues à celles que la musique verse à l'oreille" (77).[m] This is a simple shifting of sensations in which the pleasure lies both in the substitution—the making of metaphors—and in his ability to manipulate experience. More complicated, and deeper than a simple shifting, is his conclusion that he could satisfy an impulse to go to England by eating what he considers to be an English style meal in a Parisian restaurant populated by visiting Englishmen: "N'était-il pas à Londres dont les senteurs, dont l'atmosphere, dont les habitants, dont les pâtures, dont les ustensiles, l'environnaient?" (178).[n] He convinces himself that he cannot do better in London than he is doing in Paris, that the series of sensations he has achieved is perfect and would only be attenuated by his actual presence elsewhere. The difference between this kind of substitution and that of the *orgue à bouche* is that the latter substitutes experience on the same plane, one sensation standing for its counterpart, while the former offers the sensations that its own counterpart would offer but offers them in a different place, a place that is an obvious but satisfying fake. Why then leave for London at all, as he had originally planned? As it is he manages to have his Paris and eat London too. Thus he can be both aloof and involved, distanced and participating, keeping his living pure, without the possibility of disappointment. Most satisfying, perhaps, is his awareness that he is in absolute control of his experience, that his creations obey him:

> Enfin quelle aberration ai-je donc eue pour avoir tenté de renier des idées anciennes, pour avoir condamné *les dociles fantasmagories de ma cervelle*, pour avoir, ainsi qu'un veritable béjaune, cru à la nécessité, à la curiosité, à l'intérêt d'une excursion? (178-79; my italics)[o]

The offspring of *natura naturans* are no more submissive to their progenitor than the offspring of his imagination are to the faculty that made them. The mind is its own place and can make a London of Paris whenever it pleases.

Yet there is terror in Des Esseintes, a subliminal sense that all his maneuverings are the spinnings of a mind that can get nowhere and must be satisfied with its talent for manipulation. The most subtle of his approximations of life is also the most poignant. Des Esseintes is fascinated by a lady ventriloquist whom he has seen perform, and he takes her as a mistress. He is less interested in her body, however, than in appeasing a craving for a special bit of self-punishment. He coaches the woman carefully and, one night after she has depleted him, he brings a Sphinx and a Chimera into their room. The lady makes the images speak to each other in the prose of Flaubert. He shivers in cold ecstasy at some of the words: "Je cherche des parfums nouveaux, des fleurs plus larges, des plaisirs inéprouvés" (145).[p] But the ironies of the situation interweave and bind him:

> Ah! c'était à lui-même que cette voix aussi mystérieuse qu'une incantation, parlait; c'était à lui qu'elle racontait sa fièvre d'inconnu, son idéal inassouvi, son besoin d'échapper à l'horrible réalité de l'existence, à franchir les confins de la pensée, à tâtonner sans jamais arriver à une certitude, dans les brumes des au-delà de l'art!—Toute la misère de ses propres efforts lui refoula le coeur. Doucement, il étreignait la femme silencieuse, à ses côtés, se réfugiant, ainsi qu'un enfant inconsolé, près d'elle. (145)[q] [15]

He has maneuvered an imitator of life, a mistress of artifice, into creating a semblance. That semblance not only sounds an elaborate prose but speaks thoughts condemning his own attempts at achieving transcendence through artifice. He uses his will and money and the talents of the maker of false voices to bring home to himself his own limitations, the final torturing inadequacy of his imagination. Living through analogy had seemed like a sufficient procedure for both breaching the walls of the circle of self and staying snugly within its confines. In one way he was like Quixote, who found satisfaction in living through fictions; in another he was like the Coleridge of *Dejection*, who received from nature only what he put into it. But unlike Quixote he is aware that what he experiences is finally of his own making; and unlike Coleridge he uses that making to torture himself, to prove to himself that he cannot fly. Des Esseintes' efforts are themselves ultimately circular, going out from himself and the woman who is his instrument and returning, eventually, to himself. He is caught within that magic circle, trapped by his own inadequacies.

The most telling of Des Esseintes' tricks is his manipulation of the turtle. He bought the beast so that the colors of its carapace would tone down the raw, unsettled colors of the carpet. When that doesn't work he has the beast gilded, and the carpet submits to the overpowering effect. Yet he is still not fully satisfied: "Des Esseintes fut tout d'abord enchanté de cet effet; puis il pensa que ce gigantesque bijou n'était qu'ébauché, qu'il ne serait vraiment complet qu'après qu'il aurait été incrusté de pierres rares" (72-73).[r] This is a crucial move. Of course Des Esseintes wants the richest sort of elaboration, a turtle's back paved with jewels as well as gold, prefiguring the streets of the final Jerusalem ("les pierreries dont on lui avait pavé le dos" [82]).[s] But there is more here, a manipulation of object and image, which gets to the center of Des Esseintes' endeavors. The most congenial metaphor for the turtle is "ce gigantesque bijou" (this gigantic jewel). Why not, then, beat nature at its own game and turn the figurative into the literal by implanting real jewels in the turtle's back? The imagination is strong enough to turn nature into art by making verbal analogues out of what nature gives it, thinking of the beast as though it were a great bauble. But the imagination can be even more forceful than that, carrying the image to a more exalted plane and giving it a special, dazzling actuality. The beast was transformed into a phrase and the phrase, in its turn, into a gem. This was not, however, a simple return to concreteness, but a progression up a scale on which turtles would be at the bottom and jewels would be at the top. The incarnation is not from word to flesh, as the old ways would have it (why go down the scale to the more vulgar?), but from flesh to word and word to jewel. Flesh is transcended by language, the unliteral and indirect, but then language is transcended by a higher sort of literalness, which has neither the resilience of flesh nor its potential for spoilage. Des Esseintes, the lover of substitutes, exchanges figuration for actuality, but an actuality that is more in keeping with his own tastes and predilections than the first one had been. He shows that he can be as literal as *natura naturans*, as concerned as it is with creation. Yet, again, *natura naturans* could never accomplish such clever, complicated gestures. It simply isn't bright or sensitive enough.

But then nature turns out to be nasty enough and takes its revenge. The change from the figurative to the literal kills the beast. Des Esseintes' highest flight, his grandest assertion of the imagination's independence and adequacy, is cut off by the intervention of the lowest stage of the literal. This episode is the precise complement of the scene with the lady ventriloquist. There he had been in despair, regressing like a hurt child to the side of the parodic mother figure, because the exaltation he wanted was not within his capacity. With the turtle he made his most refined attempt to show how the mind can manipulate every aspect of experience. But *natura naturans*, the crassest of those aspects, rejects the imposition and ends the game. The turtle's fate prefigures the threat of death at the end of the novel. It is a private lesson for Des Esseintes, but he did not yet know that he was being schooled.

At the end he knows something, of course, though he never comes to see the full extent of his previous ignorance. His mockery of nature's analogy making in the episode with the exotic plants ignored the patent fact that his own mode of living was also a brazen analogy making, as intense and obsessed as that of any of his predecessors. Des Esseintes' compulsion to live through simulation and semblance is, finally, an extension of the romantic impulse to figuration, to seeing man (as Werther does) as the little lord of the microcosm making images out of that which moves him. Of course the differences between Des Esseintes and his predecessors remain, and they are crucial. In the organic world of Werther there are no gaps or discontinuities; that kind of nature abhors a lacuna. It is a world based on the Great Chain of Being, emphasizing plentitude, continuity, and gradation, tolerating no barriers because it functions through a harmonious se-

290 ◆ *Nocuous Nourishment*

quence of linkages.[16] Werther assumes that the mirroring capacities of art and the human soul depend on that sequence
for order and inspiration. But that is a basis for creativity Des
Esseintes could never accept. In fact, one of the defining acts
of the decadents is the attempt to break up parts of that
linkage. The connection with the Divine tends to remain. Indeed, the religious imagery woven through *A Rebours* is one
of the major creators of the novel's tensions, and similar effects
appear in Wilde and others. The major link they seek to frac-
ture is, of course, the one with nature. If they could not do
away with nature entirely, they could try to load its products
with dissembling paraphernalia, as Des Esseintes did with the
unfortunate turtle. Alternatively they might deal only with
selected elements of nature, the more gracious representatives
of the whole, such as its light. Des Esseintes' curious dining
room admits the light of nature through colored glass, and
then only very darkly: "le jour traversait donc, pour éclairer
la cabine, la croisée, dont les carreaux avaient été remplacés
par une glace sans tain, l'eau, et, en dernier lieu, la vitre à
demeure du sabord" (48).[t] By the time the light reaches him
it is far from its point of origin and very different from its
original state.

   This purified light stands for all those stimuli strained
through a myriad of filters before they get to Des Esseintes.
Once they reach him he liberates the stimuli from any relation
to their source, keeping them locked up within his enclosure
to mirror and mimic each other. The microcosm has become
all. Nature has meaning only as a horn of plenty whose fruits
are fastidiously picked over by this most careful of shoppers.
The intricate affiliation of microcosm and macrocosm that
had been assumed for the romantic enclosure has been replaced by simple contiguity, and affiliation is now found only
among the elements within the microcosm rather than among
a series of elements of which the microcosm is one. Thus the
strange, dislocated independence of the *orgue à bouche* and
the perfumes he orchestrates into symphonies: these effects
build upon an exchange of stimuli that have already reached

the microcosm and are now comfortably ensconced within it. Whatever they derived from nature has long since been separated from its source. Wordsworth's ennobling interchange, the marriage of the cosmoses within and without, has given way to an onanistic interchange within the enclosed world of the recipient. In its turn the new form of relationship builds up immense pressures. Once inside his house and his self, the stimuli work on Des Esseintes with vehemence. His senses are driven to expand their scope and content as they are pushed into more and more exquisite combinations and analogies. Held tightly within the enclosure of a self that will not return what it receives, the senses are forced to expand within its confines, feeding on each other's substance and growing fat by that feeding until they push at the walls of a container that does not know how to give. Mario Praz quotes Gustave Moreau (a favorite of Huysmans) as claiming two defining principles for his painting, the Necessity of Richness and the Beauty of Inertia.[17] Yet the latter, an opulent lassitude, is only one more decadent mask, a false face of passivity, for Des Esseintes actually lives in a frantic, diligent luxuriance, which he is forever pushing to new limits. This activity takes place in a field whose constricted limits are both its glory and its deadly limitation.

Here too Des Esseintes links up with his predecessors, for what happened to Werther very nearly happened to him. Both books seem to have much the same plot, though with an ending available to Des Esseintes that was simply not there for Werther. In both cases the container could hold no more, and it had either to explode in the crack of a pistol shot or assume a new shape permitting it to give. Barbey d'Aurevilly's well-known comment about *A Rebours* helps us to link up, as well as to distinguish, a number of critical junctures in literary history:

Un jour, je défiai l'originalité de Baudelaire de recommencer les *Fleurs du mal* et de faire un pas de plus dans le sens épuisé du blasphème. Je serais bien capable de porter à l'auteur d'*A Rebours* le même défi: "Après les *Fleurs du mal*—dis-je à Baudelaire,—il ne vous reste plus, logiquement, que la bouche d'un pistolet ou les pieds de la croix." Baudelaire choisit les pieds de la croix.

Mais l'auteur d'*A Rebours* les choisira-t-il?[u] [18]

The ending of Huysmans' novel leaves no doubt about his hero's craving for certainty and peace, and the direction it would take.[19] Werther took no such step, and his creator could never have done so. For Goethe's hero there was only termination, for Des Esseintes there was an exhausted reemergence. For both there was that bitter parody of self-sufficiency in which one consumes oneself, living off oneself because nothing else seems sufficiently nourishing. Des Esseintes had guessed that the question of nourishment was somehow at the heart of his contranaturalism. Toward the end, when he was very weak, his doctor prescribed a peptone enema as the most suitable mode of feeding. Des Esseintes accepts it with relish, seeing it as the climax of his penchant for artifice. But more, the enema spites *natura naturans*; his temptation to offend it has never let up: "enfin quelle décisive insulte jetée à la face de cette vieille nature dont les uniformes exigences seraient pour jamais éteintes" (256).[v] Here, he thinks, is the high point of his quest for independence. But Huysmans knew better, knew that all along Des Esseintes had been stuffing himself with himself in the ultimate version of self-sufficiency: "Il vivait sur lui-même, se nourrissait de sa propre substance, pareil à ces bêtes engourdies, tapies dans un trou, pendant l'hiver" (108).[w] To use Baudelaire's words from *Les Paradis artificiels*, this is an "épouvantable mariage de l'homme avec lui-même."[x] [20] Autonomy can go no further than this, and it can never be more terrifying.

In his essay on *Nature* Emerson worried about some implications of idealism, and they are precisely the problems that the later figures in the history we have been examining ought to have been worrying about:

Idealism is a hypothesis to account for nature by other

principles than those of carpentry and chemistry. Yet, if it only deny the existence of matter, it does not satisfy the demands of the spirit. It leaves God out of me. It leaves me in the splendid labyrinth of my perceptions, to wander without end.[21]

Emerson was concerned with the idealist denial of the actuality of matter, how that seemed to cut him off from flesh-and-blood people ("denying substantial being to men and women") and leave him only with himself, inside of himself. He did not feel comfortable with its potential for entrapment. After all, the romantic journey within was generally imaged as a terrestrial journey, on the sea, into mines, up a mountain. If there was only a wandering around inside, treading the corridors of one's private labyrinth, then one would, in effect, get nowhere at all, ending only in self-devouring. It was accepted doctrine that the ego had to put something out there in order to realize itself. One needed to act outside in order to enact meaningful events inside.

But these issues were more than the parochial problems of idealists. Given different shapes they affected most versions of the romantic tradition. The best minds among the decadents—Pater, Huysmans, Wilde—knew of them, worried them through, dramatized them. Des Esseintes' idea of living by figuration was not good enough, though we can see why he tried it out. In *Dorian Gray* Wilde tested a different possibility. Dorian was fascinated and perhaps somewhat repelled by Des Esseintes' experiment, and though he felt that the book could have been written about himself, he acts very differently than does Des Esseintes. Wilde's novel is a sardonic fairy tale in which the hero's main wish is granted: "Ah! in what a monstrous moment of pride and passion he had prayed that the portrait should bear the burden of his days, and he keep the unsullied splendour of eternal youth!"[22] Dorian, like Julien Sorel and unlike Des Esseintes, wants an elaborate involvement with the world. Like everyone else, he wants to keep his selfhood from being touched by the vicissitudes of experience.

He falls into a dazzling, deadly compromise. The chamber of the self, away where the world cannot invade it, is inhabited by a figure that does his dying for him. Dorian soars in society and declines by proxy through literal figuration. The parody of Huysmans, the precise reversal of his hero's situation, could not be more precise or incisive. But there are other twists involved: the novel implies that it is art that ought to be autonomous and inalterable, not man. *Dorian Gray* is based on the ancient distinction of kind and durability between life and art. Dorian acts as though those distinctions had now been reversed, though in fact, of course, they had not. At the end the portrait returns to its traditional relation to temporality, that is, its independence from it. Dorian, like so many others at different times and in different ways, revives a facet of Don Quixote. Cervantes' rider turns out to be a mad prefiguration of the decadent impulse to live life as though it were art; in Dorian's case, claiming for himself the independence that his contemporaries felt was proper peculiarly to art. Art turns out to be for its own sake after all; it is certainly not for man's. Wallace Stevens's query about a Keatsian pastoral tradition—"Is there no change of death in Paradise? / Does ripe fruit never fall?"—is finally the appropriate one for Dorian Gray, who relished Keats. Paradises and Palaces of Art were the right idea, but for art, not for man.

Decadence is an epilogue, the last words and rounding out of a sequence that had begun on the Ile de Saint-Pierre and in the green enclosure of Madame de Wolmar. Julie's garden became Ellison's eclectic Paradise, and that domain turned into Des Esseintes' dining room and the sequestered schoolroom where Dorian Gray kept his likeness. Julie's tactful touch of the human was transformed into Ellison's more forceful imposition, and the latter into the full and deadening humanization of Des Esseintes. Julie's Elysium and Ellison's Arnheim had been difficult to get into, but one could always get out of them to touch at the world. Des Esseintes had to be carried from his shelter, and Dorian died within his own. The protagonists of Huysmans and Wilde worked with compromises, approximations; but like the sequestered aristocrats in *The Masque of the Red Death*, they carried their antagonists deeply inside.

Emerson's worries about the labyrinth were justified, though not for himself. For the decadents there was, after all, no way out of oneself. The potential for entrapment, which had unnerved Saint-Preux, was realized and not just for an occasional Werther, but for much of an entire generation. How ironic it is that a masterly reading of this dead end should come in a study of rebirth, Walter Pater's *The Renaissance*:

> Experience, already reduced to a group of impressions, is ringed round for each one of us by that thick wall of personality through which no real voice has ever pierced on its way to us, or from us to that which we can only conjecture to be without. Every one of those impressions is the impression of the individual in his isolation, each mind keeping as a solitary prisoner its own dream of a world.[23]

Notes

CHAPTER ONE

1 Samuel Richardson, *Clarissa: Or, the History of a Young Lady* (London: Everyman's Library, 1967), I, 2. Further references, including volume number, will be in the text.

2 Margaret Anne Doody, *A Natural Passion: A Study of the Novels of Samuel Richardson* (Oxford: Clarendon Press, 1974), p. 134.

3 Ian Watt, *The Rise of the Novel* (Berkeley: University of California Press, 1967), pp. 188-89.

4 *The Correspondence of Samuel Richardson*, III (London: Richard Phillips, 1804), 252-53.

5 The word "Paradise" comes from the Old Persian *pairidaēza*, meaning a park or enclosure. We need the phrase "paradisal enclosure" because the enclosing is not implicit in the English "Paradise" and not all Paradises since Ancient Persia have been enclosed.

6 Watt, *The Rise of the Novel*, pp. 222-25; Christopher Hill, "Clarissa Harlowe and her Times," in *Essays in Criticism*, 5 (1955), rpt. in *Samuel Richardson: A Collection of Critical Essays*, Twentieth Century Views, ed. John Carroll (Englewood Cliffs, N.J.: Prentice-Hall, 1969), pp. 113-14.

7 Daniel Defoe, *The Life and Adventures of Robinson Crusoe*, ed. Angus Ross (Harmondsworth: Penguin English Library, 1965), p. 192. Further references will be in the text. For a view that Crusoe is content in his self-sufficiency see W. B. Carnochan, *Confinement and Flight* (Berkeley: University of California Press, 1977), pp. 30ff.

8 John Milton, *Complete Poems and Major Prose*, ed. Merrit Y. Hughes (New York: Odyssey Press, 1962), *Paradise Lost*, XII, 587. Further references will be in the text.

9 For a lengthy comparison of Richardson and Rousseau, including quotations from contemporary analyses, see Joseph Texte, *Jean-Jacques Rousseau and the Cosmopolitan Spirit in Literature*, trans. J. W. Matthews (London: Duckworth, 1899), Book Two, pp. 208-54.

10 Mornet sees the effect of Richardson mainly in "le 'doux coloris d'innocence' et les tonalités qu'il y voulut" ("the 'sweet coloring of

innocence' and the tonalities that he sought for it"). See his edition of the novel (Paris, 1925), I, 95.

[11] Jean-Jacques Rousseau, *La Nouvelle Héloïse*, in *Œuvres Complètes de Jean-Jacques Rousseau*, II, ed. Bernard Gagnebin and Marcel Raymond (Paris: Gallimard, 1959), 199. Further references will be in the text.

[12] To call a garden "Elysium" was not unusual in the eighteenth century. For material especially relevant to Rousseau see H. F. Clark, "Eighteenth Century Elysiums. The Role of 'Association' in the Landscape Movement," in *Journal of the Warburg and Courtauld Institutes*, 6 (1943), 165-89; Eva Maria Neumeyer, "The Landscape Garden as a Symbol in Rousseau, Goethe and Flaubert," in *Journal of the History of Ideas*, 8 (1947), 187-217; Peter Willis, "Rousseau, Stow and *Le Jardin anglais*: speculations on visual sources for *La Nouvelle Héloïse*," in *Studies on Voltaire and the Eighteenth Century*, 90, ed. Theodore Besterman (Banbury: The Voltaire Foundation, 1972), 1791-98.

[13] The necessity of having an autonomous *azile* within oneself turns up at several points in *Rousseau Juges de Jean-Jacques*, e.g., *Œuvres Complètes*, I, ed. Marcel Raymond (Paris: Gallimard, 1964), 745. See also, in the same volume, the third of the *Lettres à Malesherbes*, 1139-40.

[14] The separate private place within an enclosure occurs in *Paradise Lost*, not only in the Bower of Adam and Eve (see IV, 690-703) but also when Satan, mad with frustration and jealousy, imagines them "Imparadis't in one another's arms / The happier *Eden*" (IV, 506-07).

[15] For a sampling of important uses of the term see the following pages in the Pléiade text: 32, 53, 100, 201, 208, 335.

[16] The history of the garden paradise through the Renaissance is traced in A. Bartlett Giamatti's *The Earthly Paradise and the Renaissance Epic* (Princeton: Princeton University Press, 1966). See also Stanley Stewart, *The Enclosed Garden: The Tradition and the Image in Seventeenth Century Poetry* (Milwaukee: University of Wisconsin Press, 1966) for an excellent discussion of the *Song of Songs*, its eroticism, and the allegorical readings thereof. Central to the situation in *Julie* is the line from the *Song of Songs*, "A garden inclosed is my sister, my spouse" (IV, 12). Wolmar, who plays a paternal role in the ménage, urges Saint-Preux to think of Julie as "votre soeur et votre amie" (424), an irony with manifold reverberations.

CHAPTER TWO

¹ For some useful comments on Satan's argument here see A. J. A. Waldock, *Paradise Lost and its Critics* (Cambridge, England: Cambridge University Press, 1966), p. 71.

² From William Hazlitt's essay "On Shakespeare and Milton" in *Lectures on the English Poets, The Complete Works of William Hazlitt*, V, ed. P. P. Howe (London: J. M. Dent, 1930), 64.

³ John Milton, *Complete Poems and Major Prose*, ed. Merrit Y. Hughes (New York: Odyssey Press, 1962), p. 99.

⁴ Ibid., p. 555.

⁵ For an excellent survey from a somewhat different point of view see Ronald Grimsley, "Rousseau and the Ideal of Self-Sufficiency," *Studies in Romanticism*, 10 (1971), 283-99.

⁶ *Œuvres Complètes de Jean-Jacques Rousseau*, III, ed. Bernard Gagnebin and Marcel Raymond (Paris: Gallimard, 1964), 144. See also the note on 1320-21.

⁷ Ibid., 154-55.

⁸ Henri Frédéric Amiel, "Caractéristique générale de Rousseau," in *J. J. Rousseau jugé par les Genèvois d'aujourd'hui* (Genève: Jules Sandoz, 1879), p. 40.

⁹ *Œuvres Complètes*, I (1964), ed. Marcel Raymond, 1149; cf. 1154.

¹⁰ Ibid., 936.

¹¹ Marcel Raymond's *Jean-Jacques Rousseau. La quête de soi et la rêverie* (Paris: Jose Corti, 1962) is indispensable for work on the *Rêveries*. There are important comments in Robert Osmont, "Contribution à l'étude psychologique des Rêveries du Promeneur Solitaire," *Annales de la société Jean-Jacques Rousseau*, 23 (Genève: A. Jullien, 1934), 7-135; and in Robert Ricatte, *Réflexions sur les "Rêveries"* (Paris: Jose Corti, 1960).

¹² *Œuvres Complètes*, I, 1005. All further references will be in the text.

¹³ *Œuvres Complètes*, IV, ed. Bernard Gagnebin and Marcel Raymond (Paris: Gallimard, 1969), 279-80; cf. 298 and fn. 2, 1335.

¹⁴ For closely related material see the chapter on Rousseau in Georges Poulet's *Les métamorphoses du cercle* (Paris: Librairie Plon, 1961).

¹⁵ *Œuvres Complètes*, I, 645.

[16] *Correspondance Complète de Jean-Jacques Rousseau*, ed. R. A. Leigh, 27 (Oxford: The Voltaire Foundation, 1976), 148.

[17] *Œuvres Complètes*, I, 753.

[18] Compare the version in the *Confessions, Œuvres Complètes*, I, 643-44.

[19] Compare Saint-Preux on the mountain in *La Nouvelle Héloïse, Œuvres Complètes*, II, 78.

[20] "Every 'construction,' and every contact with a 'centre' involves doing away with profane time, and entering the mythical *illud tempus* of creation": Mircea Eliade, *Patterns in Comparative Religion* (New York: World Publishing, 1963), p. 378.

[21] *L'œil vivant* (Paris: Gallimard, 1961).

CHAPTER THREE

[1] *The Life and Opinions of Tristram Shandy, Gentleman*, ed. James A. Work (New York: The Odyssey Press, 1940), p. 206. All further references will be in the text.

[2] *Letters of Laurence Sterne*, ed. Lewis Curtis (Oxford: Clarendon Press, 1935), p. 77.

[3] See the complex moment of lucidity in Quixote's comments at the end of chapter seventeen in part two.

[4] See not only Mann's essay on Quixote but also Hans Eichner, "Thomas Mann und die deutsche Romantik," in *Das Nachleben der Romantik in der modernen deutschen Literatur*, ed. Wolfgang Paulsen (Heidelberg: Lothar Stiehm, 1969), pp. 152-73; and Oskar Seidlin, "Laurence Sterne's *Tristram Shandy* and Thomas Mann's *Joseph the Provider*," in his *Essays in German and Comparative Literature* (Chapel Hill: University of North Carolina Press, 1961), pp. 182-202.

[5] See for example Robert Gorham Davis, "Sterne and the Delineation of the Modern Novel," in *The Winged Skull*, ed. Arthur Cash and John Stedmond (Kent, Ohio: The Kent State University Press, 1971), pp. 21-41.

[6] Curtis, *Letters*, p. 81.

[7] There are numerous indications in the novel that wordless gestures can touch areas that words have no way of reaching.

[8] Denis Diderot, *Correspondance*, IV, ed. Georges Roth (Paris: Les editions de minuit, 1958), 189.

⁹ See John Traugott, *Tristram Shandy's World* (Berkeley: University of California Press, 1954).

¹⁰ For a useful analysis of such imagery see Frank Brady, "*Tristram Shandy*: Sexuality, Morality, and Sensibility," in *Eighteenth Century Studies*, 4 (1970), 41-56.

¹¹ Two of the most important studies of this change are Erich Kahler, *The Inward Turn of Narrative*, trans. Richard and Clara Winston (Princeton: Princeton University Press, 1973); and George Lukács, *The Theory of the Novel*, trans. Anna Bostock (Cambridge, Mass.: MIT Press, 1971). Hegel, of course, lurks in the background of any study of this increasing subjectivization.

¹² "Conjectures on Original Composition," in *English Critical Essays (Sixteenth, Seventeenth, and Eighteenth Centuries)*, ed. Edmund Jones (London: Humphrey Milford, 1940), p. 337.

¹³ *Charakteristen und Kritiken I, (1796-1801)*, ed. Hans Eichner, Kritische Friedrich-Schlegel-Ausgabe, II (Munich: Ferdinand Schöningh, 1967), 318.

¹⁴ Eichner, *Charakteristen und Kritiken I*, 173.

¹⁵ Ibid., 262; see also *Ideen*, no. 69, 263.

¹⁶ Ibid., 183.

¹⁷ Ibid., 159.

¹⁸ Ibid., 318-19.

¹⁹ Ibid., 331.

²⁰ Ibid., 331.

²¹ From his 1818 lectures in *The Complete Works of Samuel Taylor Coleridge*, IV, ed. W. G. T. Shedd (New York: Harper & Brothers, 1844), 281. See also *Aids to Reflection*, 137, in *Works*, I, ed. Shedd.

²² Coleridge, "Lecture Nine" in *The Complete Works*, IV, 278. The sentence is slightly misquoted; see *Tristram Shandy*, p. 229.

²³ Ibid., 282.

²⁴ Ibid., 282.

²⁵ Ibid., 282.

²⁶ Ibid., 268.

²⁷ Ibid., 268.

²⁸ See Anthony Close, *The Romantic Approach to "Don Quixote"* (Cambridge: Cambridge University Press, 1978).

²⁹ Eichner, *Charakteristen und Kritiken I*, 312.

³⁰ See Friedrich Schlegel, *Literary Notebooks, 1797-1801*, ed. Hans Eichner (London: The Athlone Press, 1957).

CHAPTER FOUR

¹ *The Poetry and Prose of William Blake*, ed. David Erdman (Garden City, N.Y.: Doubleday, 1965), p. 656.

² See the poem beginning "With happiness stretched across the hills" in Blake's letter to Thomas Butts of 22 November 1802 in Erdman, *William Blake*, p. 692. Compare the poem in the letter to Butts of 2 October 1800 (Erdman, pp. 683-84), where Blake has a vision of nature transformed into its true, anthropomorphic status: that imaginative process is actually very different from Blake's use of correspondences, since in the latter nature is utilized but does not change its ontological qualities.

³ Erdman, *William Blake*, p. 590.

⁴ Novalis, *Die Lehrlinge zu Sais* in *Schriften*, ed. Paul Kluckhohn and Richard Samuel (Stuttgart: W. Kohlhammer, 1960), I, 105.

⁵ Kluckhohn and Samuel, *Schriften*, p. 100.

⁶ Letter of 3 February 1818 to John Hamilton Reynolds in *The Letters of John Keats, 1814-1821*, ed. Hyder Edward Rollins (Cambridge, Mass.: Harvard University Press, 1958), I, 224-25.

⁷ Erdman, *William Blake*, p. 271.

⁸ Ibid., p. 545.

⁹ Ibid., p. 229.

¹⁰ Ibid., p. 123.

¹¹ Ibid., pp. 653-54.

¹² Ibid., p. 270.

¹³ Ibid., p. 37.

¹⁴ *The Collected Works of Ralph Waldo Emerson*, ed. Robert E. Spiller and Alfred R. Ferguson (Cambridge, Mass.: Belknap Press, 1971), I, 19. Further references to this edition are in the text.

¹⁵ Ralph Waldo Emerson, *Journals of Ralph Waldo Emerson*, ed. Edward Waldo Emerson and Waldo Emerson Forbes (Boston and New York: Houghton Mifflin, 1911), V, 421. In this passage the things of nature add up to a "Sanskrit cipher," i.e., a variation of the metaphor of hieroglyphics.

¹⁶ *The American Transcendentalists: Their Prose and Poetry*, ed. Perry Miller (Garden City, N.Y.: Doubleday, 1957), p. 53. Cf. the quotation above from Blake's *Milton*.

¹⁷ See Stanley Vogel, *German Literary Influences on the American Transcendentalists* (New Haven: Yale University Press, 1955).

[18] See my essay "The Hedging Consciousness in Coleridge's Conversation Poems," *The Wordsworth Circle*, 4 (1973), 124-38.

[19] Letter of 10 September 1802 to William Sotheby in *Collected Letters of Samuel Taylor Coleridge*, ed. Earl Leslie Griggs (Oxford: Clarendon Press, 1956), II, 864. In Book Fourteen of *The Prelude*, Wordsworth attributes nature's "apt illustrations of the moral world" to the work of the Fancy.

[20] Hölderlin, *Sämtliche Werke*, ed. Friedrich Beissner, IV (Stuttgart: W. Kohlhammer, 1961), 95. Further references to this edition are in the text. All quotations are from the second version of the play.

[21] From Appendix C to *The Statesman's Manual* in *Lay Sermons*, ed. R. J. White (Princeton: Princeton University Press, 1972), pp. 74-75.

[22] Letter of 27 October 1818 to Richard Woodhouse in Rollins, *Letters of John Keats*, I, 387.

[23] Letter of 3 February 1818 to John Hamilton Reynolds in Rollins, *Letters of John Keats*, I, 224.

[24] *The Complete Works of William Hazlitt*, ed. P. P. Howe (London: J. M. Dent, 1930), IV, 88. Further references to this essay are in the text.

[25] Kluckhohn and Samuel, *Schriften*, p. 105.

[26] Letter of 21 (27?) December 1818 to George and Tom Keats in Rollins, *Letters of John Keats*, I, 193. Of the many interpretations of the phrase the most elaborate and convincing is the reading by Walter Jackson Bate. See his *John Keats* (Cambridge, Mass.: Belknap Press, 1963), especially chapter ten.

[27] *Lectures on the English Poets* in *Complete Works*, ed. P. P. Howe (London, 1930), V, 48.

[28] Letter of 10 June 1818 to Benjamin Bailey in Rollins, *Letters of John Keats*, I, 292.

[29] *Werke*, ed. Benno von Wiese (Weimar, 1962), XX, 433.

[30] Howe, *Lectures on the English Poets*, 156.

[31] Letter of 21 September 1818 to Charles Wentworth Dilke in Rollins, *Letters of John Keats*, I, 368-69. Cf. the letter of 27 October 1818 to Richard Woodhouse, p. 387.

[32] Letter of 13 July 1802 to William Sotheby in Griggs, *Letters of Coleridge*, II, 810.

[33] *Biographia Literaria*, ed. J. Shawcross (London: Oxford University Press, 1907), II, 16. Compare these further comments on Shakespeare:

in his very first productions he projected his mind out of his own particular being, and felt and made others feel, on subjects [in] no way connected with himself, except by force of contemplation, and that sublime faculty, by which a great mind becomes that which it meditates on.

(From Samuel Taylor Coleridge, *Shakespearean Criticism*, ed. Thomas Raysor [London: J. M. Dent, 1960], II, 187-88.) For more comments by Coleridge and others see Meyer Abrams, *The Mirror and the Lamp* (New York: W. W. Norton, 1958), pp. 244-49. For a suggestion about the possible influence of Coleridge on Keats's concept of negative capability see the edition of the *Biographia* by George Watson (London: J. M. Dent, 1960), p. 256, fn. 3.

[34] *Specimens of the Table Talk of the Late Samuel Taylor Coleridge* in *The Complete Works of Samuel Taylor Coleridge*, ed. W. G. T. Shedd (New York: Harper & Brothers, 1884), VI, 312.

[35] Shedd, *Table Talk*, p. 479. We should remember, however, that in Coleridge's distinction of the humorist from the man of humor the former is fully evident in his work, and that is part of what makes him an inferior type.

[36] Letter of 27 October 1818 to Richard Woodhouse in Rollins, *Letters of John Keats*, I, 386-87.

[37] *Naive*, 424.

[38] Ibid., 481.

[39] Spiller and Ferguson, *Collected Works of Emerson*, 19.

[40] Ibid., 31.

[41] Wordsworth, *The Prelude*, ed. Ernest de Selincourt, 2nd ed., rev. Helen Darbishire (Oxford: Clarendon Press, 1959), X, 415.

[42] My remarks here are not meant to present anything like a complete picture of romantic irony but to show how significant elements within the mode echo characteristics and concerns of other romantic forms of the engagement of mind and nature. The literature of romantic irony is vast and includes a considerable variety of interpretations of the phenomenon. The most comprehensive study is that of Ingrid Strohschneider-Kohrs, *Die romantische Ironie in Theorie und Gestaltung* (Tübingen: Max Niemeyer, 1960). Significant modern studies include Ernst Behler, *Klassische Ironie, romantische Ironie, tragische Ironie* (Darmstadt: Wissenschaftliche Buchgesellschaft, 1972); René Bourgeois, *L'Ironie romantique* (Grenoble: Presses Universitaires, 1974); Raymond Immerwahr, "Romantic

Irony and Romantic Arabesque prior to Romanticism," *GQ*, 42 (1969), 665-85; Immerwahr, "The Subjectivity or Objectivity of Friedrich Schlegel's Poetic Irony," *GR*, 26 (1951), 173-91; Helmut Prang, *Die romantische Ironie* (Darmstadt: Wissenschaftliche Buchgesellschaft, 1972); Peter Szondi, "Friedrich Schlegel und die romantische Ironie," *Euphorion*, Dritte Folge, 48 (1954), 397-411.

[43] *Charakteristen und Kritiken I, (1796-1801)*, ed. Hans Eichner, Kritische Friedrich-Schlegel-Ausgabe, II (Munich, 1967), 263.

[44] Eichner, *Charakteristen und Kritiken I*, 263.

[45] Ibid., 262.

[46] Ibid., 172.

[47] See, in Eichner, *Charakteristen und Kritiken I, Athenaeum Fragmente*, No. 305, the illusion of self-destruction (217).

[48] Letter of 21 (27?) December 1817 to George and Tom Keats in Rollins, *Letters of John Keats*, I, 193-94.

[49] Eichner, *Charakteristen und Kritiken I*, 160.

[50] Ibid., 152.

[51] Letter of 22 November 1817 to Benjamin Bailey in Rollins, *Letters of John Keats*, I, 185.

CHAPTER FIVE

[1] From Hazlitt's essay "On Shakespeare and Milton," in *Lectures on the English Poets, The Complete Works of William Hazlitt*, V, ed. P. P. Howe (London: J. M. Dent, 1930), 64.

[2] Hölderlin, *Sämtliche Werke*, I, ed. Friedrich Beissner (Stuttgart: W. Kohlhammer, 1946), 265.

[3] William Wordsworth, *The Prelude*, ed. Ernest de Selincourt, 2nd ed., rev. Helen Darbishire (Oxford: Clarendon Press, 1959), II, 32-33.

[4] Friedrich Schiller, *Werke*, ed. Benno von Wiese (Weimar: H. Böhlaus, 1962), XX, 415-16.

[5] Ibid., 414.

[6] There are important comments on nostalgia and form in Sidney Tillin, "Notes on Narrative and History Painting," *Artforum*, May 1977, 41-43.

[7] From "Schillers Theorie der modernen Literatur," in *Goethe und seine Zeit* (Berlin: Aufbau, 1950), p. 147.

[8] Schiller, *Werke*, 449, note.

[9] William Blake, *The Poetry and Prose of William Blake*, ed. David

Erdman (Garden City, N.Y.: Doubleday, 1965), p. 581. From Blake's annotations to Lavater.

[10] See Book Nine of the *Confessions* in *Œuvres Complètes*, I, (Paris: Gallimard, 1964), ed. Marcel Raymond, 430-31.

[11] Hölderlin, *Sämtliche Werke*, I, 239.

[12] Ibid., p. 240.

[13] Hölderlin, *Sämtliche Werke*, II (Stuttgart, 1951), 165.

[14] *Goethes Werke*, VI, ed. Benno von Wiese and Erich Trunz (Hamburg: Christian Wegner, 1965), 74.

[15] Von Wiese and Trunz, *Werther*, 84.

[16] Ibid., 85.

[17] Ibid., 9.

[18] Ibid., 10.

[19] *Œuvres Complètes*, I, 1002.

[20] Ibid., 1075.

[21] Von Wiese and Trunz, *Werther*, 85.

[22] I, i. 127, in *The Complete Poetical Works of Byron*, ed. Paul Elmer More (Cambridge, Mass.: Houghton Mifflin Company, 1933). Further references to act, scene, and line numbers will be in the text.

CHAPTER SIX

[1] Although the bibliography of individual figures is, of course, extensive, studies of wider aspects of the tradition of the romantic hero are still comparatively rare. Among the most useful books is Peter Thorslev's *The Byronic Hero: Types and Prototypes* (Minneapolis: University of Minnesota Press, 1962). See also Thorslev's "The Romantic Mind is its own Place," *Comparative Literature*, 15 (1963), 250-68; George Ross Ridge, *The Hero in French Romantic Literature* (Athens, Georgia: University of Georgia Press, 1961); Maurice Z. Shroder, *Icarus: The Image of the Artist in French Romanticism* (Cambridge, Mass.: Harvard University Press, 1961); Victor Erlich, *The Double Image: Concepts of the Poet in Slavic Literatures* (Baltimore: Johns Hopkins University Press, 1964); Edmond Estève, *Byron et le romantisme français*, 2nd ed., (Paris: Boivin, 1929); André Monglond, *Le préromantisme français* (Grenoble: B. Arthaud, 1930). There are several important essays in the special issue of *Studies in the Literary Imagination*, 9 (1976), ed. Lilian R. Furst and James D. Wilson.

² William Wordsworth, *The Prelude*, ed. Ernest de Selincourt, 2nd ed., rev. Helen Darbishire (Oxford: Clarendon Press, 1959), II, 175.

³ "Nun hast du dich zusammengenommen in dich, siehst dich vor dir aufhören in deinen Händen, ziehst von Zeit zu Zeit mit einer ungenauen Bewegung dein Gesicht nach. Und in dir ist beinah kein Raum; and fast stillst es dich, dass in dieser Engheit in dir unmöglich sehr Grosses sich aufhalten kann; dass auch das Unerhörte binnen werden muss und beschränken den Verhältnissen nach. Aber draussen, draussen ist es ohne Absehen" (Now you have pulled yourself together within yourself, you see yourself end in your hands, from time to time you trace the outline of your face with an uncertain gesture. And within you there is scarcely any room; and it almost quiets you that in this narrowness within you nothing very large can possibly dwell; that even the unheard-of must become inward and restrict itself to the circumstances; but outside, outside it is endless). See *Die Aufzeichnungen des Malte Laurids Brigge* (Insel-Verlag, n.d.), p. 83. For important comments on this and related matters in Rilke see Priscilla Washburn Shaw, *Rilke, Valéry and Yeats: The Domain of the Self* (New Brunswick: Rutgers University Press, 1964). See also my essay "Time and the City in Rilke's *Malte Laurids Brigge*," *Contemporary Literature*, XI (1970), 324-39.

⁴ *PMLA*, 40 (1925), 874-80. Miss McIntyre builds her definition on that of Clarence Boyer in *The Villain as Hero in Elizabethan Tragedy* (London: Routledge, 1914).

⁵ See also Miss McIntyre's related article "Were the 'Gothic Novels' Really Gothic?," *PMLA*, 36 (1921), 644-67, in which the point is made that Gothic fiction continues the gorier aspects of Renaissance dramatic style. Her argument is based on the concept of a romantic revival, which in its turn implies a systole-diastole theory of the movement of literary history.

⁶ For further discussion of Schedoni and of *The Italian* see my edition of the novel (London, 1968).

⁷ A more acceptable view of the heroic genealogy and of the nature of the romantic hero appears in Louis I. Bredvold's *The Natural History of Sensibility* (Detroit, 1962), pp. 95-98. But Bredvold tends to identify the character with a Satanic figure "exhibiting fiendish pleasure in cruelty" (p. 96), a pleasure found nowhere in any romantic hero, and the argument leads from this point into what is to my mind a narrowly exclusive and not quite accurate view of the

characteristics of the romantic hero, a view tending to confine him too closely to the attributes of the Gothic villain.

8 Cf. Thorslev, *Byronic Hero*, pp. 88-89, for a view of another, closely related dichotomy, the urge to lose one's self in an absolute, as opposed to the assertion of one's own specific individuality.

9 *Goethes Werke*, Hamburger Ausgabe, VI, ed. Benno von Wiese and Erich Trunz (Hamburg: Christian Wegner, 1965), 10-11.

10 Ibid., 10-11.

11 Ibid., 63.

12 Henry Mackenzie, *The Man of Feeling*, ed. Brian Vickers (London: Oxford University Press, 1970) p. 25.

13 Ibid., p. 125.

14 Ibid., p. 131.

15 "Der Widersinn in ihren Sitten vergnügte mich, wie eine Kinderposse, und weil ich von Natur hinaus war über all' die eingeführten Formen und Bräuche, spielt' ich mit allen, und legte sie an und zog sie aus, wie Fastnachtskleider" (The absurdity of their manners amused me like a children's prank, and because I was by nature above their established forms and customs I played with them all, and put them on and took them off like carnival outfits).

16 Schiller, *Werke*, III, ed. Herbert Stubenrauch (Weimar: H. Böhlaus, 1953), 6.

17 Schiller, *Die Räuber*, 6.

18 Schiller's Karl Moor is quite possibly in the background of Byron's Corsair. But Byron avoids some of the difficulties by giving to the band of pirates the language, attitudes, and decorum of a higher, more sophisticated and genteel class than even the remotest probability would allow. My remarks just below on Shelley point out a similar approach in some of his poems.

19 Apocalyptic mythography is in no sense an evasion of contemporary realities, as Hölderlin's later odes and Blake's major and minor epics make clear.

20 Ed. Bonamy Dobrée (London: Oxford University Press, 1970), pp. 216-17.

21 Compare the "unprofitable dust" of the poet in Wordsworth's "A Poet's Epitaph."

22 *Werther*, 97.

23 Ibid., 117.

24 Chateaubriand, *Œuvres romanesques et voyages*, ed. Maurice Regard, I (Paris: Gallimard, 1969), 145.

[25] *René*, 145.
[26] Ibid., 146.

CHAPTER SEVEN

[1] *Œuvres Complètes de Jean-Jacques Rousseau*, IV (Paris: Gallimard, 1969), ed. Bernard Gagnebin and Marcel Raymond, 327. All further references will be in the text.

[2] Jean-Louis Lecercle, *Rousseau et l'art du roman* (Paris: Armand Colin, 1969), p. 346.

[3] *The Italian*, ed. Frederick Garber (London: Oxford University Press, 1968), p. 412.

[4] Radcliffe, p. 413.

[5] *Emile*, clxiv ff.

[6] William Wordsworth, *The Prelude*, ed. Ernest de Selincourt, 2nd ed., rev. Helen Darbishire (Oxford: Clarendon Press, 1959), III, 111-12. All further references will be in the text.

[7] The passage these lines conclude was at one time published under the title "French Revolution as It Appeared to Enthusiasts at Its Commencement."

[8] William Wordsworth, *Home at Grasmere*, ed. Beth Darlington (Ithaca: Cornell University Press, 1977), D text, 805-06. The designations "B text" and "D text" refer to states of the manuscript. All further references will be incorporated in my text.

[9] The most important essay is by Kenneth R. Johnston, " 'Home at Grasmere': Reclusive Song," *Studies in Romanticism*, 14 (1975), 1-28.

[10] See Mircea Eliade, *Patterns in Comparative Religion* (New York: World Publishing, 1972), pp. 231-33.

[11] Cf. the analogies in art history in Panofsky's "*Et in Arcadia Ego:* Poussin and the Elegiac Tradition," *Meaning in the Visual Arts* (Garden City, New York: Doubleday, 1955), pp. 295-320.

[12] Henry David Thoreau, *A Week on the Concord and Merrimack Rivers* (Boston: Houghton Mifflin Company, n.d.), p. 405.

CHAPTER EIGHT

[1] Stendhal, *Romans et Nouvelles*, ed. Henri Martineau, I (Paris: Gallimard, 1952), 344. All further references will be in the text.

² For a wide-scale study of this naturalizing see Meyer Abrams, *Natural Supernaturalism* (New York: W. W. Norton, 1971).

³ Jean-Jacques Rousseau, *La Nouvelle Héloïse*, in *Œuvres Complètes de Jean-Jacques Rousseau*, II, ed. Bernard Gagnebin and Marcel Raymond (Paris: Gallimard, 1959), 471.

⁴ *La prison romantique* (Paris: Jose Corti, 1975).

CHAPTER NINE

¹ Edgar Allan Poe, *The Complete Works of Edgar Allan Poe*, ed. J. A. Harrison, (New York: Crowell and Co., 1902), IV, 193-94. Further references will be in the text.

² See especially Nina Baym, "The Function of Poe's Pictorialism," *The South Atlantic Quarterly*, 65 (1966), 46-54; and Richard Wilbur, "The House of Poe," in *Poe: A Collection of Critical Essays*, ed. Robert Regan (Englewood Cliffs, N.J.: Prentice Hall, 1967), pp. 98-120.

³ John Keats, *The Letters of John Keats, 1814-1821*, ed. Hyder Edward Rollins (Cambridge, Mass: Harvard University Press, 1958), I, 184.

⁴ Edgar Allan Poe, *Collected Works of Edgar Allan Poe*, I, ed. Thomas Mabbott (Cambridge, Mass.: Belknap Press, 1969), 214.

⁵ Ibid., 236-37.

⁶ *Eureka* in *Edgar Allan Poe: Selected Prose, Poetry and Eureka*, ed. W. H. Auden (New York: Holt, Rinehart and Winston, 1950), p. 514. Further references will be in the text.

⁷ Poe, *Complete Works*, IV, 202.

⁸ Poe, *Collected Works*, I, 315.

⁹ Poe, *Complete Works*, VIII, 281.

¹⁰ Ibid., IV, 250.

¹¹ Ibid., II, 240.

¹² Ibid., VI, 175.

¹³ Ibid., II, 258.

¹⁴ The *Oxford English Dictionary* defines "viable" not only as "capable of living" but also as "able to maintain a separate existence."

¹⁵ Poe, *Complete Works*, IV, 148.

¹⁶ Ibid., VI, 176.

¹⁷ From *Marginalia* in Edgar Allan Poe, *The Complete Poems and*

Stories of Edgar Allan Poe, ed. Arthur Quinn (New York: Knopf, 1951), II, 1049.

18 Poe, *Complete Works*, IV, 205.

19 Tate's famous essay seems to be radically mistaken about Poe and to be far closer to Tate's reading of the world than to Poe's.

20 Poe, *Complete Works*, VI, 212.

21 Ibid, VI, 256.

CHAPTER TEN

1 Herman Melville, *Moby Dick*, ed. Harrison Hayford and Hershel Parker (New York: W. W. Norton, 1967), p. 147. All further references will be in the text.

2 Nathaniel Hawthorne, *Mosses from an Old Manse*, The Centenary Edition of the Works of Nathaniel Hawthorne (Columbus: Ohio State University Press, 1974), p. 98. All further references will be in the text.

3 Frederick Crews speaks of the story's "equation of poison with sexuality" and argues that Giovanni's ambivalence is based on that unnerving combination. See his *The Sins of the Fathers: Hawthorne's Psychological Themes* (New York: Oxford University Press, 1966), p. 119. See also Roy Male's related comment that the poison is in Beatrice's "combination of sexual attractiveness and angelic purity" in *Hawthorne's Tragic Vision* (Austin: University of Texas Press, 1957), p. 55.

4 William Blake, *The Four Zoas, Night the First*, in *The Poetry and Prose of William Blake*, ed. David Erdman (Garden City, New York: Doubleday, 1965), p. 299.

5 Blake, *The Poetry and Prose*, p. 351.

6 Ibid., p. 119.

7 Ibid., p. 155.

8 Ibid., p. 354.

9 "Salon de 1846," in *Œuvres Complètes*, ed. Y.-G. le Dantec (Paris: Gallimard, 1954), p. 659.

10 Quotations are from Charles Baudelaire, *Œuvres Complètes*, and will be incorporated in the text.

11 *Correspondance*, ed. Claude Pichois, I (Paris: Gallimard, 1966), 248.

12 Oscar Wilde, *Decay of Lying* in *The Works of Oscar Wilde* (London: Spring Books, 1977), p. 825.

[13] Joris-Karl Huysmans, *A Rebours* (Paris: Fasquelle, 1970), p. 126. All further references will be in the text.

[14] *Goethes Werke*, Hamburger Ausgabe, VI, ed. Benno von Wiese and Erich Trunz (Hamburg: Christian Wegner, 1965), 9.

[15] For the compatability of Des Esseintes' dandyism and a nostalgia for *l'au-delà* ("the beyond") see Fernande Zayed, *Huysmans. Peintre de son époque* (Paris: Nizet, 1973), pp. 410-11. It is surely erroneous to assert, as Zayed does, that the point is prefigured in Baudelaire's comments on the dandy in *Le peintre de la vie moderne*. For Baudelaire the dandy's spirituality is admittedly self-directed, self-contained, not an attempt to transcend self, but to enclose one's longings within the confines of self. Dandyism does, after all, end in "une espèce de culte de soi-même" ("a kind of cult of oneself" [*Œuvres Complètes*, p. 907]). The dandies are "à la fois les prêtres et les victimes" ("at once the priests and the victims"). The values of the dandy necessarily circle in upon himself because he is a self-engendered artifact and his selfhood is the only remaining weapon against the crassness of the age.

[16] See A. O. Lovejoy, *The Great Chain of Being* (Cambridge, Mass.: Harvard University Press, 1942).

[17] *The Romantic Agony*, trans. Angus Davidson (New York: Meridian, 1956), pp. 289-90.

[18] *Le roman contemporain* (Paris: A. Lemerre, 1902), pp. 281-82.

[19] For a contrary view, arguing that religion is only one idea among the many tried out in the novel, see Pierre Cogny, *J.-K. Huysmans à la recherche de l'unité* (Paris: Nizet, 1953), especially pages 104-05.

[20] Baudelaire, *Œuvres Complètes*, p. 463.

[21] Ralph Waldo Emerson, *The Collected Works of Ralph Waldo Emerson*, ed. Robert E. Spiller and Alfred R. Ferguson (Cambridge, Mass.: Belknap Press, 1971), I, 37.

[22] *Dorian Gray* in *The Works of Oscar Wilde*, p. 501.

[23] (New York: Boni and Liveright, 1919), p. 196.

Translations

ᵃ the most sociable and the most affectionate of men.

CHAPTER ONE

ᵃ the surroundings are lonely but agreeable and varied.

ᵇ Hateful prejudice has no access whatever into this happy region. The peaceful resident still keeps the simple manners of the earliest times.

ᶜ But if Julie, pure and chaste, succumbed anyway, how will she raise herself after her fall?

ᵈ No, if you want me to be peaceful and content, give me a shelter that is even more secure, where I can escape from shame and repentance.

ᵉ As I compared so pleasant an abode to the objects which surrounded it, it seemed that this deserted place should have been the shelter of two lovers who alone had escaped the upheaval of nature.

ᶠ nothing is there which I have not arranged.

ᵍ peace reigns in the depths of her heart as in the shelter which she has named.

ʰ When this fearful Julie pursues me I take refuge near Madame de Wolmar and I am peaceful; where will I flee if this shelter is taken from me?

ⁱ O what a winter we will spend together, if the hope of our reunion does not deceive me. Each day prepares for it by bringing here one of those privileged souls who are so dear to each other, who are so worthy of loving each other, and who seem to await only you in order to do without the rest of the universe.

ʲ a healthy soul, a heart free of the disturbance of the passions.

ᵏ The order which he has put into his house is the image of that which reigns in the depths of his soul, and seems to imitate in a small household the order established in the government of the world.

ˡ souls of a certain stamp.

ᵐ O Julie, what a fatal present from heaven is a sensitive soul!

ⁿ This tie, so dreaded, delivers me from a servitude still more dreadful, and my husband becomes dearer to me for having given me back to myself.

º One would say that, since nothing on earth can satisfy the need to love which devours her, this excess of sensibility is forced to return to its source.

ᵖ beauty, there indeed is your final shelter.

CHAPTER TWO

ᵃ His modest needs are found so readily at hand, and he is so far from the degree of knowledge necessary to desire the acquisition of still greater knowledge, that he can have neither foresight nor curiosity.

ᵇ the generalization of his self.

ᶜ I want to strive so that, in learning to appraise oneself, one can have at least one item of comparison; so that each can know himself and another, and that other will be me.

ᵈ He described it as he felt it himself.

ᵉ I saw the sky, some stars, and a bit of greenery. That first sensation was a delicious moment. I still felt my own existence only through that. I was born in that moment into life.

ᶠ It seemed to me that I filled with my slight existence all the objects which I saw.

ᵍ I had no distinct notion of my separate being.

ʰ I did not know who I was or where I was.

ⁱ We are born capable of learning but knowing nothing, familiar with nothing. The soul chained in these imperfect and half-formed organs does not even have the feeling of its own existence.

ʲ in the middle of the lake of Bienne.

ᵏ a form almost round.

ˡ *loves* to circumscribe himself.

ᵐ it was impossible for me to leave without assistance and without being clearly seen, and ... I could only have communication and correspondence through the cooperation of the people who surrounded me.

ⁿ I could have wished that this shelter had been made a permanent prison for me, that I had been confined there for my entire life.

º Ah, I said to myself, how gladly I would exchange the freedom to leave here, which I don't care about at all, for the assurance of being able to stay here forever.

[p] successively from all the most remote, most solitary shelters in which he had imprisoned himself.

[q] a peaceful captivity.

[r] alone and naked.

[s] and there, stretching out my entire length in the boat with my eyes turned toward the sky, I let myself go and drift slowly at the water's will, sometimes for several hours, plunged into a thousand confused but delicious reveries which, though they had no well-determined or constant object, still seemed, in my opinion, to be a hundred times preferable to all that I had found sweetest in what is called the pleasures of life.

[t] of a sufficient, perfect and full happiness, which leaves in the soul no void which it feels the need of filling.

[u] What does one enjoy in a situation like this? Nothing external to oneself, nothing except oneself and one's own existence, as long as that state lasts one is sufficient to oneself like God.

[v] without movement life is only a lethargy . . . an absolute silence offers an image of death.

[w] slight and sweet ideas.

[x] the movement which does not come from outside occurs then inside of us.

[y] if there is a state . . . in which time is nothing for her [the soul], in which the present lasts forever yet without marking its duration and without any trace of succession, without any other feeling of privation or enjoyment, of pleasure or pain, of desire or fear than that alone of our existence.

[z] a place solid enough for it to repose there completely and assemble there its entire being.

[aa] in a fertile and solitary Island, naturally circumscribed and separated from the rest of the world.

[bb] a thousand confused but delicious reveries.

[cc] the ornament and the garment of the earth . . . its wedding dress.

[dd] a retreat so hidden that I never in my life saw a wilder sight.

[ee] thinking that I was there in a refuge unknown to the whole universe.

[ff] I compared myself to those great travellers who discover a desert Island, and I said to myself complacently: without doubt I am the first mortal to have penetrated here; I saw myself almost as another Columbus.

[gg] a movement of pride.

ʰʰ I learned thus through my own experience that the source of true happiness is within us, and that men cannot make truly miserable a person who knows how to will to be happy.

CHAPTER THREE

ᵃ this book so mad, so wise and so gay . . . the Rabelais of the English.

ᵇ artistically ordered confusion.

ᶜ It is equally deadly for the mind to have a system and not to have one. Therefore it must decide to unite both.

ᵈ Versatility requires not only a comprehensive system but also a sense for the chaos outside of it, just as mankind requires a sense for something beyond mankind.

ᵉ The romantic mode of poetry is still in a state of becoming; indeed, that is its genuine essence, that it is always becoming and can never be completed. . . . It alone is infinite just as it alone is free, and it acknowledges as its primary law that the will of the poet can tolerate no law over itself.

ᶠ an artistically ordered confusion, this charming symmetry of contradictions, this wonderful eternal alternation of enthusiasm and irony.

ᵍ a quite definite and essential form or mode of expression of poetry.

ʰ the divine wit, the imagination of an Ariosto, Cervantes, Shakespeare.

CHAPTER FOUR

ᵃ Does not the whole of nature, as well as the face and gestures, the pulse and colors, express the condition of each of those higher, wonderful beings whom we call men? Does not the rock become a specific Thou at the moment when I speak to it? And what else am I but the stream when I look down wistfully into its waves and lose my thoughts in its flow?

ᵇ you honor me . . . and do right therein; for nature is mute.

ᶜ the ground would appear dead if someone did not attend to it, waking life, and mine is that field.

ᵈ What then would the sky and ocean be, and the islands and stars, and all that lies before the eyes of men, what would it be, this dead lyre, if I did not give it tone and language and soul? What are the gods and their spirit if I do not proclaim them? Speak now, who am I?

ᵉ To be alone and without the gods is death.

ᶠ Led astray by my familiarity with later poets into first seeking out the poet in his work, to find *his* heart, to reflect in common with *him* on his theme; in short, to view the object in the subject, I found it intolerable that the poet would nowhere let himself be grasped and would nowhere account to me.

ᵍ Every true genius must be naive, or else it is no genius. Its naiveté alone makes it into a genius.

ʰ only that confusion is a chaos out of which a world can spring.

ⁱ Irony is clear consciousness of eternal agility, of infinitely full chaos.

ʲ Versatility requires not only a comprehensive system but also a sense for the chaos outside of it, just as mankind requires a sense for something beyond mankind.

ᵏ constant alternation of self-creation and self-destruction.

ˡ the freest of all licenses because through it one transcends oneself.

ᵐ Within, the mood which surveys everything and lifts itself infinitely beyond all that is limited, even beyond its own art, virtue or genius.

CHAPTER FIVE

ᵃ "Hyperion's Song of Fate": Fateless as the sleeping babe breathe the heavenly ones; chastely preserved in modest bud their spirit blooms eternally, and their blessed eyes gaze in still, eternal clarity.

ᵇ This sensitivity to nature manifests itself most strongly and commonly under the impetus of such objects as stand in a close relationship to us and bring closer to us a glance backward upon ourselves and the unnaturalness in us, [such objects] as for example, children and childlike peoples.

ᶜ existence according to its own laws, the inner necessity, the eternal unity with itself.

ᵈ He continually subjectivizes his explanations and accordingly always makes modes of feeling and thought out of objective matters of fact.

ᵉ I look only at the dominant modes of feeling in these poetic kinds.

ᶠ The poets are holy vessels in which the wine of life, the spirit of heroes, is preserved. But the spirit of this youth, the swift one—would it not shatter the vessel that sought to contain it? Let the poet leave him untouched like the spirit of nature: such material turns the master into a boy. He cannot live and last in a poem; he lives and lasts in the world.

ᵍ It's life you seek, you seek, and a divine fire gushes and gleams at you from deep in the earth, and in your shuddering desire you throw yourself down into Etna's flames. So did the exuberance of the queen melt pearls into wine, and indeed she might! but if only you had not sacrificed your wealth, oh Poet, deep in the effervescing chalice! Yet you are holy to me as the might of the earth that took you away, bold dead one! And I would follow the hero into the depths if love did not hold me back.

ʰ Thus, since the summits of time are heaped all around, and the dearest ones live nearby, weakening on the most separate mountains, then give us innocent water, oh give us wings, to go over and return with most faithful mind.

ⁱ alone is the source of all things, all strength, all bliss, all misery.

ʲ the source of all misery is buried within me, as formerly the source of all bliss.

ᵏ the holy, enlivening power, with which I created worlds around me.

ˡ I couldn't draw now, not a stroke, and I have never been a better painter than in these moments.

ᵐ I no longer want to be led, encouraged or inspired, this heart storms enough on its own.

ⁿ to the time when, losing all hope here below and finding no further nourishment for my heart here on the earth, I accustomed myself little by little to feeding it with its own substance and to seeking all its sustenance within myself.

Chapter Six

ᵃ the humble people . . . we are not equal, nor can we be.

ᵇ people of social distinction will always keep a cold distance from common folk, as if they felt they would lose something by coming close.

ᶜ Ah, I will gladly let others go their own way, if only they will let me go mine.

ᵈ a bitterness against the unidealistic world.

ᵉ You cannot be saved, unhappy one! I see clearly, we cannot be saved.

ᶠ And what does it mean that Albert is your husband? Husband! That is for this world—and for this world it is a sin that I love you, that I would tear you out of his arms into mine? A sin? Very well, and I punish myself for it.

ᵍ Presumptuous youth who believed that man can suffice to himself! Solitude is bad for one who does not live with God.

ʰ [Solitude] redoubles the powers of the soul, at the same time that it takes away all reason for their activity.

ⁱ It is said that, urged by the two old men, he returned to his wife but found no happiness there.

Chapter Seven

ᵃ is not to gain time but to lose it.

ᵇ in a remote province, in a small island of innocence miraculously preserved since the age of gold.

ᶜ make your paradise on earth while waiting for the other.

ᵈ I was touched in thinking how many benefits Emile and Sophie can spread around them from their simple retreat, how they can enliven the countryside and reanimate the extinguished zeal of the unfortunate villager. I seem to see the population multiplying, the fields growing fertile, the earth taking on a new adornment, multitude and abundance transforming tasks into holidays, the cries of joy and blessings rising from the midst of the games around the amiable couple who have revived them. The golden age is considered a chimera, and it will always be so for one whose taste and heart are spoiled. It is not even true that one regrets it since such regrets are always in vain. What then must be done to give it life again? Just one thing, but that is impossible; that would be to love it.

ᵉ it already seems reborn around Sophie's dwelling.

ᶠ Emile is not made to remain solitary always; a member of society, he must fulfill its duties. Made to live with men, he ought to know them.

ᵍ I have sought in our travels to find some corner of the earth where I could be absolutely mine; but in what place among men does one no longer depend on their passions?

CHAPTER EIGHT

ᵃ Speech has been given to man to hide his thought.

ᵇ Julien reached such a degree of perfection in this sort of eloquence, which has replaced the rapidity of action seen in the Empire, that he finally became bored with the sound of his own voice.

ᶜ Julien, already very badly indisposed, came to think that on the other side of the dining room wall there were some poor prisoners on whose portion of meat one had perhaps made a petty profit in order to buy all this tasteless luxury with which they wanted to dazzle him.

ᵈ Only a fool, he said to himself, gets angry with others: a stone falls because it is heavy. Will I always be a child? When will I acquire the good habit of giving these people just the right amount of my soul for their money? If I want to be esteemed both by them and by myself I must show them that my poverty is doing business with their wealth but that my heart is a thousand leagues away from their insolence, and placed in a sphere too high to be reached by their petty marks of disdain or favor.

ᵉ Scarcely was I inside when, the door being concealed by alders and hazel trees which leave only two narrow passages on the sides, I could no longer see, as I turned around, where I had entered, and seeing no door at all, I found myself there as if fallen from the clouds.

ᶠ However insensitive the soul of this ambitious youth was to this kind of beauty, he could not keep himself from stopping from time to time to look at so vast and imposing a spectacle.

ᵍ Hidden like a bird of prey amidst the bare rocks crowning the great mountain, he could see from a great distance anyone who approached him.

ʰ he was *almost* sensitive *for a moment* to the ravishing beauty of the woods amidst which he was walking.

ⁱ he found himself standing on an immense rock and quite certain of being separated from all men. This physical position made him smile, it painted to him the position which he was burning to reach in the moral sphere.

ʲ twenty leagues of country.

ᵏ hidden like a bird of prey.

ˡ here . . . men cannot hurt me.

ᵐ in the midst of this vast darkness.

ⁿ solitary in this mountain.

° sacred fire . . . sublime energy.

ᵖ Julien could not contain his joy. He had to go down to the garden. His room, in which he had locked himself, seemed too narrow for him to breathe.

Chapter Ten

ᵃ stupid grains.

ᵇ An eclectic does not know that the first concern of the artist is to substitute man for nature and to protest against it. This protest is not made with a preconceived opinion, coldly, like a code of laws or a rhetoric; it is tempestuous and naive, like vice, like passion, like appetite.

ᶜ from cursed condiments the excitement one must find within oneself.

ᵈ What is a paradise that one buys at the price of one's eternal salvation? . . . by the assiduous exercise of the will and the permanent nobility of the intention, we have created for our use a garden of true beauty.

ᵉ You will see in this tableau a somber and solitary walker, plunged into the moving wave of the multitudes.

ᶠ I am the vampire of my heart.

ᵍ I have even always thought that in *Nature*, flourishing and re-juvenated, there was something impudent and vexing.

ʰ the masterpeice of artifice . . . a bit of stovepipe, cut into the shape of a pike point by a chimney attendant.

ⁱ When she was not able to imitate the work of men, she was reduced to copying the inner membranes of animals, to borrowing the vivid tints of their rotting flesh, the magnificent horrors of their gangrenes.

ʲ Ah, if only you could express it again, if you could breathe onto the paper what lives in you so warmly and fully, so that it would become the mirror of your soul, as your soul is the mirror of infinite God!

ᵏ Like those Japanese boxes that fit one inside the other, this room was inserted within a larger room, which was the real dining room built by the architect.

ˡ The shadow of this coif passing before him in the twilight gave him the impression of a cloister, reminded him of those silent, devout villages, those dead neighborhoods hidden deep in the corner of an active and lively city.

ᵐ sensations analogous to those which music pours into the air.

ⁿ Was he not in London, whose odors, atmosphere, people, foods, and utensils surrounded him?

ᵒ Really, what aberration must I have had when I tried to deny my old ideas, to condemn *the docile fantasies of my brain*, to believe like a true ninny in the necessity, the value, the interest of a trip abroad?

ᵖ I seek new perfumes, fuller blossoms, untried pleasures.

q Ah, it was to him that this voice, mysterious as an incantation, spoke; it was to him that she told of her fever for the unknown, her unsatisfied longing for the ideal, her need to escape from the horrible reality of existence, to pass beyond the boundaries of thought, to grope after a certitude without ever getting there, in the mists of the beyond of art—all the wretchedness of his own efforts made his heart ebb. Gently he embraced the silent woman at his side, taking refuge with her like a child needing consolation.

ʳ Des Esseintes was at first delighted with this effect; then he thought that this giant jewel was no more than sketched, that it would not be really complete until it had been incrusted with rare stones.

ˢ the precious stones with which its back had been paved.

ᵗ thus, the daylight, to light up the cabin, passed through the window, the panes of which had been replaced by plain glass, the water, and, finally, the fixed glass of the porthole.

ᵘ One day I challenged Baudelaire's originality to begin the *Fleurs du mal* again and to take yet one further step in the exhausted meaning of blasphemy. I would be quite capable of putting to the author of *A Rebours* the same challenge: "After the *Fleurs du mal*," I said to Baudelaire, "there remains to you, logically, only the mouth of a pistol or the feet of the cross." Baudelaire chose the feet of the cross. But will the author of *A Rebours* choose them?

ᵛ finally what a decisive insult thrown in the face of this old nature whose uniform demands would be forever extinguished.

ʷ He lived on himself, fed himself on his own substance, like those torpid beasts, crouched in a hole in winter.

ˣ terrifying marriage of man with himself.

Index

terdingen, 271; *Die Lehrlinge zu Sais,* 93-95, 98, 107, 115

Osmont, Robert, 299n
Ossian, 139

Panofsky, Erwin, 309n
Pater, Walter, 174, 213, 283, 293; *The Renaissance,* 295
Poe, Edgar Allan, 206, Chapter Nine *passim,* 259, 268-69, 274-75, 294; *The Black Cat,* 235-36, 243, 256; *The Cask of Amontillado,* 237-41, 243; *The Colloquy of Monos and Una,* 232, 252; *A Descent into the Maelstrom,* 236, 256; *The Domain of Arnheim,* 245-55, 256-57, 259-60, 269, 271, 278; *Eleonora,* 225-29; *Eureka,* 231-32; "The Haunted Palace," 232; *The Island of the Fay,* 220-26, 251; *Landor's Cottage,* 254-55, 259-60, 269; *The Landscape Garden,* 245-49; *Ligeia,* 238-40; *Marginalia,* 246; *The Masque of the Red Death,* 233-35, 295; *Mellonta Tauta,* 253; *MS Found in a Bottle,* 236; *Murders in the Rue Morgue,* 241-42; *The Philosophy of Furniture,* 257, 269; *The Poetic Principle,* 247; *The Premature Burial,* 236; *The Purloined Letter,* 242-44; *A Tale of the Ragged Mountains,* 249-50; *The Tell-Tale Heart,* 235-36, 256; "To F—," 230-31; "To One in Paradise," 229-30
Poulet, Georges, 299n
Prang, Helmut, 305n

Rabelais, François, 67, 70, 75
Radcliffe, Ann, *The Italian,* 153-54, 164, 176-77; *The Mysteries of Udolpho,* 159, 164

Raymond, Marcel, 299n
Ricatte, Robert, 299n
Richardson, Samuel, x, 61, 73-74, 159, 193, 206; *Clarissa,* Chapter One *passim,* 46, 158, 170, 179, 210-11, 213, 219, 246, 259
Richter, Jean Paul Friedrich, 78, 85
Ridge, George Ross, 306n
Rilke, Rainer Maria, *Die Aufzeichnungen des Malte Laurids Brigge,* 152
Rimbaud, Arthur, 163
Rousseau, Jean-Jacques, 73, 75, 88, 103, 107, 110, 124-26, 128, 132, 146, 168, 170, 173, 203, 206, 210, 217-18, 232, 235, 240, 258-59, 273, 275, 283; *Confessions,* 39-42, 45, 47, 206; *Discourses,* 40-41, 60, 131; *Emile,* 45, 56, Chapter Seven *passim,* 259, 268; *Emile et Sophie, ou les Solitaires,* 178-80, 200-201; *La Nouvelle Héloïse,* 17-32, 41, 131, 151, 172, 178, 198-99, 213, 263-64, 267, 275, 294; *Les Rêveries du Promeneur Solitaire,* ix, 39, 43-44, 46-57, 89, 145, 197-99, 254, 274; *Rousseau, Juge de Jean-Jacques,* 41-42, 47

Sade, Marquis de, 31
Schiller, Friedrich, 206; *Die Räuber,* 88, 128, 153-54, 160-64, 169; *Uber naive und sentimentalische Dichtung,* x, 104, 109-110, 112-13, 119, 122, 124-29, 145, 180, 205-206, 243
Schlegel, Friedrich, 78, 87, 115-16, 137; *Athenaeum,* 79; "Brief über den Roman," 90; *Gespräch über die Poesie,* 78, 85, 89; *Ideen,* 79
Schroder, Maurice, 306n

LIBRARY OF CONGRESS CATALOGING IN PUBLICATION DATA

Garber, Frederick.
The autonomy of the self from Richardson to Huysmans.

Includes bibliographical references and indexes.
  1. Literature, Modern—18th century—History and
criticism.   2. Literature, Modern—19th century—
History and criticism.   3. Self in literature.
I. Title.
PN751.G37   809'.03   81-47131
ISBN 0-691-06481-4   AACR2

DATE DUE